RITUAL AND
PILGRIMAGE IN
THE ANCIENT
ANDES

RITUAL AND PILGRIMAGE IN THE ANCIENT ANDES

THE ISLANDS OF THE SUN AND THE MOON

Brian S. Bauer and Charles Stanish

University of Texas Press　Austin

First edition, 2001

Requests for permission to reproduce material from this work should be sent to Permissions, University of Texas Press, Box 7819, Austin, TX 78713-7819.

(∞) The paper used in this book meets the minimum requirements of ANSI/NISO Z39.48-1992 (R1997) (Permanence of Paper).

ISBN 0-292-70889-0 hardcover
ISBN 0-292-70890-4 paperback

Library of Congress Cataloging-in-Publication Data
Bauer, Brian S.
    Ritual and pilgrimage in the ancient Andes : the islands of the sun and the moon / Brian S. Bauer and Charles Stanish. — 1st ed.
        p.   cm.
Includes bibliographical references (p.   ) and index.
    ISBN 0-292-70889-0 (alk. paper) — ISBN 0-292-70890-4 pbk. : (alk. paper)
    1. Incas—Titicaca Lake Region (Peru and Bolivia)—Religion. 2. Inca mythology —Titicaca Lake Region (Peru and Bolivia) 3. Incas—Titicaca Lake Region (Peru and Bolivia)—Rites and ceremonies. 4. Pilgrims and pilgrimages—Titicaca Lake (Peru and Bolivia) 5. Shrines—Titicaca Lake Region (Peru and Bolivia)—History. 6. Titicaca Lake Region (Peru and Bolivia)—Antiquities. I. Stanish, Charles, 1956– II. Title.
    F3429.3.R3 B36   2001
    985'.36—dc21   00-010612

To the people of the
Islands of the Sun (Titicaca)
and the Moon (Coati)

La veneración de la Isla del Sol "fué tan grande, que de todas partes acudían en peregrinación a él, donde era muy extraordinario el concurso que siempre había de gentes extranjeras; con que vino a ser tan célebre y famoso, que vivirá su memoria entre los indios todo lo que ellos duraren."

The veneration of the Island of the Sun "was so widespread that people came to this place on pilgrimage from everywhere. And there was always a large gathering of people there from far away. Thus this place became so famous that its memory will live on among the Indians as long as they last."

BERNABÉ COBO (1653)

CONTENTS

THIS BOOK brings together ethnographic, textual, and archaeological data to describe the nature and history of the Islands of the Sun and the Moon, located in Lake Titicaca (Bolivia). In the early sixteenth century AD, these islands were among the most sacred places in the Inca world. However, within a few years after the conquest of Peru by the Spanish Empire, the islands became a looting ground for treasure hunters, and their Inca temples became quarries for cut stones to build churches on the mainland. By the eighteenth century, the islands had fallen into the hands of a few powerful landowners, and their sacred status was nearly forgotten.

From 1994 to 1996 we directed an archaeological research program to understand the history of the islands. Our research included a systematic survey of both the islands as well as test excavations at a number of their archaeological sites. The survey of the islands (1994–1995) located more than 180 prehispanic sites that span from 2000 BC to the time of European contact in the 1530s. The survey results greatly improved our understanding of the islands' history and documented that the Inca were the last of several complex polities to occupy them. The test excavations (1995–1996) yielded detailed information on several of the most important sites on the islands and helped to refine the ceramic sequences for the region. Furthermore, during the 1995 field season, we directed archaeoastronomy research on the islands and identified the remains of two towers that marked the June solstice sunset as seen from the Sanctuary area on the Island of the Sun. In conjunction with this field research, we also examined historical texts from the sixteenth and seventeenth centuries that describe the pilgrimage route to the islands.

The survey and excavation data provide a fascinating corroboration of key early colonial documents describing the Islands of the Sun and the Moon as an important pilgrimage center in the Inca Empire. They also furnish significant insights into the pre-Inca use of the islands and raise the compelling possibility that the religious significance of the islands is of great antiquity. These results are relevant to broader anthropological problems concerning the role that pilgrimage centers hold in the development of premodern states.

This work was made possible by a number of foundations, institutions, and individuals. We gratefully acknowledge the support of the Wenner-Gren Foundation for Anthropological Research, The Field Museum of Natural History, The National Science Foundation, the Office of Social Science Research (The University of Illinois at Chicago), and The Institute for New World Archaeology. The Institute for the Humanities (The University of Illinois at Chicago) provided Brian Bauer with a Faculty Writing Fellowship as well as travel funds to visit the American Museum of Natural History. Charles Stanish's work was funded in 1997 by the College of Letters and Sciences, University of California, Los Angeles. The Dudley Observatory supported the archaeoastronomy research on the islands that was directed by David Dearborn. Patricia Dodson is gratefully acknowledged for her support over the many years. Luis and Mary Vásquez are acknowledged for their contributions to our work as well. Other supporters include Robert Donnelly, Carl and JoAnn Cipolla, Cara Cipolla Kretz, Gayle Bauer, William Bauer, Martina Munsters, and anonymous donors.

Several colleagues have provided gracious assistance and advice over the years, including Mark Aldenderfer, Bennet Bronson, Cecilia Chávez, Clark Erickson, Paul Goldstein, Jonathan Haas, Larry Keeley, Chapuruka Kusimba, Joyce Marcus, Michael Moseley, Don Rice, Katharina Schreiber, Helaine Silverman, Edmundo de la Vega, Alaka Wali, and Karen Wise. Stanish offers a personal thanks to Ken and Ligia Keller and their family for their generous help and support over the years. He also thanks Lupe Andrade and her family for their support during his work in Bolivia. Margot Beyersdorff, Jean-Jacques Decoster, Javier Flores Espinoza, and Anne Cruz provided advice on the translations.

We gratefully acknowledge the help of Craig Morris and Sumru Aricanli of the American Museum of Natural History for providing access to the Bandelier Collection, as well as Richard Burger at Yale University and Ramiro Matos M. at the Museum of the American Indian, Smithsonian Institution. We would also like to thank Johan Reinhard, who worked on the Island of the Sun before us and helped us develop our initial contacts there.

We thank the Instituto Nacional de Arqueología, Javier Escalante M., Carlos Ostermann, and Oswaldo Rivera S. as well as members of our research teams, including Lisa Cipolla, Mary Futrell, Joshua Terry, Alan Covey, Elizabeth Klarich, Christopher Cackett Keller, and Despina Margomenou. We are also grateful to Esteban Quelima, of Challa, for his excavations at Titinhua-yani, and to Matthew Seddon for his excavations at Chucaripupata. We were also aided by Santiago Mendosa Huanca and Heriberto Ticona Ticona, of Challapampa, and Felix Mamani, of Coati. Most importantly, we thank the people of the Islands of the Sun and the Moon who welcomed us into their communities and allowed the project to be conducted across their fields.

RITUAL AND PILGRIMAGE IN THE ANCIENT ANDES

1 | INCA SHRINE WORSHIP IN THE ANDES

HIGH IN THE central Andes of South America, in the great lake called Titicaca, lie two small islands. In Inca times (AD 1400–1532), they were dedicated to the Sun and the Moon and they housed elaborate temples for the Inca sky deities. Known as the Islands of the Sun and the Moon, they were also the home for large numbers of "chosen women" and "colonists" selected from around the empire. These imperial attendants devoted their lives to maintaining the temples on both of the islands as places of worship.

According to Andean traditions, the heavenly bodies first rose into the sky from these two islands. As the origin points of the universe, they were two of the most sacred locations in the Inca Empire and were the final destination for thousands of pilgrims from across the realm. Bernabé Cobo (1990:94 [1653: Bk. 13, Ch. 18]), an especially astute Spanish chronicler who lived and traveled throughout Peru in the early seventeenth century, wrote that the veneration of the shrines was "so widespread that people came to this place on pilgrimage from everywhere. And there was always a large gathering of people there from far away. Thus this place became so famous that its memory will live on among the Indians as long as they last."[1]

The Islands of the Sun and the Moon are known by the people of the region as Titicaca and Coati respectively. In this book, we will journey to these sacred islands to explore their histories and their ancient past. We will trace the route that the pilgrims traveled to the shrines and seek to answer questions of how and why these islands became two of the most revered locations of the Andes. We will also examine the roles that such state-sponsored pilgrimage centers played in the growth and development of Andean empires like the Inca and their predecessors.

We are able to investigate the Inca use of these islands and their more ancient past through two independent sets of information. The first consists of Spanish accounts written after the European invasion and the subsequent collapse of the Inca Empire. These documents were written by a number of chroniclers, including state officials, literate soldiers, educated citizens (both native and Spanish), and most importantly, by the priests of the many Catholic orders that quickly established themselves along the shores of Lake Titicaca.

Our second major source of information on the prehispanic use of the islands is the material remains left on them by their former inhabitants. The Inca invested considerable amounts of time, labor, and materials to construct state facilities on the islands, and they left a wealth of offerings in the sanctuaries. The Inca also built several villages and settled them with hundreds of colonists from around the empire. The remains of the state facilities, sanctuaries, and villages survive today. Likewise, the museums of the world contain objects recovered from the islands over the last five centuries.

By combining the available historical and archaeological information about the islands, we can reconstruct many of the activities that took place on them during Inca rule. Furthermore, careful study of the historical and archaeological materials from the Islands of the Sun and the Moon provides evidence that they were important pilgrimage centers in pre-Inca times. For example, Cobo (1990:93 [1653: Bk. 13, Ch. 18]) indicates that the islands were venerated by the people of the region "before they were subjugated by the Inca kings."[2] Moreover, elaborate offerings have been recovered over the centuries from the most important pre-Inca sites on the islands. In other words, the historical and archaeological information indicates that the Inca viewed these islands as sacred places and that the worship of the islands may have predated the Inca Conquest of the Lake Titicaca region.

The most extensive study of the islands was conducted in 1895 under the direction of Adolph Bandelier, a Swiss anthropologist and archaeologist working for the American Museum of Natural History in New York. Bandelier worked, however, at a time when the outlines of Andean cultural history were just emerging. He knew little of the Inca occupation of the region and even less about the pre-Inca cultures of the Lake Titicaca Basin. Furthermore, even though the early colonial documents and Bandelier's archaeological research suggest that the human occupation of the islands extends back at least a millennium, little archaeological work on them has been done in recent times. As a result, the antiquity of this Andean pilgrimage center is poorly understood. The nature of the Inca's use of the Islands of the Sun and the Moon remains to be fully investigated, and critical issues concerning the character and function of the pre-Inca occupations on the islands remain unaddressed.

From 1994 to 1996, almost exactly one century after Bandelier worked on the Islands of the Sun and the Moon, we initiated an extensive review of the historical sources pertaining to them and directed an archaeological study of their prehispanic remains. The overall goals of the research were first, to examine the historical documents about the Inca occupation and use of the islands; second, to assess the accuracy of these documents; and third, to determine the extent to which the Inca center was founded on, and developed from, earlier religious traditions of the Lake Titicaca region. The fieldwork included systematic surveys of both the islands, the mapping of their major sites, and test excavations at several of their most important Inca and pre-Inca sites. This book presents the results of our historical and archaeological work and offers a comprehensive description of one of the most important religious pilgrimage centers in the ancient world.

The End of Empire

In 1531, Francisco Pizarro and a small force of men landed on the northern shores of the Inca Empire. Word of these strangers, and of their horses, ships, weapons, and hunger for gold, quickly spread throughout the realm. But Pizarro and his soldiers were preceded by a plague of European diseases that had ravaged the empire, and the ruling Inca, Huayna Capac, and his appointed heir had just died. The largest empire ever to develop in the Western Hemisphere was in a state of civil war as two half brothers, Atahualpa and Huascar, battled for control. As Atahualpa emerged victorious, he was told of intruders on the edge of his newly won empire. Seeking advice on the sudden and unprecedented arrival of unknown peoples, Atahualpa sent a group of priests to consult the great oracle of Pachacamac located on the central coast of Peru. The shrine, a source of political counsel for generations of kings, predicted that Atahualpa would defeat the strangers and retain the empire. The prediction proved to be ill advised, as within a short time, the Spaniards had captured Atahualpa. Eight months later, after providing one of the richest ransoms in history, Atahualpa was executed. The Spaniards attracted a large number of native allies who sought to free themselves from Inca rule, and within a few months and after several decisive battles, the empire began to collapse. In 1533, the Spaniards entered and occupied Cuzco, the Inca capital located in the central highlands of modern Peru. By 1572 the remnants of the Inca nobility had either been assimilated into Spanish colonial society or exterminated. The conquistadors and the Spanish monarchy that they represented were the undisputed rulers of the empire.

At its height on the eve of European contact, the Inca Empire stretched from southern Ecuador to central Chile, comprising much of what is now Peru, Bolivia, and parts of northern Chile and northwestern Argentina (Map 1.1). On the perimeter of this vast state were Inca forts, and imperial armies could be raised at a moment's notice to quell rebellions over the huge territory. Within the provinces, Inca administrators built roads, storehouses, cities, and temples.

Historical sources and archaeological data suggest that the Inca expansion began sometime in the late fourteenth or early fifteenth century. Within a few generations the Inca had extended beyond their traditional heartland of the Cuzco region to dominate hundreds of different ethnic groups, many of which had been rulers in their own right before their domination by the Inca.[3] They quickly conquered the lands between Cuzco and the Lake Titicaca region to the southeast. The empire then spread to the northwest and eventually incorporated a population of at least six million.

The great city of Cuzco was the political and religious center of the Inca Empire. Known as the center or "navel" of the world, it was home to the dynastic order that ruled the realm. Inca mythology tells that the city was founded by the first Inca, Manco Capac, who began a noble lineage that ran unbroken for some eleven generations (Table 1.1). Traditionally, the Inca are thought to have aggressively expanded the geographical limits of their state under Pachacuti Inca Yupanqui, the ninth ruling Inca. A warrior-king of legendary proportions, Pachacuti is frequently credited with reorganizing much of Cuzco as well as its social and political institutions. It is also said that Pachacuti made the first imperial conquests in the Lake Titicaca Basin to the southeast. According to oral accounts recorded by the Spaniards, Topa Inca, second son to Pachacuti, assumed the role of Inca at the death of his father. Decades later, Huayna Capac, the eldest son of Topa Inca, inherited the rule and continued expanding the

Facing page

MAP 1.1. Empire of the Inca. In 1532, the Inca Empire was the largest empire to develop in the New World. Its capital city, Cuzco, lay near its center, while the important area of Lake Titicaca was to the southeast, between what is now Peru and Bolivia.

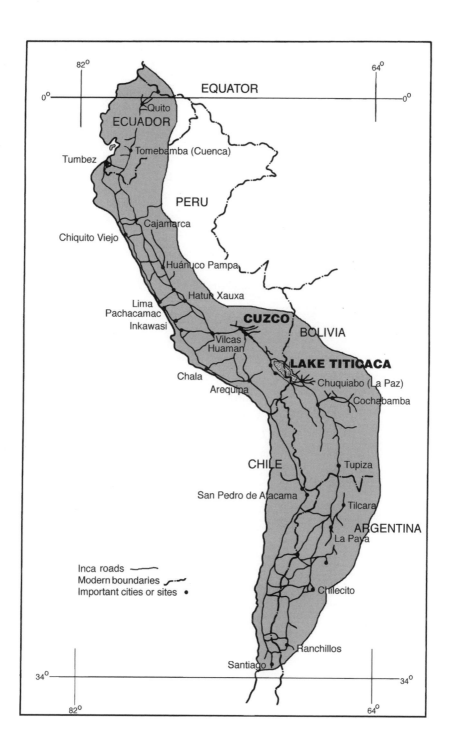

82° 64°

EQUATOR

0° 0°

Quito

ECUADOR

Tumbez Tomebamba (Cuenca)

PERU

Cajamarca

Chiquito Viejo

Huánuco Pampa

Hatun Xauxa

Lima
Pachacamac
Inkawasi

CUZCO

Vilcas
Huaman

BOLIVIA

LAKE TITICACA

Chala Chuquiabo (La Paz)

Arequipa Cochabamba

CHILE Tupiza

San Pedro de Atacama

Tilcara

ARGENTINA

La Paya

Inca roads
Modern boundaries
Important cities or sites •

Chilecito

Ranchillos

Santiago

34° 34°

82° 64°

empire until his sudden death, about the time that Pizarro began exploring the shores of the Inca Empire.

The authority and power of the reigning Inca was, in theory at least, absolute, and was passed down from generation to generation. In reality, the reigning Inca was like other monarchs of archaic states in that he was subject to the political pressures of the ruling elite. Legitimacy was profoundly important for the rulers of the state, particularly a new Inca emperor. Much effort was expended in securing a consensus from the nobility that a new ruler had a legitimate right and was fit to rule. For instance, within the dynastic order of the

Table 1.1. Traditional List of Inca Kings. Cuzco was the ancestral home of the thirteen dynastic rulers who are said to have reigned before the arrival of the Spaniards in 1531.

	Ruler
(1)	Manco Capac
(2)	Sinchi Roca
(3)	Lloque Yupanqui
(4)	Mayta Capac
(5)	Capac Yupanqui
(6)	Inca Roca
(7)	Yahuar Huacac
(8)	Viracocha Inca
(9)	Pachacuti Inca Yupanqui
(10)	Topa Inca Yupanqui
(11)	Huayna Capac
(12)	Huascar
(13)	Atahualpa
	(European Invasion of 1531)
(14)	Manco Inca
(15)	Paullu Inca

Inca, it was considered best if the principal wife of the ruling Inca was a close relative, preferably a sister. Furthermore, the ruling elite gained semidivine status through the state cults that associated the ruling Inca with the Sun, and his sister-wife, called the Coya (queen), with the Moon. The nobility of the state carefully followed the prescribed ritual behavior, which both demonstrated and legitimated their right to rule.

The Shrines of the Incas

Besides worshipping the Sun and the Moon, the peoples of the Andes revered an immense host of objects (such as individual mountains, caves, springs, lakes, and rocks) that were believed to be endowed with powerful "animas." These sacred objects are known in Quechua, the language of the Inca, as *huacas* (shrines). At the time of the Spanish invasion, there were thousands of smaller *huacas,* scores of major *huacas,* and perhaps a dozen great *huaca* sanctuaries that received pilgrims from across the Andean world.

The most powerful shrines required conspicuous amounts of goods for their maintenance and were attended by hundreds, if not thousands, of individuals. These *huacas* were often established by the Inca state to be largely self-sufficient, and they controlled considerable allotments of agricultural land and camelid herds. Offspring of the animals and produce from the fields were sacrificed to the shrine and were used to support its attendants. The Inca themselves worshipped many such *huacas*. However, their cosmology placed paramount importance on the Sun and the Moon.

The Inca state invested substantial energy and resources in developing a religion that served, among other things, to unify their far-flung empire. Throughout the Andes, Inca priests established temples at major *huacas* that were dedicated to the state religion. These religious monuments existed side by side with local shrines and served to emphasize the enormous power the Cuzco nobility held over the lives of their subjects. Conquered peoples were not required to abandon their own *huacas* or religious beliefs, but they were compelled to acknowledge the superiority of the Sun and the Moon, as well as their earthly descendants in Cuzco, the ruling Incas.

The most powerful shrines of the empire were also the final destinations for pilgrims. As centers of religious importance with profound political and cultural implications, these shrines were heavily invested in by the Inca state. Splendid altars and temples were built for elaborate public rituals involving costly sacrificial objects and multitudes of people. Occasionally, human sacrifices were offered to these shrines as well. Furthermore, permanent support personnel were sent to the shrine. Since the primary role of the attendants was to maintain the shrine, they were exempt from all other tax and tribute owed to the state. This special status placed them above the commoner population of the empire but below the nobility.

The Great Sanctuaries of the Empire

Hundreds of important Inca *huacas* were located around the empire. However, a very select few stood out as shrines of pan-Andean significance. The three most important sanctuaries of the Inca Empire were the Coricancha in the city of Cuzco, the temple of Pachacamac on the central Pacific coast, and the Islands of the Sun and the Moon in Lake Titicaca.

The Coricancha

The most famous sanctuary in the Inca Empire was the Coricancha, called the Templo del Sol (Temple of the Sun) by the Spaniards. The Coricancha translates as "Golden Enclosure," a name that perhaps derives from the gold sheets that were attached to its walls. This great sanctuary was located on a slight rise in the heart of Cuzco, near the confluence of two small rivers that flowed through the city. It was built out of the exquisitely cut stone blocks for which the Inca are justifiably famous. The Coricancha was actually a series of buildings that were most likely temples to various deities. Together, these temples, a plaza area, and adjoining terraces formed an impressive architectural complex that dominated the center of the city and was visible from a great distance. The importance of this complex is reflected in the fact that, according to some accounts, it was where the first mythical Inca couple built their house and began the process of creating a great empire (Photo 1.1).

The Coricancha contained the finest gold and silver objects of the empire. Because of this, the temple was sacked by the Spaniards even before they established a secure rule over the Andes. Nevertheless, we know something about the organization of the complex and the activities that occurred within its confines from the various literate Spaniards and natives who lived in Cuzco during the Early Colonial Period. The Coricancha was made up of a group of buildings dedicated to various deities: the Sun, the Moon, the Stars, the Thunder, the Rainbow, and the creator god Viracocha. The most important shrines in the complex, however, were those of the Sun and the Moon. Their

PHOTO 1.1. The Coricancha. The Coricancha (Golden Enclosure) was the focal point for the major ceremonies of the imperial city of Cuzco. It housed a series of temples, including shrines to the Sun and to the Moon. Today the church and monastery of Santo Domingo stand above the Inca remains.

images were housed in separate chambers adorned with gold and silver respectively. Cobo offers the following description of the Temple of the Sun:

> The most important and most sumptuous temple of this kingdom was the one located in the city of Cuzco; this temple was held to be the chief center or capital of their false religion and the most venerated sanctuary that these Indians had, and for that reason, it was visited by all of the people of the Inca empire, who came to it out of devotion on pilgrimages. This temple was called Coricancha, which means "house of gold," because of the incomparable wealth of this metal which was embedded in the temple's chapels and walls, its ceilings and altars. (Cobo 1990:48–49 [1653: Bk. 13, Ch. 12])[4]

The Coricancha was of such significance to the Inca that imperial coronations were held within it (MacCormack 1990:13). The central icon of the Coricancha was a highly venerated gold image of the Sun called Punchao (sunlight), which by the end of the empire had become almost synonymous with Inca rule. It was before this statue that the great Pachacuti was crowned emperor, taking the royal headband that was in the hand of the statue (MacCormack 1990:12). Various early colonial writers state that the image was in the shape of a man (Sarmiento de Gamboa 1906 [1572]; Molina 1943 [ca. 1575]). Likewise we are told that the Coricancha also housed the silver image of the Moon, which was in the form of a woman (Molina 1943 [ca. 1575]; Garcilaso de la Vega 1966 [1609]). These were without a doubt the two most sacred idols of the late prehispanic Andean world.

After the fall of the Inca Empire, the monastery of Santo Domingo was built on the site of the Coricancha, and much of the original compound was destroyed. Substantial Spanish alterations have drastically changed the architecture of the complex. Nevertheless, a fair amount of it remains, and examples of its superb Inca stonework can still be seen.

The Coricancha was originally a local shrine of the pre-imperial Inca peoples. A number of separate archaeological excavations have been conducted in and around the temple area over the past two decades by Cuzco archaeologists, including Luis Barreda Murillo, Arminda Gibaja Oviedo, Alfredo Valencia Zegarra, and, most recently, Raymundo Béjar Navarro. They have each recovered exceptionally high quality Early Inca pottery (ca. AD 1000–1400), indicating that the special character of the site extends back before the establishment of the empire.

The importance of the Coricancha cannot be underestimated. The indigenous name for the Inca Empire, Tawantinsuyu (the four parts together), was derived from the four great spatial divisions that together made up the realm. These four quarters, or *suyus*, radiated from the Coricancha as the center of the Inca world. The northwest quarter of the empire was referred to as Chinchaysuyu, and the northeast was named Antisuyu. The two southern quarters included Collasuyu to the southeast and Cuntisuyu to the southwest. The Inca Empire was seen as the sum of these four parts, and for the Inca, the Coricancha marked the most sacred spot in the universe. Furthermore, it housed the images of the Sun and the Moon and represented the location of imperial coronations, where candidates to the throne were granted the power of the empire.

Pachacamac (Maker of the World)

Another important shrine, called Pachacamac, was located on the coast a short distance south of modern-day Lima. This large center is consistently described in the chronicles as an area of immense religious importance.[5] For example, Cobo writes:

In magnitude, devotion, authority and richness, the Temple of Pachacama was second only to the magnificent (Cuzco) Temple of the Sun. Since it was a universal sanctuary, people came to the Temple of Pachacama on pilgrimages from all over the Inca empire, and there they made their votive offerings. (Cobo 1990:85 [1653: Bk. 13, Ch. 17])[6]

In the center of the complex was a series of massive adobe platforms, the largest of which contained a temple that housed the creator god Pachacamac. Pilgrims, both noble and common, made offerings and received advice at this universally recognized oracle.

After the incorporation of Pachacamac into the Inca Empire, the oracle remained an important *huaca*. The chronicles suggest that the emperors Topa Inca, Huayna Capac, Huascar, and Atahualpa each visited the shrine seeking advice. We are also told that the Inca constructed various state installations at Pachacamac, including a Temple of the Sun and lodgings for the priests, attendants, and guards. Furthermore, quarters were constructed for the chosen women of the state who served in the temple, and lodgings were built for the pilgrims who visited the Sanctuary (Cieza de León 1976:334–337 [1553: Pt. 1, Ch. 72]; Cobo 1990:85–90 [1653: Bk. 13, Ch. 17]).

Francisco Pizarro sent his brother, Hernando, to investigate Pachacamac. On his arrival at the oracle, Hernando Pizarro learned that pilgrims from as far away as 300 leagues (approximately 1,600 kilometers) visited the principal image of Pachacamac. He also learned that the lords of the surrounding polities came annually to make sacrifices to the shrine. The official report from this expedition tells of Hernando Pizarro's encounter with the *huaca* or idol of Pachacamac:

> The captain went along with them and said that he wanted to see the idol that they had . . . It was in a good house well painted in a very dark, smelly, very small room. They have a very dirty idol made of wood. They say it is their god, the one that nurses and supports and maintains them. At the foot of it they had offered some gold jewels. It is so venerated that only the pages and servants that it appoints serve him; and no other dares to enter, or are worthy of touching the walls of its house . . . They come to this devil in pilgrimage of 300 leagues with gold and silver and clothes, and those who arrive go to the watchmen and make their requests, and he enters, and speaks with the idol, and he says that it is granted. (Xérez 1985:136–137 [1534]; authors' translation)[7]

Hernando spent almost a month in the town and temple area of Pachacamac looking for gold. He then returned to the highlands with the spoils and added them to Atahualpa's ransom.

Systematic archaeological research at Pachacamac began in 1896 with Max Uhle's (1903) investigations. Historical and archaeological work on this pilgrimage center has continued throughout the twentieth century. It is now known that the occupation of Pachacamac is of great antiquity, and it is widely speculated that the site was already a pilgrimage center during the period of Wari control (AD 600–900) of the coast (Schreiber 1992:106; Morris and von Hagen 1993:121), well before the Inca occupation.

Islands of the Sun and the Moon

Upon initial contact with the Inca Empire, the Spaniards were told that the Sun first emerged from a sacred rock on an island in Lake Titicaca (Photo 1.2). They also learned that the founding couple of the Inca Empire rose from this island. Furthermore, informants told the Spaniards that the island housed a

PHOTO 1.2. The Island of the Sun. The southeast end of the island (foreground) is closest to the mainland. The Sacred Rock is located on the extreme northwest end of the island (upper center). (Photograph courtesy of Johan Reinhard.)

PHOTO 1.3. According to Inca mythology, the Sun first emerged from a large rock on the Island of the Sun. This rock, also called the Titikala, can still be seen. Note the road leading to the rock as well as the Inca ruins in the foreground. The plaza area, where offerings were made to the rock, can be seen at the center left.

series of temples that was part of a religious complex on the southern shores of the lake and that the largest temple stood beside the revered rock (Photo 1.3).

The first Europeans to view Lake Titicaca were two members of Francisco Pizarro's forces who arrived at the lake in late December 1533 or early January 1534. From their report, and others that followed, we learn that there were indeed two sacred islands, one called Titicaca (Island of the Sun) and the other Coati (Island of the Moon). Cobo visited the islands about eighty years after Pizarro's explorations and interviewed many of the local inhabitants. He provides a fine introduction to the sacred islands:

> On the basis of its reputation and authority, this sanctuary was the third most important one for these Peruvian Indians. (Notice that for our purposes here we are treating it as if it were a single entity.) Actually, it comprised two magnificent temples, which were located on two separate islands of Lake Chucuito [Titicaca].[8] And since both islands are close to the town of Copacabana, we use

this name to make reference to the sanctuary. One of these islands was called Titicaca, and the other Coata [Coati]. The former was dedicated to the Sun, and the latter to the Moon. (Cobo 1990:91 [1653: Bk. 13, Ch. 18]; parentheses in original)[9]

Cobo's descriptions of the Islands of the Sun and the Moon agree with, and are partially derived from, those of Ramos Gavilán (1988 [1621]). Cobo and Ramos Gavilán visited the Lake Titicaca region during the same decade, although they belonged to different religious orders and lived in separate towns. Ramos Gavilán resided in Copacabana, a town that was controlled by the Augustinians and that continues to the present day to be a major Christian pilgrimage destination. Cobo spent time in Juli, a major Spanish religious center initially established by the Dominicans, but later taken over by the Jesuits.[10] Both of these authors furnish extensive eyewitness accounts of the Inca remains on the islands and relate how pilgrimages were conducted to them. Most important, Ramos Gavilán and Cobo offer detailed descriptions of the Inca shrine complex on the Islands of the Sun and the Moon in the century following the Spanish Conquest. These two chroniclers represent what we believe to be the most accurate and essential sources for the early prehistory of the islands.

According to Ramos Gavilán and Cobo, the religious complex on the Island of the Sun included the Sacred Rock called Titikala (where the Sun and the Moon were born), a temple to the Sun and other sky deities, and a large labyrinthine structure that housed the "chosen women" of the state who attended the shrine. In addition, Ramos Gavilán and Cobo describe a large temple on the Island of the Moon that is now called Iñak Uyu. They also state that the political and ideological importance of the islands was immense and that the Inca Empire invested huge resources in maintaining various temples, storehouses, and roads on the Copacabana mainland as well.

The Imperial Cults of the Sun and the Moon

To understand the importance that the Islands of the Sun and the Moon had for the Inca, we must examine the imperial cults that developed around them. Like most Andean peoples, the Inca observed and explained the world around them through symbols of gender (Silverblatt 1987:40). According to Inca cosmology, the Sun as well as the Moon held important gender-related roles. The Sun was largely associated with the ruling Inca and masculinity. The Moon, on the other hand, was affiliated with the royal wife of the Inca (Coya) and femininity. As Silverblatt (1987:54) writes, "The coya, as daughter of the Moon and representative of all womankind, enjoyed the same relation to her divine mother that the Inca had with its father the Sun. Like gendered mirrors, the Inca worshipped the Sun assisted by the male high priests of the empire, as the Coya prayed to the Moon, accompanied by her 'sorceresses,' or select priestesses." The Inca used this same gender pairing to explain the relation between the heavenly bodies. For example, the early chronicler Blas Valera writes:

> The Moon was the sister and wife of the Sun, and Illa Tecce [the creator god] has given her part of his divinity, and made her mistress over the sea and winds, over the queens and princesses, and over the process in which women give birth; and she is queen of the sky. They called the Moon "Coya," which means queen. (Valera 1950:136 [ca. 1585]; translation by Silverblatt 1987:47)[11]

At the time of the European invasion, solar and lunar worship with gender-based elements was widespread throughout the Andean world. This is illustrated by the 1656 testimony of Hernando Hacaspoma, who, while being questioned during an anti-idolatry campaign in Cajatambo (in the north-central highlands of Peru), tells of the creation of men and women in the remote Lake Titicaca region:

> . . . all men adored the Sun as their creator because there was a tradition of their ancestors that the Sun raised men in the east in Titicaca and he raised them with loin cloths, that they call *carbolic,* and he ordered the women to adore the Moon as the mother and creator of women and who provides them food and gives them clothing. (in Duviols 1986:151; authors' translation)[12]

By the end of Inca rule there was an inseparable link between the ruling emperor and the Sun. As the central figure at all public ceremonies for Sun worship, the ruling Inca stood as the sole mediator between the populations of the Andes and the cosmological forces of the heavens (Bauer and Dearborn 1996). The Inca elite usurped direct access to the generally acknowledged powers of the Sun, taking it as both ancestor and patron. The inseparable relation that existed between the Sun and the Inca elite was clearly portrayed in the Punchao, the central Sun idol of the Coricancha. The close relationship between the ruling Inca and the Sun was reinforced by the fact that the Punchao contained a substance made from the dried hearts of previous Inca kings in its center (Toledo 1924:344–345 [1572]).

The worship of the Sun by the Inca is universally noted in the chronicles, and there are abundant references to, and descriptions of, the solar cult. In contrast, descriptions of lunar worship by the Inca are exceedingly rare and are generally brief. We know, for example, from Polo de Ondegardo that offerings were made by women to the Moon at the time of childbirth and during lunar eclipses, but there are few detailed accounts describing the rituals involved. Nevertheless, the chroniclers do make it clear that the role of lunar worship was the task of women and that it was both a widespread and an important aspect of Andean culture. Molina, for example, describes the adoration of the Moon within the confines of the Coricancha in Cuzco:

> They also took out an image of a woman, which was the huaca [shrine] of the Moon, which was called Pacsamama (Moon Mother). Women were entrusted with this image, and consequently when it was taken out of the house of the sun, which is where they had her shrine, where the belvedere of Santo Domingo is now, women carried (the image) on their shoulders. The reason why women were responsible for it was because they said it was a woman, which is what the statue resembled. (Molina 1943:49–50 [ca. 1575]; translation by Silverblatt 1987:55)[13]

Garcilaso de la Vega offers another rare description of the Temple of the Moon in the Coricancha. In this passage he stresses the linkages between the Moon, silver, and the royal wife of the Inca:

> One of these halls was dedicated to the Moon, the wife of the Sun, and was the one nearest the principal chapel of the temple. All of it and its doors were lined with plates of silver, which by their white color showed it to be the hall of the Moon. Her image and portrait was placed like that of the Sun and consisted of a woman's face drawn on a silver plate. They used to enter this hall to visit the Moon and commend themselves to her as the sister and wife of the Sun and mother of the Incas and all their progeny. Thus they called her Mamaquilla, "Mother Moon." They did not offer sacrifices to her as they did to the Sun. On either side of the figure of the Moon were the bodies of dead queens, arranged in order of antiquity. (Garcilaso de la Vega 1966:181–182 [1609: Vol. 1, Bk. 3, Ch. 21])[14]

Within the colonial accounts of Inca religious activities the importance of the Moon is eclipsed by descriptions of solar worship. The gender-based identity of lunar worship is, perhaps, the greatest factor in the scarcity of descriptions concerning the Moon cult. An indigenous informant "justified" this in 1621 to Rodrigo Hernández Príncipe stating:

> The reason why the Indians did not pay much attention to women when they wrote their histories is an ancient tradition. Because not even the Inca paid much attention to the worship of the Moon, being the responsibility of women. (in Duviols 1986:466; authors' translation)[15]

As solar worship dominated the records of the Spaniards, so did the Island of the Sun overshadow that of the Moon. This bias in the sixteenth- and seventeenth-century literature is not surprising, given the strong patriarchal organization of Spanish religion and society. Nevertheless, a careful analysis of the available historical accounts makes it clear that the Islands of the Sun and the Moon were both important centers of solar and lunar worship. People traveled long distances and suffered great hardships to view these islands and to participate in the rituals carried out in Copacabana. The celebrated reputation that these shrines had earned was a major impetus for the Inca state to assert their political control over them and to invest considerable resources in their maintenance. In turn, the construction of imperial facilities on the islands helped to raise the status of their shrines as well as the status of the people who controlled them. Like other important pilgrimage centers, these shrines served the state, as the state served them.

Pilgrimage Centers and the State: A Theoretical Perspective

The existence of a pilgrimage center constructed by a large empire such as the Inca in the southern end of Lake Titicaca raises a number of interesting theoretical issues. In particular, it focuses our attention on the relationship between the formation and expansion of preindustrial states and the development of large, multiregional pilgrimage centers. It furthermore requires us to consider the role that state ideologies played in the maintenance and promotion of large pilgrimage complexes.

Ideology is at once the most elusive and powerful of tools used by early states to project their authority. It is elusive because it is intensely personal and is imbued with different meanings. At the same time, precisely because it is so personal, and thus capable of reaching the individual, it can be one of the most powerful means to assert the authority of the ruling elite. Viewed in this way, pilgrimages and large state-controlled shrines played important roles in defining and legitimizing the power of the elite within early states by designating the elite as the rightful "owners" of the shrine. Pilgrimages and large state-controlled shrines also played critical roles in legitimizing and reinforcing the social and political status of non-elite individuals as they participated in rituals at the shrine, and they contributed to the development of a multiregional religion that provided a unifying theology to the state.

From this perspective, a pilgrimage center provides an ideal opportunity to materially depict a state ideology. It is a classic example of a hegemonic ideology "materialized" in the sense defined by DeMarrais, Castillo, and Earle (1996). Selected natural features, culturally modified forms, architecture, artifacts, and ritual activities are converted into a comprehensive metaphor for transmitting the ideals of the state religion and society. This is particularly significant in the Andes, where nonstate "folk" religions had a tradition rich in metaphors of social creation from inanimate, natural objects. As MacCormack (1990:8) describes, "The Andes abounded with myths of origin . . . Each kin group, however small, thus knew the place whence their first ancestor had come forth . . . The primary Andean process of generation was the transformation of rocks and of inanimate matter in general into human beings." MacCormack correctly notes that general Andean themes underlie and unify the mythohistories of most Andean ethnic groups. In particular, she describes how the specific locations from which ancestral kin, including those of the ruling Inca elite, were believed to have emerged were classified by the indigenous populations of the Andes as sacred places (MacCormack 1990:8). In doing so, she identifies a strong linkage between the "great tradition" of Inca state religion and earlier, more modest folk traditions. In effect, when a local shrine is co-opted by a state, the social, ideological, and political significance surrounding that sacred area is increased dramatically. This is because the local shrine and its underlying beliefs become incorporated into a much larger ideological system shared by thousands of others.

Furthermore, the mere fact that a pilgrimage center associated with the dominant state exists on or near an older sacred site sends a powerful message of cultural dominance or legitimate succession. From the Delian League and Rome in the classical world through the fragmented states of medieval Christendom in Europe to the pilgrimages in the Hindu and Moslem states, elites have reworked a particularly "sacred" area into the endpoint of a physical and spiritual journey that transformed a pilgrim from a member of a local ethnic group or village into a participant in a larger state system. In the same way that a local set of beliefs is merged with a ~~larger ideological system~~, an individual is transformed from being a member of a village to being a member of a large regional cultural reality built around a state, its institutions, and its ruling elite.

The Inca, in fact, were experts at this type of ideological manipulation, drawing on earlier traditions and creating new ones to suit the needs of their empire. The Inca use of the Islands of the Sun and the Moon and the adjoining Copacabana area for state ideological purposes has to be understood on several levels. First, the co-option of this renowned shrine complex from the local population in the fifteenth century was an unambiguous display of the might and authority of Inca rule. Furthermore, the use of gendered symbols such as the Sun (male) and the Moon (female) and the sanctification of natural features of the landscape, such as the sacred outcrops, were consistent with "traditional" Andean conceptions of proper ritual that developed long before the expansion of the Inca Empire. Moreover, the actual pilgrimage and ritual acts performed by the pilgrims had both political and personal meanings. The act of participating in the pilgrimage reinforced the status of the pilgrims, whether commoners or members of the elite. In this sense, it was a profoundly political act. On the other hand, there is little doubt that for many pilgrims the journey held deep religious meanings that were not consciously perceived by them as overtly political. These three levels of meaning—the openly political and conscious, the subtly unconscious that reinforced values of the Inca state, and the deeply felt religious sentiment by some participants in the pilgrimage—represent the range of meaning associated with this great ritual complex.

Pilgrimages and pilgrimage centers worldwide have traditionally been understood by two broad classes of theory. One theoretical perspective begins with Emile Durkheim (1965). As Eade and Sallnow (1991:4) note, "This Durkheimian approach to pilgrimage is sometimes given a Marxist slant. Here, the cults are implicated in the generation and maintenance of ideologies which legitimize domination and oppression." In this view, religion and ideology are not inherently sacred products of the human mind, collective or otherwise, but are the products of competing social forces (Coleman and Elsner 1995:199). As Coleman and Elsner (1995:229, n. 14) suggest, this viewpoint sees "the sacred as society divinised." From this perspective, state-sponsored and state-controlled pilgrimage centers are constructions by the elite to perpetuate class distinction, political authority, ideological legitimacy, and divine sanction of the existing social order.

One of the great examples of a state leader creating a pilgrimage center to aid in the maintenance of empire is that of Constantine after his legalization of Christianity. Glenn Bowman (1991) argues that the first pilgrimage center in Christendom was "consciously created as such by the emperor Constantine to provide physical anchorage for the written texts of the newly adopted state religion with which he hoped to unify the empire" (in Eade and Sallnow 1991:1). Another salient example is the cathedral of Santiago de Compostela in northwest Spain. Santiago (St. James) was renowned as a fighter against the Moors, and the ideological power of his putative remains in the cathedral was intimately tied to Christian efforts to retake the Holy Land in the Crusades (Coleman and Elsner 1995:106). A pilgrimage to this shrine most certainly served to immerse the pilgrim in the ideology of anti-Islamic expansion and western European military campaigns.

The second class of theory is what Eade and Sallnow refer to as a "Turnerian" approach. For Victor Turner (e.g., 1979; Turner and Turner 1960), such religious constructions actually served to subvert the established social order (Eade and Sallnow 1991:5). Turner viewed such cults not as hegemonic devices that reinforced existing statuses, but as counterhegemonic institutions. In this perspective, shrines challenged the authority of the state by setting up alternative and competing religious icons that conformed to religious orthodoxy but did not need to be controlled by a hierarchy.

There are hundreds of examples of such "counterhegemonic" shrines in history and ethnography. Medieval European Christianity is replete with cases of pilgrimage shrines that were created outside of, and in many cases antithetical to, the interests of the Church. In the Americas as well, many pilgrimage centers developed in a context of popular dissatisfaction with the social order. The famous case of Padre Cicero Romão Batista, a late-nineteenth-century indigenous priest from northeastern Brazil, illustrates how a shrine can be created by individuals outside of the authority of ecclesiastical or state officials. Padre Cicero befriended socially unacceptable people and thus was already under suspicion by the church hierarchy when a "miracle" occurred during mass. He was subsequently dismissed by the Church and went into politics. However, years after his death, the town where he conducted his ministry attracted thousands of pilgrims. The pilgrimage was outside the control of the Church authorities, and it served to counter the interests of the status quo. As related by Robinson (1997:42), Padre Cicero's town "remains a Holy City, the new Jerusalem, the centre of the world, the land of Salvation" for the thousands who travel there. It survives as a nominally Christian shrine, worshipped according to official Church doctrine, but in reality it serves to defy the very authority that it imitates.

Numerous local pilgrimage destinations and shrines around the Andes can also be interpreted as popular expressions of resistance by the local peoples against political forces beyond their immediate control or, at the very least, as local shrines controlled by non-elite populations. There was, in fact, a multitude of sacred places in the Andes at the time of the Spanish invasion. These *huacas* varied in size and significance from local places or objects venerated by a single family to regionally important shrines observed by many, if not most, of the people who lived around them. These *huacas* may have been "pilgrimage destinations" in a limited sense, but they were largely worshipped and maintained by a relatively small and culturally homogeneous group of people in a confined geographical area. In these instances, the Turnerian perspective works well, and it explains the varied social, political, ideological, economic, and cultural forces that revolve around the shrines.

The Inca shrine complex in the southern Lake Titicaca Basin, however, was profoundly different from these local shrines. Along with the multitude of local *huacas* in the Andes that are understandable in a Turnerian framework, there were a few select *huacas* that were centers of pan-Andean religious importance (e.g., the Coricancha, Pachacamac, and the Islands of the Sun and the Moon). Although these great *huacas* also served as local shrines for the people who lived near them, they were principally famous as the destination for long-distance pilgrimages. The fact that long-distance pilgrimages were made to these shrines distinguished them from local *huacas* or even from regionally important shrines. With the largest shrines of the empire there was not only a quantitative difference in the number of people who visited the shrines and the resources that were dedicated to them, but there was a qualitative difference in the role of the *huaca* within the state and society. The pilgrimage complex in the southern Lake Titicaca Basin essentially became a state institution, albeit one with local roots. This final destination point, the complex on the Islands of the Sun and the Moon, was designed to project certain meanings associated with Cuzco-Inca culture and a political ideology that was foreign to the basin.

The shrine complex on the Islands of the Sun and the Moon is a clear example of a massive state investment by the Inca in religion. We believe that a Durkheimian approach is the most appropriate theoretical tool for understanding such an enormous Andean pilgrimage center. In effect, we approach the problem of the origin and maintenance of the sacred islands as one tied to the development of complex polities in general. The Inca shrine was designed to project certain meanings associated with Inca culture and political ideology. That is to say, the experience of the pilgrims as they traveled through the Copacabana area was carefully orchestrated and controlled by the Inca state. We argue that the role of the Lake Titicaca shrine complex was more akin to Constantine's efforts in the Holy Land and to the Spaniards' use of the cathedral of Santiago de Compostela than it was to the large-scale visitation and worship of the thousands of local shrines that dotted the Andean religious and geographical landscape.

In the case of the island sanctuaries and a few select shrines in the Inca Empire, the Durkheimian framework is the most relevant for understanding the nature and function of state ideology in a sacred place. From this perspective, the development of multiregional pilgrimage complexes (with temples, support buildings, attendants, and so forth) only occurs in the context of state levels of organization. In the first instance, this is because only states have the capacity to mobilize labor, provision the attendants, and maintain the infrastructure of such a large complex. Furthermore, these kinds of pilgrimage complexes serve huge regions, integrate numerous ethnic groups, and therefore fit precisely into the ideological needs of multiethnic, regional state organizations.

It is from this perspective that we explore the sites on the Islands of the Sun and the Moon in Lake Titicaca. Our ultimate goal is to understand the antiquity of this pivotal pilgrimage center and the role of sacred sites in the development, legitimization, and organization of complex societies in the Andes. Given, however, that the Inca were foreign invaders into the Lake Titicaca region, it is necessary to define the historical and cultural context into which the Inca expanded. In doing so, we will find that the Inca were but the last in a series of complex polities to control the island sanctuaries.

2 | THE LAKE TITICACA BASIN AND ITS PREHISTORY

THE LAKE TITICACA BASIN lies between the Cordillera Real and the Cordillera Blanca in the southern Andes. Between these two mountain ranges are the deep blue waters of Lake Titicaca at 3,810 meters above sea level (m.a.s.l.). The lake drainage is over 50,000 km² in size and stretches between the two cordilleras from east to west and from the pass of La Raya in the north to the large desert salt flats of Uyuni and Coipaso in the south (Roche et al. 1991:84). The lake itself covers an area of around 8,500 km². This unique geographical and ecological region has nurtured the development of civilizations for several thousand years.

In the first section of this chapter, we provide a brief overview of the people and the geography of the Lake Titicaca Basin. In the second section, we outline the prehistory of the region, including the arrival of the first hunter-gatherers, the development of the first sedentary villages, the rise of complex polities, the development of the Tiwanaku state, and the emergence of a series of complex "kingdoms" along the lakeshore just prior to the arrival of the Inca.

The Lake Titicaca Basin

Most of the population of the Titicaca Basin today lives within a few kilometers of the lake. Away from the lake, populations thin rapidly into sparse settlements of herders and marginal farmers. This settlement pattern is a direct result of the geography of the basin. The large body of water raises ambient temperatures near the lake and extends the growing season along the lakeshore. This thin strip of land is one of the most productive areas of land in the Andean highland, and it has long attracted human settlement.

Many islands are also found in the lake. The largest islands, such as Amantaní and Taquile near the Peruvian town of Puno, Pariti located in the southern lake, and the Islands of the Sun and the Moon found off the shores of Copacabana, support modern communities (Map 2.1). In contrast, the smaller islands are generally uninhabited. These islands are usually owned by nearby

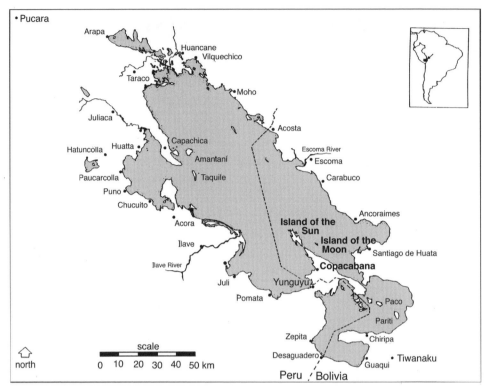

MAP 2.1. Lake Titicaca. The Islands of the Sun and the Moon are located off the Copacabana Peninsula in the southern part of the lake. The lake itself covers an area of around 8,500 km².

communities and are used for fishing stations, groves of trees, and some cultivation or the pasturing of animals.

The cold, open, and rugged territory surrounding Lake Titicaca has long fascinated travelers, naturalists, and scholars. The altitude and the low rainfall in the dry season (May to September) create an arid environment for most of the year. This austere landscape blooms, however, with the rains that begin in October and November. Red, blue, and yellow flowers of agricultural plants grow among the green pastures and transform the region from a high-altitude desert into a rich and productive agricultural landscape (Photos 2.1 and 2.2). The hill slopes above the lake support large areas of potato cultivation, and the higher elevations (above 4,000 m.a.s.l.), called the *puna,* are covered with

PHOTO 2.1. The floodplain near Lake Titicaca provides rich farmlands.

PHOTO 2.2. Today, as in the past, most of the inhabitants of the region live near the lake.

PHOTO 2.3. Llamas and alpacas on the Island of the Sun. Camelids have long been an important part of the Lake Titicaca economy.

tough highland grasses that furnish pasturage for Andean camelids, particularly llamas and alpacas (Photo 2.3).

The early Spanish chronicler Pedro de Cieza de León provides one of the first detailed written accounts of the region by an outsider. It is a description that still evokes the images that a modern traveler sees and feels in the high altiplano landscape:

> The region of the Collas is the largest of all Peru, and in my opinion the most thickly settled. It extends from Ayaviri as far as Caracollo. To the east lie the mountains of the Andes, to the west the promontories of the snow-capped sierras and their flanks, which descend to the Southern Sea. Aside from the territory occupied by their settlements and fields, there are great unsettled regions full of wild flocks. The lands of the Colla are all level, and through them run many rivers of good water. In these plains there are beautiful broad meadows always thick with grass, and part of the time very green, though in summer they turn brown as in Spain. The winter begins, as I have written, in October and lasts until April. The days and nights are of almost equal length, and this is the coldest region of all Peru, aside from the high, snow-capped sierras, because of its elevation. It is so high that it is almost equal to the sierras. The fact of the matter is that if this land of the Colla were a low-lying valley like that of

Jauja or Chuquiabo, where corn could be raised, it would be considered one of the best and richest of much of these Indies . . . But as it is so cold, corn cannot grow nor any kind of tree; on the contrary, none of the many fruits produced in other valleys can be raised here. (Cieza de León 1976: 270 [1553: Pt. 1, Ch. 99])[1]

Cieza de León's description of the region as both "green" and "cold" captures the paradox of a high, intertropical climatic zone tempered by a huge body of water. The high altitude and montane qualities of the region, such as low temperatures and humidity, alter its tropical character toward conditions more typical of alpine areas (Dejoux and Iltis 1991:11). Yet the intense rainfall in a restricted summer season creates a highland landscape that blooms with natural plants and agricultural fields.

Mean annual rainfall in the Lake Titicaca Basin is highly variable and ranges from approximately 500 to 1,500 mm/yr., with the driest areas found in the south and the wetter regions in the north. The median annual temperatures vary between 7° and 10°C (Roche et al. 1991:86–87). Although the basin as a whole has a fairly cold climate, the median temperatures at the lake edge are often higher than 8° C (Boulangé and Aquize 1981). In general, temperatures are higher near the lake and become progressively colder away from the water. This, of course, is a function not only of the water mass but also of the elevation, which increases with distance from the lakeshore.

The Past Climate of the Basin

The climate of the Titicaca Basin has varied throughout prehistory. Recent research indicates that substantial changes in rainfall and temperature have occurred over the past millennia. Even in this century, the lake level has fluctuated more than six meters (Roche et al. 1991:84). One of the principal reasons for such fluctuations is the large drainage area for the lake. Small changes in rainfall and other hydrological patterns in this vast region can have substantial effects on the lake level. In addition, the cross-section of the lake is like a funnel with long, shallow sides and a deep, narrow center. Due to this topographical feature, small fluctuations in the total lake volume can dramatically affect its size.

The data on the paleoecology of the Lake Titicaca Basin come from several projects. For example, the Quelccaya ice cap, located roughly midway between Cuzco and the northern side of the lake, has yielded important insights into climate change in the Andes (Thompson et al. 1985; Shimada et al. 1991). Likewise, two separate series of limnological cores sunk in the southern end of the lake under the ORSTOM-UMSA[2] project (Wirrmann et al. 1990; Wirrmann et al. 1991; Ybert 1991) and the Proyecto Wila Jawira (Binford et al. 1996) have served to further increase our understanding of the past climate in the region.

Thompson et al. (1985) have reconstructed "wet" and "dry" periods from approximately AD 540 to the present using ice cores from Quelccaya. The standard is based on modern conditions, so a wet or dry period represents a time when the precipitation was substantially greater or lesser than the present. Their data indicate a series of alternating wet/dry periods of around 100–200 years duration throughout the sequence. Most significant for the Lake Titicaca region, there were wetter periods in the first half of the seventh century AD and from the mid-eighth century to the mid-eleventh century AD (Ortloff and Kolata 1993:199). The latter part of the seventh century AD was drier, and there was also an appreciably drier period from the mid-thirteenth to the beginning of the fourteenth century AD.

The ORSTOM-UMSA project furnishes data on lake-level changes during the Holocene (Wirrmann et al. 1990:119–123; Wirrmann et al. 1991:65–67). The period that is of interest to us is from approximately 2000 BC, the date for which we have the first evidence of human occupation on the Island of the Sun, to the Early Colonial Period. Their data suggest a gradual rise in the lake level to around 10–45 meters below the present level by about four thousand years ago. For the next two thousand years the lake continued to rise to approximately 10 meters below present levels. According to these reconstructions, the lake did not reach modern levels until after the beginning of the first millennium AD and before AD 1000.[3]

The existence of an appreciably colder period dating from approximately the late fifteenth to the mid nineteenth century, known as the Little Ice Age (L.I.A.), is accepted by almost all paleoclimatologists and carries important implications for understanding the later prehistory and history of the Lake Titicaca Basin (Thompson et al. 1986; Thompson et al. 1988). Thompson and Mosley-Thompson (1987:105) suggest that this period began around AD 1490 but that the most extreme effects did not begin until the early sixteenth century. Both the beginning and the end of the L.I.A. were very abrupt, as indicated by distinct and dramatic increases in the climate indices in the ice cores. The end of the L.I.A. is placed at AD 1880, with the modern climate characterized by increased annual mean temperatures (Thompson and Mosley-Thompson 1987:107). The Little Ice Age is particularly important for our study of the Islands of the Sun and the Moon because it characterized the climate in which the Inca state expanded into the Lake Titicaca region.

The Ecological Zones of the Lake Titicaca Basin

At first glance, the vast Lake Titicaca Basin appears to be a relatively uniform environmental zone characterized by a large, slightly saline lake, with a high-altitude landscape. From a human geographical perspective, however, the region is a highly complex mosaic, composed of various distinctive ecological zones. Each of these zones has unique resources for supporting human populations.

The economic mainstays of the Lake Titicaca populations are agriculture and pastoralism, augmented by fishing (Photos 2.4 and 2.5) and, more recently, by commercial exchange. Indeed, agriculture, herding, and lake exploitation have been the three main economic activities of the Lake Titicaca Basin during most of its prehistory. As mentioned above, the richest agricultural areas of the region are near the lake. Today this is where the majority of the region's people live, and prehispanic settlement patterns indicate that these areas were always the most heavily settled. The lake edges, both on the mainland as well as on the largest islands, have been favored areas for settlement for millennia, precisely because they are the optimal locations to engage in all three of these economic pursuits.

The majority of the agricultural fields in the Lake Titicaca Basin are located on terraced hillsides. Most of the water for the fields comes from the rains, although on occasion spring water is brought to them via small canals. The major crops are tubers (particularly the tremendous variety of potatoes that grow in the region) as well as beans, quinoa, and barley. Some maize is also produced in protected pockets along the mainland lake edge and on the largest islands.

As one moves from the lakeshore into the higher puna, the climate rapidly becomes colder and drier. Less than 300 meters above the lake level, the terrain changes from a relatively rich lacustrine landscape to treeless rolling hills covered with hardy grasses. Although this area supports thousands of llamas, alpacas, cattle, sheep, and other domestic animals, is it sparsely inhabited by humans. Most of the modern settlements in this region consist of isolated hamlets and small villages; however, there are also a few large towns along the major roads.

PHOTO 2.4. Boats can be made from local lake reeds. In prehistoric times some were small, like these craft, but others were large enough to hold sixty people. (Photograph by George Dorsey in 1891. Courtesy of the Field Museum of National History, negative CSA77427.)

Precontact Languages of the Lake Titicaca Basin

The largest indigenous language group in the Lake Titicaca Basin is known as the Aymara. The greatest concentration of modern Aymara speakers is along the lakeshore, particularly on the west and south sides.[4] Urbanized Aymara speakers are also concentrated in two large cities, Puno and Juliaca, and in many small towns, villages, and hamlets throughout the area.[5]

Most of the larger towns on the Peruvian side are listed in sixteenth-century documents as former prehispanic settlements. These include Hatuncolla, Chucuito, Acora, Ilave, Juli, Pomata, Zepita, and Desaguadero. On the Bolivian side, the towns of substantial size include Escoma, Ancoraimes, Guaqui, Tiwanaku, and Copacabana (see Map 2.1). Most of these settlements were populated by Aymara speakers in the sixteenth century, and they most likely represent the forced clustering of Aymara speakers under Inca rule during the late fifteenth and early sixteenth centuries.

The second most common indigenous language in the Lake Titicaca Basin is Quechua, the language of the Inca Empire. There are dozens of areas in the basin where Quechua is spoken. Quechua speakers are found in abundance in

PHOTO 2.5. Reed boat in Lake Titicaca. (Photograph by Carlos and Miguel Vargas, ca. 1928. Courtesy of Roxana Chirinos Laso.)

the north, but their presence declines substantially south of Puno. Colonial documents indicate that there were also substantial pockets of Quechua speakers in the gold-producing Carabaya region to the east of the lake and in various pockets to the south, particularly in the Cochabamba region.

Other languages mentioned in the colonial documents include Pukina and Uruquilla. Pukina is now extinct, although a small group of itinerant curers, known as the Kalawaya, may speak a modified form of the language. Sixteenth-century documents indicate that Pukina was widely spoken in the South Central Andes. It was, in fact, one of the *lenguas generales,* or "general languages," of Peru, along with Quechua and Aymara. The distribution of Pukina in the sixteenth century covered a crescent-shaped area centered in the north of the Lake Titicaca Basin. One arm reached to the southwest as far as the present Chilean/Peruvian border on the coast, and the other reached to the southeast to about Ancoraimes on the eastern side of the lake. Uruquilla is also called Uro-Chipaya in some texts, although this is not an appropriate term according to modern linguistic research. This language was restricted to a few small pockets in the far southern basin, most notably near the Desaguadero River.

In the sixteenth century, the distribution of Quechua, Aymara, Pukina, and Uruquilla speakers in the Lake Titicaca Basin was a mosaic produced by Inca resettlement policy, earlier migrations, and pre-Inca conflict and alliance patterns. Data derived from church documents and adapted from Cook (1975) help us define these distributions. The Quechua distribution in the Lake Titicaca Basin is the least problematic to explain. The concentration of Quechua speakers in the north most likely reflects an ancestral distribution of Quechua established before Inca expansion into the region. The scattering of Quechua in the eastern, western, and southern basin correlates to the road system. This uneven distribution of Quechua speakers is most likely a result of Inca resettlement policies, which included the movement of large numbers of *mitimaes* (colonists) into the lake region.

Pukina poses a much more difficult linguistic and historical problem. There is no comprehensive lexicon and little of its grammar and vocabulary is known. The correlation of the Uru "ethnic" group with the Pukina or Uruquilla language has been a common hypothesis in the anthropological and linguistic literature from the late nineteenth century up to the present (e.g., Brinton 1891; de la Grasserie 1894; Métraux 1970 [1936]; La Barre 1941:499).[6] However, this position has been questioned by more recent scholarship. Most significantly, Torero (1987) states that there is no connection between Pukina and the other three languages (Quechua, Aymara, and Uruquilla) and that people classified as Uru spoke all of these languages. Bouysse-Cassagne (1987) has presented corroborating evidence that language and ethnicity were indeed very fluid and that there is no direct correlation between Uru and Pukina.[7] Browman (1994) presents a detailed discussion of the relationship between these languages. He notes that the terms "(H)uchusuma" and "Ochosuma" also refer to the Uru (Browman 1994:237). We accept this later linguistic research and view Uru as a social category and Pukina and Uruquilla as distinct languages.[8]

An Overview of the Lake Titicaca Basin Prehistory

The Earliest Peoples

The earliest human occupations of the Lake Titicaca Basin date to the Early Archaic Period before 6000 BC and probably several millennia earlier (Table 2.1). Aldenderfer (1998) has discovered Archaic hunters and foragers at the site of Asana, in the upper Moquegua drainage just west of the Lake Titicaca Basin, beginning at 7500 BC. Following Aldenderfer, we divide the Archaic into Early, Middle, and Late Periods, with dates of 9000–6000, 6000–4000, and 4000–2000 BC respectively (Aldenderfer 1998:51).

The Archaic peoples were groups of hunters and gatherers that lived off wild animals, particularly camelids, deer, and fish, as well as a wide variety of wild plants. Until recently, the Early and Middle Archaic populations of the Lake Tit-

Table 2.1. The General Chronologies of the Lake Titicaca Basin and of the Islands of the Sun and the Moon

Lake Titicaca Basin		Islands of the Sun and the Moon	
Early Colonial	(AD 1532–1572)	Early Colonial	(AD 1532–1572)
Inca	(AD 1400–1532)	Inca	(AD 1400–1532)
Altiplano	(AD 1100–1400)	Altiplano	(AD 1100–1400)
Tiwanaku	(AD 400–1100)	Tiwanaku	(AD 400–1100)
Upper Formative	(500 BC–AD 400)	Late Titinhuayani	(500 BC–AD 400)
Middle Formative	(1300–500 BC)	Early Titinhuayani	(1300–500 BC)
Early Formative	(2000–1300 BC)	Early Formative	(2000–1300 BC)
Late Archaic	(4000–2000 BC)	Late Archaic	(4000–2000 BC)
Middle Archaic	(6000–4000 BC)		
Early Archaic	(9000–6000 BC)		

icaca Basin were poorly understood and in many areas unknown. Recent research has located various Early and Middle Archaic sites in the Ilave drainage and beyond (Aldenderfer 1991). The Late Archaic Period populations are better known. Like their predecessors, they were small groups that hunted, fished, and harvested wild plants. They appear, however, to have been semi-sedentary, engaging in some forms of early horticulture and incipient animal domestication.

The establishment of the first sedentary villages in the region transformed the Archaic Period lifeways. The next period, referred to as the Early Formative, begins around 2000 BC and ends at 1300 BC. The Early Formative cultures developed successful agricultural systems, maintained domesticated animal herds, consistently exploited the lake resources, and established permanent villages. Of course, there is no discrete beginning to the Formative, just as there is no definitive end to the Archaic, but critical changes in the lifeways of the Lake Titicaca Basin peoples mark this transition. Browman aptly noted that after around 2000 BC, there are substantial shifts in the archaeological record, including the adoption of pottery, the use of new architectural styles, and the increased dependence on domesticated plants (1984:119). To these changes we can now add an increase in population size, greater sedentism, a shift in lithic technologies from large to small bifacial points, and an apparent increase in lake exploitation.

The development of fully sedentary villages, subsisting predominantly on agricultural and lacustrine resources, was a long and uneven process. Various archaeologists stress different characteristics as important in this process. We argue that the development of permanent residential structures that were aggregated in villages is the defining characteristic of Early Formative lifeways, as distinct from those of the Late Archaic. Also important are the cultural concomitants of sedentary village life. The existence of permanent villages implies a reliance on stable food sources as well as population levels above those of most hunter-gatherer societies.

In the Lake Titicaca Basin, the Early Formative hamlets and small villages were undifferentiated settlements of no more than a few dozen households. Intensive archaeological surveys in the greater Juli area and reconnaissance work throughout the northern and southern sides of the lake have revealed numerous Early Formative sites distributed largely along the rivers and the lake edges (Stanish et al. 1997). We hypothesize that other early villages were spread throughout the entire basin, with river and lake edges as favored locations.[9]

The Middle Formative Period begins with the establishment of ranked societies at approximately 1300 BC, and it ends around 500 BC. During this period, there is evidence of corporate labor projects that were well above the capacities of individual households. This is a major cultural feature associated with the development of moderately ranked or simple chiefly societies. The results of increasingly complex labor organization are particularly evident in the remains of corporate architecture at sites such as Qaluyu, Chiripa, Tiwanaku, Pucara, Tumatumani, and Titimani. These and other major settlements of the Lake Titicaca region are also associated with the development of specialized ceramic and stone art traditions. The ceramics are more elaborate in this period and include decorated fiber-tempered Chiripa wares to the south and non-fiber-tempered Qaluyu ones to the north. Alongside these complex pottery styles were other recently defined ones, such as Early Sillumocco in the southwest region (Stanish and Steadman 1994; Steadman 1994, 1995).

It is significant that the first recognizable site-size ranking occurred during the Middle Formative Period. Many polities are distinguished by a two-tiered, site-size distribution—regional centers and villages. The regional centers were most likely the residences of emergent elite groups or chiefly lineages. These settlements are distinguished by their large size, their corporate architecture, and the concentration of specialized craft production that took place at them. Aspects of craft specialization at the regional centers are reflected especially well in the surviving pottery and the stone stelae. Furthermore, certain kinds of elite or ceremonial architecture develop in the form of small rooms with plaster floors, canals, and other structures showing evidence of nondomestic activities (e.g., see Hastorf 1998). In contrast, the village sites are composed entirely of simple domestic structures. Each of these small sites was affiliated with a regional center via a variety of cultural mechanisms.

The later part of the Middle Formative Period in the Lake Titicaca Basin was characterized by the development of numerous small polities. These include the cultures represented by the Cusipata Phase of Pucara, the Early Sillumocco near Juli, Chiripa Mamani, Kalasasaya, Early Ckackachipata, and others (Chávez 1988; Stanish et al. 1997; Hastorf 1998). The Middle Formative was a time of an emergent elite that shared a regional Lake Titicaca Basin ideology, which is evident in the production of a distinctive stone art style named Yaya-Mama by Sergio and Karen Chávez (Chávez and Chávez 1975). Most frequently represented on stone stelae and slabs, this style has been found on monoliths at numerous sites throughout the southern lake region.

The Middle Formative Period ends and the Upper Formative Period begins in the Lake Titicaca Basin with the emergence of the first markedly ranked societies. In general, an economic hierarchy paralleled the adoption of hereditary social and political ranking. This process was uneven and occurred at different times throughout the region. In the Tiwanaku/Chiripa and Pucara areas in the extreme southern and northern ends of the Lake Titicaca Basin, markedly ranked societies developed early, perhaps around 500 BC. In other areas, such complex societies did not develop until several hundred years later. In general, however, by the turn of the millennium, most of the Lake Titicaca Basin was dominated by large chiefly societies of varying levels of complexity. Nevertheless, from the earliest times, the societies in the far southern and northern basin were precociously larger and more complex than their contemporaries elsewhere in the region.

The settlement patterns of the Upper Formative are correspondingly more complex than those of the Middle Formative. Many of the regional centers of the Middle Formative disappeared, but a few continued and dramatically increased in size. These Upper Formative primary centers contained large (generally more than 10 × 10 m) sunken courts constructed with stone slabs. It is likely that these courts developed out of the smaller elaborate rooms of the Middle Formative. They also included large plaza areas and architecturally enhanced hilltops that may have served as pyramid-like structures. Stelae were placed in the courts or the plaza areas. Usually, the elite/ceremonial architectural structure was built on top of a hill. The flanks of the hills, in turn, were surrounded by domestic structures.

Most of the primary centers of the Upper Formative covered areas of between five and fifteen hectares. We have identified more than a dozen of these primary centers in the Lake Titicaca Basin, including Chiripa (Hastorf 1998) and Taraco (Kidder 1943) as well as Incatunuhuiri near Ichu (Kidder 1943); Palermo near Juli (de la Vega 1997; Stanish et al. 1997); Cerro Mincheros near Puno (Stanish et al. 1998); Wanina and Paucarcolla–Santa Bárbara in the Capachica Pampa (Stanish et al. 1998); and Titimani in the Santiago de Huata Peninsula of Bolivia (Portugal Ortiz 1988).

Along with these primary centers, two substantially larger sites developed in the region during the Upper Formative: Pucara to the north of the lake and Tiwanaku to the south. We refer to these two exceptional settlements as *primate* centers due to their size. In the case of Pucara, the site extended over an area of about 150 hectares. We do not know the extent of Tiwanaku during this period, but it is safe to assume that it was at least as large as Pucara. These sites were home to hundreds, and probably thousands, of inhabitants, including elite, attached retainers, craft specialists, and resident farmers and herders.

The Upper Formative was a period of extensive competition and interaction. Evidence of conflict between Upper Formative groups is reflected in the remains of human sacrifices, as well as in the art of the time, which includes trophy-head depictions. Ceramic distribution patterns also suggest that exchange relationships intensified between sites and polities during this period. In sum, the Upper Formative was a time of intense political and economic development characterized by fluid relationships between competing and, perhaps at times, allied polities throughout the Lake Titicaca region.

Sometime around AD 200, the Pucara polity collapsed and there was a shift to agropastoral economies in the north. The reasons for this collapse are not known, but a serious drought in the second century AD may have been partially responsible (Binford et al. 1996). A drought could have destroyed the raised-field systems in the northern area that had long supported its growing populations. Raised fields are an intensive agricultural technique first developed in the region by at least 800 BC, and possibly earlier (Erickson 1987, 1988, 1993; Stanish 1994). They were an integral part of the Lake Titicaca Basin economies for more than a millennium. Relict raised fields are found throughout the basin along rivers and the lake edge, where the topography permits.

During this same period, the northern basin polities also ceased to produce stone stelae and fancy pottery, hallmarks of complex elite organization. In fact, the concomitant collapse of complex elite organizations and the rise of agropastoral economies are understandable in the context of a drought. Pastoralism can be a practical solution to drought conditions, but it works against the concentration of wealth by an elite and is inimical to the aggregation of large, dense populations.

The fall of the Pucara polity, in part due to the severe contraction of their raised-field systems, facilitated the emergence of Tiwanaku as an unrivaled regional power. However, there does not appear to be a direct relationship between the demise of Pucara and the expansion of Tiwanaku. Recent carbon dates for the establishment of Tiwanaku sites outside the Tiwanaku Valley suggest that the center's expansion did not occur until at least the sixth century, and probably not even until the seventh (e.g., Seddon 1998 for the Island of the Sun). Yet, Pucara ceased to be a major center after AD 250 (Mujica 1978, 1985, 1987, 1988; Lynch 1981; Steadman 1995). It currently appears that Tiwanaku expanded into a political and economic landscape in the northern lake area that was characterized by Pucara-derived agropastoral polities, with a few stronger and nucleated polities along the rivers and lake edge (e.g., Taraco) where raised-field agriculture was still possible.

The Emergence of the Tiwanaku State

The Upper Formative Period in the Lake Titicaca Basin was a culturally dynamic time. By the end of this period dozens of complex chiefdoms of varying sizes and complexities existed in the Lake Titicaca region. Within this cultural context, Tiwanaku developed as an integrated political entity around the middle of the first millennium AD.

Tiwanaku was an expansionistic state with the capacity to incorporate other polities, both in its core territory of the southern Lake Titicaca Basin as well as throughout the south central Andes (Map 2.2). Its economy was based on local agriculture (both raised fields and rain-fed fields), camelid herding, lake exploitation, as well as commodity production; it also included external mechanisms such as the creation of long-distance exchange and colonial relationships. Ideology, particularly as expressed in art and architecture, played an important part in the construction of the Tiwanaku phenomenon as well. The Tiwanaku state was able to mobilize labor on a large scale and to construct monumental structures in its capital city as well as in a series of secondary centers situated across the Lake Titicaca region and beyond.

The capital of Tiwanaku was located in a wide valley, about two dozen kilometers from the southern lakeshore. This monumental site was one of the first ruins to capture the attention of the early chroniclers (Photo 2.6). The early Spanish historians commented on its impressive stone monuments and speculated on the importance of the site in Andean prehistory. By the turn of the nineteenth century, Tiwanaku had been described by many scholars, including Squier, Uhle, and Bandelier.

This vast planned urban center represented the greatest concentration of people south of Cuzco prior to the Spanish Conquest. Current estimates suggest that the total settlement of Tiwanaku covered around 4–6 km^2 and held a population of 30,000 to 60,000 (Kolata and Ponce Sanginés 1992:332). However, as the capital city of an expansionist state, Tiwanaku was more than a mere concentration of artisans, commoners, and political elite. It also held the major ceremonial architecture of the state. An artificial pyramid, known as the Akapana, dominated the center of Tiwanaku. This monumental construction measured approximately 200 × 250 meters at its base and was more than 16.5

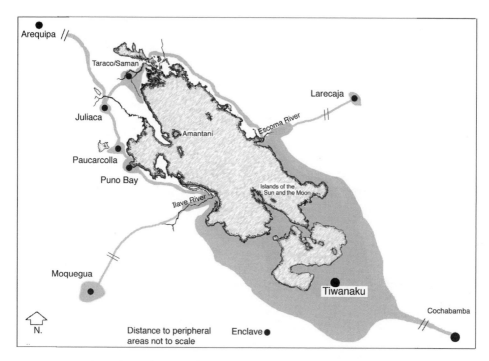

MAP 2.2. Hypothesized areas under direct Tiwanaku control at its height circa AD 800–900.

meters high (Manzanilla 1992:22; Escalante Moscoso 1994). Its exterior was faced with six large stone terraces. The Akapana was by far the largest construction in Tiwanaku and was most certainly one of the principal political and sacred areas of the capital.

Immediately north of the Akapana is a walled enclosure known as the Kalasasaya. It measures about 120 × 130 meters and is elevated slightly above the ground surface (Kolata 1993:143). The enclosure includes a sunken court, several monolithic stelae, and a series of structures of unknown function. Below the Kalasasaya is the semi-subterranean Sunken Court, which is a square, stone-lined construction measuring approximately 27 meters on each side. Its walls were built partially below the ground surface and were decorated with tenoned heads. As in the Kalasasaya, stelae were found in the Sunken Court (Photo 2.7). It is believed that together the closely spaced Akapana, Kalasasaya, and Sunken Court formed a political-religious complex in which elites conducted important rituals that promoted the powers of the state.

PHOTO 2.6. Aerial photograph of Tiwanaku. (Photograph courtesy of Johan Reinhard.)

PHOTO 2.7. A view from the center of the Sunken Court at Tiwanaku looking toward the large entranceway to the Kalasasaya.

At its height around the ninth century AD, Tiwanaku cast its influence over an area that extended nearly 400,000 square kilometers. Within its heartland were a number of large secondary centers, such as Lukurmata (Bermann 1994) on the southern lakeshore; Palermo, Sillumocco-Huaquina, and Tumatumani near Juli (Stanish et al. 1997); and Pachiri north of the capital (Bennett 1934, 1936). Each of these secondary centers carried hallmarks of Tiwanaku state architecture, including sunken courts and stelae. In the case of Sillumocco-Huaquina, a mound may even have been built in the form of a small-scale Akapana (de la Vega 1997).

Many other important areas, located a great distance from the Lake Titicaca region, were also controlled by Tiwanaku. Settlements in these areas represent state colonies, and distinctive Tiwanaku art and architectural style were reproduced within them. For example, the Omo site in the Moquegua Valley is a graphic example of the colonization of the Pacific coastal valleys by the Tiwanaku state (Goldstein 1993). Other areas of Tiwanaku control outside the Lake Titicaca heartland include the Cochabamba region of Bolivia (Anderson and Céspedes Paz 1998), the Larecaja region to the east of the lake (Faldín 1990), and possibly the area of Arequipa in southern Peru, near the major obsidian source of Chivay (Burger et al. 1998).

The development and expansion of Tiwanaku is particularly well documented through the sudden spread of its pottery styles across the Lake Titicaca Basin. The distribution of high-quality Tiwanaku pottery outside a well-defined core area constitutes a radical change from the ceramic distribution patterns of the Upper Formative. In the earlier periods, stylistic borrowing took place throughout the Lake Titicaca region, and borrowed ceramic styles were combined with local innovations. In contrast, during the Tiwanaku Period all pottery styles were based on Tiwanaku canons.[10]

Other indications of Tiwanaku control of provincial territories are the changes in settlement patterns that took place as local systems were incorporated into the expanding state. For instance, in the Juli-Pomata area, the establishment of new sites, the intensification of agricultural production, and the formalization of the road system accompanied the Tiwanaku occupation. These changes indicate that the region was incorporated directly into the Tiwanaku domain. The state consolidated its power over the region through a series of changes in communities' locations and subsistence systems and by the expansion of regional trade and communication.

Although Tiwanaku was an expansionistic state, it was not nearly as complex or as hierarchical as the Inca Empire. The best model for Tiwanaku at the present time is one of a directly controlled heartland that extended north to the Ilave River on the west shore of Lake Titicaca and to the Escoma River on the east (Stanish n.d.). Beyond these territories the Tiwanaku state created enclaves. To date, we have identified several such enclaves around the lake, including the Puno Bay, the Paucarcolla-Juliaca region, and the Taraco area as well as three distant enclaves in Moquegua, Larecaja, and Cochabamba (Stanish and de la Vega 1998). The precise nature of these enclaves is not known, but several features are common to each. First, all of the Lake Titicaca Basin enclaves are on the major road that borders the lake. Second, all enclaves are associated with raised-field systems and major sources of water. The colonies outside the Lake Titicaca region are located in prime agricultural land and are also on major road systems. In short, Tiwanaku created a network of strategically located, surplus-producing colonies that furnished the state with the goods that maintained its complex political economy.

Why Did Tiwanaku Collapse?

After the rapid expansion of the Tiwanaku state, there appears to have been a gradual, centuries-long retraction of Tiwanaku influence across the south central Andes. Ortloff and Kolata (1993) have argued that the proximate cause of the Tiwanaku collapse was a drought that destroyed the raised-field systems in the core territory. Environmental disaster alone, however, cannot account for the complete collapse of state systems. In fact, the Quelccaya ice cores also indicate a short but severe drought from AD 650–730, which corresponds to a period of Tiwanaku expansion (Thompson et al. 1985). As with Pucara, the drought would have greatly affected Tiwanaku's intensive agricultural production. But, unlike Pucara, the end of the Tiwanaku state witnessed the virtual collapse of all Tiwanaku artistic iconography, settlement patterns, economic systems, and political organization. By inference, we can presume a profound cultural shift occurred between the Tiwanaku and post-Tiwanaku periods in the entire Lake Titicaca region.

History and ethnography teach us that other factors, including political fractionalization, ruptures in trade networks, and the rise of competing polities, usually are concomitants to the environmental and economic declines of first-generation states such as Tiwanaku. These and other factors were also most likely critical in the decline of Tiwanaku influence throughout the region. Goldstein, for instance, argues that the fall of Tiwanaku in the Moquegua Valley, as represented by the regional center of Omo, was associated with a violent episode: "The downfall of the system came from within. All indications suggest that the sudden and deliberate destruction of the Omo site in the tenth century came at the hands of rebellious Tiwanaku provincials, rather than any outside agent" (Goldstein 1993:42). The causes and effects of the Tiwanaku collapse are numerous and remain to be explored with future research.

The Rise of the Aymara *Señoríos*

A curious parallel to the collapse of Pucara is that in the post-Tiwanaku periods there was a renewed emphasis on agropastoral economies, but this time throughout the basin. Raised-field systems were essentially gone by the fifteenth century, if not earlier, and with their decline went the capacity to aggregate populations and concentrate wealth production (Stanish 1994). It was in this period of cultural and economic change that the great Aymara polities developed.

The fall of Tiwanaku provided the context for the development of a network of independent polities frequently called the Aymara *señoríos,* or "kingdoms." These polities formed along the shores of Lake Titicaca after the fall of Tiwanaku and continued until the Inca Conquest of the region in the fifteenth century. We refer to this time of regional development as the Altiplano Period (AD 1100–1400), after Lumbreras (1974a) and Hyslop (1976). The Aymara *señoríos* relied on rain-fed terrace agriculture and, more extensively, on camelid herds for their economic mainstay. The earlier cultures of the region were pastoral as well, but the Altiplano Period populations intensified the use of the puna grazing lands and created a more dispersed settlement system to maintain their large herds. It is safe to say that it was during this period that the modern Aymara economic way of life, characterized by a heavy reliance on animal herds, farming, lake exploitation, and trade, came into being.

Historical and linguistic information permit us to define several of the political divisions within the circum–Lake Titicaca region during the sixteenth century. Map 2.3, adapted from several sources including Julien (1983), Bouysse-Cassagne (1986), Saignes (1986), and Torero (1987), illustrates the distribution of these divisions during the Early Colonial occupation. Julien (1983) has convincingly argued, however, that these sixteenth-century divisions reflect the former Inca boundaries, which in turn reflected, to a fairly high degree, the immediate pre-Inca cultural landscape.

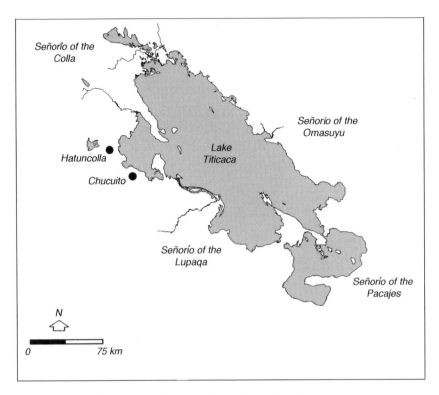

MAP 2.3. Major Aymara *señoríos* of the Lake Titicaca region during the sixteenth century. The Colla and the Lupaqa controlled most of the area along the west side of the lake. Their capitals were Hatuncolla (Colla) and Chucuito (Lupaqa).

The Colla and the Lupaqa were the two largest and most powerful polities in the Lake Titicaca Basin during the immediate pre-Inca period. The Colla controlled a region from somewhere slightly south of Puno to the area of the Canas and Canchis in the north. The capital of the Colla is often said to be the town of Hatuncolla, although it appears that the actual Altiplano Period site was a pre-Inca settlement behind the modern town in a south-southwesterly direction.

The Lupaqa area bordered the Colla in the north and perhaps extended as far south as the Desaguadero River. The Lupaqa also apparently controlled the Island of the Sun prior to the Inca Conquest, although the evidence for this remains somewhat tenuous and is addressed below.[11] The Lupaqa capital was located in the Chucuito area.

The Altiplano Period settlements focused on a series of major hilltop fortified sites, called *pucaras,* each of which was surrounded by many smaller satellite communities.[12] Each *pucara* and its associated settlements most likely formed a single polity that periodically allied with others in times of political necessity. Trade was brisk between these communities, but so was internecine warfare. Such a pattern is not uncommon in the archaeological and ethnographic record. In fact, the coexistence of trade and conflict appears to be a common feature of such societies.

The Altiplano Period is known as a time of extensive regional conflict. Indeed, one of the cultural hallmarks of this time is the development of the *pucaras* that were built, with a few notable exceptions, throughout the Lake Titicaca Basin. One of the largest hilltop fortified sites, Pukara Juli, is surrounded by five fortification walls, totaling more than sixteen kilometers in length (Hyslop 1976; de la Vega 1990; Stanish et al. 1997). Early Europeans mention these impressive sites as they describe the pre-Inca times of the region (Cieza de León 1976:273 [1553: Pt. 1, Ch. 100]; Cobo 1979:140 [1653: Bk. 11, Ch. 13]). These hilltop fortified sites stand as monuments to the endemic warfare of the region during the immediate post-Tiwanaku period.

The Aymara *señoríos* have traditionally been portrayed as a series of powerful state-level polities. However, recent archaeological work by Kirk Frye has challenged this model. His survey and excavations in the Chucuito area indicate that the Lupaqa did not consolidate political power *until* the Inca Period (Frye 1997). Furthermore, he found substantial architectural, organizational, and artifactual differences between the major pre-Inca fortified hilltop sites. Based upon these data, Frye concludes that the political organization of the Altiplano Period was one of chiefly societies.

Similar conclusions about Altiplano Period political organization are supported by data from the Moquegua Valley to the west. Various sources, including Diez de San Miguel, Cieza de León, and Cobo, strongly suggest that the Lupaqa controlled substantial landholdings in the Moquegua Valley before the expansion of the Inca into the lake region. Yet, archaeological research indicates that the major Lupaqa influence in the Moquegua Valley occurred in conjunction with Inca control of the highlands, rather than before it (Stanish 1985, 1989b, 1992). The Moquegua and Chucuito data corroborate each other and suggest that for most of their existence the Altiplano Period *señoríos* were nonstate-level chiefly societies. The data also suggest that the development of complex political organization among the lakeshore Aymara polities was a *di-*

rect result of Inca influence in the Lake Titicaca region. Perhaps the rapid development of the *señoríos* into large political institutions was induced by the threat of Inca military conquest. Whatever the case, with the arrival of the Inca in the Lake Titicaca region and the fall of the area's indigenous polities, the cultural landscape changed forever.

3 | INCA AND EARLY COLONIAL ACTIVITIES IN THE LAKE TITICACA BASIN

EARLY COLONIAL PERIOD writers furnish us with a large body of information on Inca and Spanish activities in the Lake Titicaca Basin. Much of this information was produced by members of the many religious orders that were established in the region during the consolidation of Spanish authority. Additional information comes from the chronicles, as well as from official reports to the Crown written in the area or elsewhere, such as in Cuzco or Lima. Other sources include reports by individuals who traveled through the region in the years following the European invasion.

We begin this chapter by reviewing two major Inca origin myths recorded in various early colonial sources. One myth tells of the emergence of the Inca dynasty, and the other recalls the first appearance of the Sun and the Moon from Lake Titicaca. We then turn our attention to the conquest of the Lake Titicaca Basin by the Inca and the later arrival of Europeans in the lake region. These data serve as necessary reference points for our exploration of the archaeological remains on the islands. The topics do not, however, exhaust the historical data available for the Lake Titicaca Basin or for the Islands of the Sun and the Moon. For example, much information exists on the colonization and organization of the Copacabana area by the Inca state, the pilgrimages that took place to the islands during late-prehispanic times, and the various monuments that the Inca built on them. These and other topics are addressed in later chapters.

Ramos Gavilán (1621) and Cobo (1653)

Although the sacred islands of Lake Titicaca are mentioned by a host of early colonial writers, there is no doubt that our two most important sources are Alonso Ramos Gavilán (1621) and Bernabé Cobo (1653).[1] Ramos Gavilán was born in the Andean city of Huamanga (now called Ayacucho).[2] After traveling and working in different regions on the coast and in the highlands of Peru, he arrived at Copacabana in 1618 and immediately began writing his chronicle. The resulting work, *Historia del Santuario de Nuestra Señora de Copacabana* (History of the Sanctuary of Our Lady of Copacabana) was completed and published in Lima in early 1621. In writing his book, Ramos Gavilán took care to interview many of the older members of Copacabana and to personally visit the Island of the Sun.

Cobo spent about a year living near Lake Titicaca. He arrived at the town of Juli in 1616, and sometime during that year he sailed around the lake and visited the Island of the Sun. He mentions that he was still in that province in 1617, when certain Spaniards went to the Island of the Moon to look for gold. Unlike Ramos Gavilán, who began writing soon after his arrival in Copacabana, Cobo continued to travel and collect information for another forty years. It was not until 1653 that he completed his work *Historia del Nuevo Mundo* (History of the New World). Certainly Cobo was a keen observer of Inca remains, but he also relied heavily on the works of earlier writers. For his chapter on the Islands of the Sun and the Moon, Cobo used the work of Ramos Gavilán, although he also added information based on his own personal observations.

It is important to note that both Ramos Gavilán and Cobo visited the Island of the Sun some eighty years after the Spanish invasion of Peru. It is unlikely that they could have talked with anyone who had actually lived in the area during Inca rule. In other words, neither they nor any of their informants were eyewitnesses to the Inca rituals that took place on the islands. Nevertheless, Ramos Gavilán and Cobo lived during a period when the islands' importance in the former Inca Empire was still widely recognized and fine offerings were still being made on both of the islands.

Lake Titicaca and the Origins of the Inca

Through the works of Ramos Gavilán, Cobo, and other early writers, a large number of Inca myths have been passed down to us. Two myths are central to understanding the Inca Sanctuary of the Lake Titicaca Basin: the Pacariqtambo Origin Myth and the Lake Titicaca Origin Myth. Although the Lake Titicaca Origin Myth is of primary interest to this study, many writers offer hybrid versions, combining elements of both myths into a single narrative.

The Pacariqtambo Origin Myth was perhaps the central narrative of the foundation of the Inca state as promulgated by their own historians and intelligentsia. Recorded in over twenty separate chronicles, this myth begins with the emergence of Manco Capac, the first Inca, and his royal brothers and their sister/wives from a cave, called Tambo Tocco, south of Cuzco in the region of Pacariqtambo. The myth describes Manco Capac's northward journey from Pacariqtambo to the Cuzco Valley and his battle with the indigenous people of the region. It recalls the triumphal occupation of the valley by Manco Capac and the establishment of a new dynastic order (Bauer 1991, 1996). Through the Pacariqtambo Origin Myth, the ruling elite of Cuzco were seen as the direct descendants of Manco Capac and as the legitimate rulers of the Inca state.

There is sufficient ethnographic, historical, and archaeological information to indicate that an impressive Inca complex called Maukallaqta, located about 35 km south of Cuzco in the modern district of Pacariqtambo, is directly linked to the Pacariqtambo Origin Myth (Muelle 1945; Pardo 1946, 1957; Bauer 1988, 1991, 1992a, 1992b, 1996). The complex may have been built by the Cuzco elite to commemorate the appearance of their mythical progenitor from a nearby cave.

Numerous chroniclers also indicate that the Inca and other peoples of the Andes believed that the creator god known as Viracocha caused the Sun and the Moon to rise from Lake Titicaca. This momentous event ended a prolonged period of darkness. Sarmiento de Gamboa, writing in Cuzco in 1572, records one such account:

> Viracocha went to this island and he ordered that the sun, moon, and stars leave from it and go to the sky to give light to the world. And this was done. And they say that the moon was created with more clarity than the sun. And that because of this the sun was jealous. When it was time to rise to the sky, he threw a handful of ash in her face, and from that it [the moon] has the softly darkened color that it now has. (Sarmiento de Gamboa 1906:26 [1572: Ch. 7]; authors' translation)[3]

Other writers, especially those who personally visited the Lake Titicaca region, record more details about this myth.[4] For example, Cobo provides this version of the creation myth:

> The shrine of the Sun, which was on the Island of Titicaca, was a large solid crag. The reason it was consecrated to the Sun and worshipped can be traced to a ridiculous story. It is said that in this province the people of ancient times tell of being without light from the heavens for many days, and all of the local in-

habitants were astonished, confused and frightened to have total darkness for such a long time. Finally, the people of the Island of Titicaca saw the Sun come up one morning out of that crag with extraordinary radiance. For this reason they believed that the true dwelling place of the Sun was that crag, or at least that the crag was the most delightful thing in the world for the Sun. Thus a magnificent temple, for those times, was constructed there and dedicated to the Sun, although it was not so magnificent as it was after the Incas enlarged it and enhanced its fame. (Cobo 1990:91–92 [1653: Bk. 18, Ch. 18])[5]

More commonly, however, writers combine the Pacariqtambo Origin Myth with the Lake Titicaca Origin Myth. They speak of the first Inca and his sister/wife appearing on the Island of Titicaca and link this appearance with the parallel emergence of the Sun and the Moon on that same island. The writers then relate how the first Incas left the Lake Titicaca region and traveled to Cuzco via Pacariqtambo. For example, Cobo gives the following account:

Another foolish tale is that . . . the Creator of the world . . . ordered the Sun, Moon, and Stars to go to the Island of Titicaca, which is located in the lake of this same name, and that from there they should go up to the sky. When the Sun was ready to leave in the form of a brightly shining man, he called the Incas, and the Sun himself spoke like an older brother to Manco Capac in the following way: "You and your descendants will subjugate many lands and peoples, and you will be great rulers. Always regard me as your father, and pride yourselves on being my sons, without ever forgetting to venerate me as such." And after he finished saying this, the Sun gave Manco Capac the royal insignia that he and his successors used from then on. And then the Sun went up to the sky with the Moon and Stars, where each one assumed its habitual place. And at once, by order of the Creator, the Inca brothers made their way beneath the earth and emerged at the cave of Pacarictambo. (Cobo 1979:104–105 [1653: Bk. 12, Ch. 3])[6]

In these accounts, rather than simply explaining the origin of the heavenly bodies, the Lake Titicaca Origin Myth explains how the first Inca (analogous to the Sun) and his sister/wife (analogous to the Moon) emerged from the island. Through such retellings Inca intellectuals successfully linked the ruling elite of Cuzco with the principal shrine of one of their most important highland provinces. The origin place of the Quechua-speaking Cuzco elite was mythologically merged with the most sacred place in the Aymara-speaking

Lake Titicaca Basin. The Islands of the Sun and Moon became the ideological beachhead of Inca expansion to the south.

The Inca Conquest of the Lake Titicaca Basin

One of the earliest and most detailed descriptions of the Inca Conquest of Collasuyu can be found in Cieza de León (1976:215 [1554: Pt. 2, Chs. 40–45]). Like Julien (1983), we privilege much of his information above that of other writers because Cieza de León traveled through the lake region in 1548 and interviewed numerous informants. According to Cieza de León, the first Inca incursion into the Lake Titicaca region was initiated by the eighth Inca king, Viracocha Inca, most likely in the middle of the fifteenth century (Table 1.1).[7] This Inca is said to have encountered two large kingdoms or *señoríos* in the western Lake Titicaca Basin—the Lupaqa and Colla—along with several smaller political groups.

Cieza de León suggests that at the time of initial Inca expansion into the Lake Titicaca region the Lupaqa and Colla were opponents deadlocked in nondecisive conflict and that Viracocha Inca negotiated with both groups. The Colla, fearing to be excluded from a regional alliance at best, or afraid of an Inca-Lupaqa alliance that would surround and crush them at worst, attacked the Lupaqa. The Colla were, however, soundly defeated, and the Lupaqa "king" negotiated a peace with Viracocha Inca.

If Cieza de León's accounts of early Inca activities in the lake region are accurate, then Viracocha Inca failed in his first attempt to conquer the region south of the Colla, settling instead for an alliance with the Lupaqa. During this early period of expansion, the Inca would not have installed direct political control over the basin, but would have established their state as the dominant, albeit not absolute, power in the area.

Cieza de León (1976:232–235 [1554: Pt. 2, Ch. 52]), as well as Sarmiento de Gamboa (1906:75–77 [1572: Ch. 37]) and Cobo (1979:138–141 [1653: Bk. 12, Ch. 13]), indicates that the "actual" incorporation of the Lake Titicaca Basin in the Inca state was accomplished several decades later by Pachacuti, the son of Viracocha Inca. Pachacuti is said to have initiated a new campaign in the area during which the Inca state once again fought and defeated the Colla.[8] Following this victory, Pachacuti is said to have pushed the limits of the empire farther south, bringing the entire Lake Titicaca region under Inca control. By Cobo's account, Pachacuti saw the site of Tiwanaku in the mid-1400s, and

Manco Inca, the son of the last undisputed Inca, Huayna Capac, was born there some two decades before the arrival of the Europeans (Cobo 1990:105, 141 [1653: Bk. 12, Ch. 15; Bk. 13, Ch. 19]).

Recent studies have documented a massive Inca presence in the Lake Titicaca Basin and have recorded the dramatic political and economic impact that the annexation of this region by the Cuzco-based empire had on its indigenous peoples (Hyslop 1976; Julien 1983; Albarracin-Jordan 1996; Stanish 1997; Stanish et al. 1997). As the lake region was incorporated into the Inca Empire, the local populations were forced to abandon their fortified hilltop sites, and the Inca established a series of centers along the major roads. The largest two settlements were Hatuncolla, the center of the Colla polity, and Chucuito, the capital of the Lupaqa.[9] Under Inca control of the region, more than 50 percent of the population was located within 500 meters of the road system, rather than being scattered across the landscape in dispersed communities surrounding the fortified hilltops (Stanish 1997). These shifts in settlement location initiated equally significant changes in economic strategies. For example, raised-field agriculture all but disappeared during Inca times, and the use of rain-fed terraces increased sharply, complemented by an increased use of puna and lake resources (Stanish 1994). Raised-field use had long been declining, due in large part to climatic changes that were occurring in the region. The Inca Period populations adapted to this environmental shift and virtually abandoned raised-field systems for more extensive techniques of rain-fed terrace agriculture and pastoralism.

Besides implementing a massive reorganization of the local populations, the Inca expanded and improved the road system of the region and constructed numerous state facilities (including temples, warehouses, and way stations). Furthermore, the Inca brought thousands of colonists (*mitimaes*) from other parts of the empire to the Lake Titicaca area. They also removed some local populations and sent them to occupy areas outside the basin. Although the policy of state-controlled colonization was common throughout the empire, it was implemented with considerable resolve in the lake region. Archaeological research suggests a marked increase in population around the lake during Inca times, much of which was the direct result of new colonists being brought into the area (Stanish 1997; Stanish et al. 1997).

In short, the occupation of the Lake Titicaca Basin by the Inca Empire resulted in profound changes in the indigenous societies. Settlements were moved, foreign colonists were brought in, and regional economies were altered. Certain groups were decimated, while selected local elites were incorporated into the imperial bureaucracy. Within this process of regional consolidation, the Inca also incorporated the Islands of the Sun and the Moon into their expansionist state. As we will see, these ideologically charged sacred places were appropriated by the Inca authorities and reworked into a great pilgrimage place that both justified conquest and extolled the legitimacy of Tawantinsuyu.

Incorporation of the Sacred Islands into the Inca Empire

There is some ambiguity in the historical sources as to when the Inca first reached the sacred islands of Lake Titicaca. Cieza de León suggests that though Viracocha Inca may have established an alliance with the Lupaqa, his son Pachacuti was the first of the noble Cuzco clan to visit and construct buildings on the islands. Cieza de León (1976:233 [1554: Pt. 2, Ch. 52]) writes, "He [Pachacuti] went out on the great lake of Titicaca, observed its islands, and ordered built on the largest of them a temple to the sun and palaces for himself and his descendants." [10] Elsewhere, Cieza de León (1976:277 [1553: Pt. 1, Ch. 101]) indicates that the labor force was drawn from mainland groups, particularly the Colla. According to him, Pachacuti's visit was followed by those of later Incas as the territory of the empire was extended into southern Bolivia, as well as northern Chile and Argentina. For example, Cieza de León states that as Topa Inca,[11] son of Pachacuti Inca Yupanqui, traveled southward from Chucuito, he, like his father, visited the Sanctuary of the Sun:

> Some of the lords of the Colla offered to go themselves with the Inca [Topa Inca Yupanqui], and with those he chose, he went out on the Lake Titicaca, and praised those who had put up the buildings his father had ordered constructed for the excellence of their work. (Cieza de León 1976:244 [1554: Pt. 2, Ch. 61])[12]

Ramos Gavilán (1988:32, 36 [1621: Bk. 1, Ch. 3]), provides a different chronology for the arrival of the Inca. He says that Topa Inca was the first royal Inca to arrive at the islands.[13] Ramos Gavilán (1988:39–41 [1621: Bk. 1, Ch. 4]) relates a legend about a Sanctuary priest who went to Cuzco to ask Topa Inca to visit the island. The priest told the royal Inca about a rock that was already widely recognized by the local population as the origin place of the Sun. It is said that Topa Inca traveled to the island, realizing that the incorporation of such a shrine into the realm would increase his power.

According to Ramos Gavilán, Topa Inca was so impressed by the Island of the Sun that he ordered its entire native population to be resettled into the village of Yunguyu, outside the larger Copacabana sanctuary. He then repopulated the Copacabana mainland and the island with people selected from across the Inca Empire. Ramos Gavilán (1988:84 [1621: Bk. 1, Ch. 4]) also relates that Topa Inca brought priests to be trained by the previous attendants of the shrine and provided an elite group of women to help maintain it. Topa Inca is believed to have constructed a series of buildings on the island, including a royal palace for himself about a league from the rock. Ramos Gavilán (1988:171 [1621: Bk. 1, Ch. 27]) states that after completing his work on the Island of the Sun, Topa Inca traveled to the Island of Coati to build a shrine dedicated to the Moon, the wife of the Sun.

Ramos Gavilán indicates repeatedly that Huayna Capac, the son of Topa Inca, also played an important role in developing Inca installations on the sacred islands. Not wanting to have been outdone by his father, Huayna Capac visited both of the islands and improved their facilities (Ramos Gavilán 1988:120 [1621: Bk. 1, Ch. 18]). Huayna Capac is also said to have sent two of his own daughters to serve in the Temple of the Sun near the sacred rock (Ramos Gavilán 1988:185 [1621: Bk. 1, Ch. 31]).[14]

Cobo furnishes additional information on the visits to the sacred islands by the royal Incas. However, because he incorporated several different sources into his chronicle, the work is at times contradictory. This is certainly the case for his accounts of the Inca conquest of the Lake Titicaca region and his descriptions of the Island of the Sun. For example, in one section Cobo (1979: 138–141 [1653: Bk. 12, Ch. 13]) indicates that Pachacuti conquered the lake region and that he was the first Inca to visit the Island of the Sun. Cobo then notes that it was Topa Inca who ordered the construction of palaces and temples there:

> The Inca [Topa Inca] continued ahead, and on the way he went to visit the temple at Titicaca. The people of the province had many rafts ready for him to make the passage to that island, where he remained for a few days and ordered the construction of a magnificent palace and other royal buildings; and, having made sacrifices to the Sun, he continued on his way. (Cobo 1979:144–145 [1653: Bk. 12, Ch. 13])[15]

In contrast, in another section of his history, using information taken from Ramos Gavilán, Cobo (1990:92–93 [1653: Bk. 13, Ch. 18]) presents a very different account, in which Topa Inca, while in Cuzco, was approached by an attendant of the island Sanctuary. In this rendering, Topa Inca was the first Inca to visit the island, where he encountered an altar and a temple already dedicated to the Sun. Unfortunately, a great deal more research must take place, both on the sacred island as well as throughout the mainland, before we can begin to critically evaluate these various accounts.

The Early Colonial History of the Island of the Sun

Given the importance of the Island of the Sun in Inca cosmology, it is not surprising that it was one of the first places the Spaniards visited once they began to gain control of the Andean highlands. The earliest eyewitness report of Lake Titicaca and its sacred islands comes from Pedro Sancho de la Hoz.[16] The original account by Sancho de la Hoz is lost; however, Giovanni Battista Ramusio (1550) published an early Italian translation in Venice. A section of the document is worth quoting at length, since it contains an account of the first two Europeans to visit the Lake Titicaca region. Francisco Pizarro sent these men in December of 1533, after the Spanish occupation of Cuzco, to explore the region and to report on its wealth. The trip lasted forty days, and the explorers returned with information on two sacred islands in Lake Titicaca. Sancho de la Hoz writes:

> The Indians say that in the province [of Collao] is a large lake of fresh water which, in its centre, has two islands. In order to learn the state of this land and its government, the Governor [Francisco Pizarro] sent two Christians to bring him a long report of it; they set out in the beginning of December. . . . The two Christians[17] who were sent to see the province of the Collao were forty days upon their journey, and, as soon as they had returned to Cuzco where the Governor was, they gave him news and a report of all that they had seen and learned, which is set forth below. . . . In the middle of the province there is a great lake, in length almost one hundred leagues, and the most thickly peopled land is around its shore; in the middle of the lake there are two islets, and on one of them is a mosque [i.e., temple] and house of the sun which is held in great veneration, and to it they come to make their offerings and sacrifices on a great stone on the island which they call Tichicasa [Titicaca], which, either because the devil hides himself there and speaks to them, or because of an ancient custom, or on account of some other cause that has never been made clear, all the people of that province hold in great esteem, and they offer there gold, silver and other things. There are more than six hundred Indians serving

in this place, and more than a thousand women who make *chicha* [corn beer] in order to throw it upon that stone Tichicasa. (Sancho de la Hoz 1917:148, 161, 163 [1534: Chs. 16 and 18])[18]

The generality of this account suggests that the two men did not visit the islands themselves, but relied on information provided by a knowledgeable informant. Nevertheless, the description, made before the Lake Titicaca area had begun to feel the impact of imperial collapse, offers critical information for understanding the nature of the Inca occupation and the ritual activities that occurred there.

The account tells of not one, but *two* important islands in the lake. One of the islands was called Tichicasa (Titicaca), and though unnamed, we can presume that the other was Coati. These earliest European explorers also indicate that there were religious buildings on the Island of Titicaca dedicated to the Sun. They note that there was a large stone on this island that was worshipped by the people of the region, and that natives came to the island to offer gold, silver, and other items. Furthermore, the report indicates that there were over six hundred (male?) individuals serving the island and more than a thousand women to make and offer corn beer to the sacred rock.

This first visit to the Lake Titicaca region was quickly followed by a large immigration of Europeans. J. Viscarra F. (1901:324) claims to have a copy of a 1620 document that describes the 1536 establishment of the first *doctrina* (missionary parish) in the region.[19] The 1620 document, said to have been written by Francisco de Gamboa (Augustinian), indicates that there were seven subdivisions of Inca Copacabana. According to the document, these seven subdivisions were united in 1536 into the *doctrina* of "the Holy Crosses" by three Spanish captains (Diego de Illescas, Pedro Anzurez, and Sebastián de Benalcazar) with a combined total of no less than 120 soldiers, as well as 5 Franciscans, 3 priests, 2 laymen, and 40 citizens of Spain. Bandelier (1910:63, 133–135) stresses that there are serious reasons to doubt the authenticity of the early foundation date (i.e., 1536). For example, the presence of such a large contingent of Spaniards—totaling almost 170 individuals—in Copacabana during the year that Cuzco was under siege by Manco Inca seems unlikely.[20] Furthermore, Bandelier presents evidence that at least two of the Franciscan priests and two of the captains were not in the Lake Titicaca region at that time.[21]

Another early reference to the Lake Titicaca region is found in a 1539 letter from Manuel de Espinal to the king of Spain. By this time the Spaniards had gained control over much of the crumbling Inca Empire. Francisco Pizarro had just killed his principal rival, Diego de Almagro, and Paullu Inca had been crowned as a puppet ruler of the kingdom. Hernando Pizarro and Paullu Inca left Cuzco to explore the Lake Titicaca region and to aid the Colla, who had requested help from the Spaniards to crush a Lupaqa rebellion. According to Manuel de Espinal, the expedition went to "an island called Titicaca, which is in Collao, where they say that there was much gold and silver, and to search everywhere for it" (1959:363 [1539]; authors' translation).[22]

Paullu Inca was a logical person to accompany Hernando Pizarro on the expedition. This Inca was held in high regard by the inhabitants of the Collao and Charcas (Callapiña et al. 1974:57 [1542/1608]), and Paullu Inca had made a similar (albeit unrewarding) trip with Almagro three years earlier.[23] Furthermore, some sources report that Paullu Inca and other noble Incas had retreated to the Island of the Sun while Atahualpa's forces besieged Cuzco, killing other descendants of Huayna Capac during the civil war (Callapiña et al. 1974:56–57 [1542/1608]).

Although no official report has survived to tell of Hernando Pizarro's journey into the Collao, years later his enemies claimed that Hernando gained a great deal of wealth during the expedition and was responsible for ten men drowning in the lake while they were searching for riches (Rodríguez Barragán 1873: 331, 455). It should be noted, however, that these charges do not specifically mention that Hernando Pizarro arrived at the Island of the Sun or the Moon. Furthermore, because they originated with enemies of Hernando Pizarro, they should not be accepted immediately at face value. On the other hand, it is known that the Spaniards, under Pizarro, were in the Lake Titicaca region in 1538, and it would be surprising if they had not sent a small force to investigate its most famous and putatively richest islands.

Ten years later, in 1548, the Copacabana region, which included the village on the mainland of the same name, its dependent hamlets, and perhaps the islands, was granted as an *encomienda*[24] to García de León. Members of the *encomienda* were immediately sent to Carabaya, a well-known gold-producing region to the northeast of the lake, and two years later to Potosí to the south, to extract precious metals for the landowner (Espinoza Soriano 1972a:1, 14).[25] In 1548 the *encomienda* included 739 taxpayers (i.e., male heads of households) and 334 elders and widows, and we are told that they were all *mitimaes*, which had been "placed there by the Lords of Cuzco to serve the House of the Sun which they had in the Lake Titicaca" (Espinoza Soriano 1972a:10 [1548]). As will be examined in more detail below, various early colonial writers mention the role of *mitimaes* in maintaining Copacabana and the sacred islands.

Around the time that the Copacabana *encomienda* was established, Cieza de León left Cuzco and traveled south into the area of the Collao. As he did so, Cieza de León recorded the legend that the Sun first emerged from the Island of Titicaca. He further suggested that it was for that reason that the island was worshipped.

> The name of this great lake of the Colla is Titicaca, from the temple that was built in the center of the lake. About this the natives had an idea that was pure superstition, and this is that they say their forebears asserted for a fact, like the other nonsense they tell, that for many days they were without light, and when they were all in darkness and gloom, there arose from this island of Titicaca the sun in all its splendor, for which reason they hold the island to be a hallowed stop, and the Incas built there the temple I have mentioned, which was one of the most venerated, in honor of their sun, bringing to it vessels and priests and great treasure. Although the Spaniards on different occasions have removed much of this, it is believed that most of it has not been discovered. (Cieza de León 1976:280–281 [1553: Pt. 1, Ch. 103])[26]

Cieza de León was a careful observer and a cautious reporter who had traveled widely in Peru. In this passage, he mentions that the Inca built a widely venerated temple, dedicated to the Sun, on the Island of Titicaca and that they brought a great wealth of offerings to this temple. Since Cieza de León does not describe any of the Inca remains on the island, we cannot assume that he actually visited it. He may have gained his information secondhand. Nevertheless, it is interesting to note that even though Cieza de León journeyed through the Lake Titicaca area only seventeen years after the arrival of the first Europeans in Peru, the Spaniards had already visited the Island of Titicaca on different occasions looking for treasure.

Spanish Activities in the Copacabana Region

Beginning in 1571, under the direction of Viceroy Francisco de Toledo,[27] the Spaniards implemented a systematic reorganization of native towns and villages across the Andes. In an effort to more efficiently extract tribute, control labor, and provide religious indoctrination to native peoples, the rural populations of the highlands were forced to abandon many of their settlements and were resettled in new towns. Resettlement efforts were conducted in the Lake Titicaca region and affected the Copacabana Peninsula (Espinoza Soriano 1972b:131–132). The resettlement of Santa Ana de Copacabana was formed in 1573, and the general census of the area by Francisco Toledo (1975:72 [1573]) indicates that it contained 4,849 inhabitants, including 953 *mitimaes* and 88 Urus. Ten years later the population is listed as 4,929 (Miranda 1925:147 [1583]).[28]

The next major event of the region was precipitated by a series of early frosts in the early 1580s, most likely a manifestation of the Little Ice Age phenomenon. In an attempt to avert widespread famine, the residents of Copacabana decided to form a confraternity dedicated to a saint other than Santa Ana (MacCormack 1984; Sallnow 1987:65). After considerable debate, they selected the Virgin and founded Our Lady of Copacabana in 1582. Francisco Tito Yupanqui, the grandson of Huayna Capac (via his father, Paullu Inca), carved an image of the Virgin that was almost immediately credited with several miracles.[29] Copacabana, like the islands before it, quickly became the most important pilgrimage center of the southern Andean highlands, a position it continues to hold today.[30] In 1589, the Augustinians gained control of this mainland temple and immediately began to construct a new sanctuary. The basilica would take a vast amount of funds and nearly eighty years to complete (Vargas Ugarte 1956, 2:268–271; Sallnow 1987:66). It still stands today as the magnificent sanctuary of Copacabana.

Mining operations at indigenous shrines of the region provided much of the wealth used to build the Basilica of Copacabana. As late as the 1620s, the shrines of the Lake Titicaca area were still seen as sources of considerable wealth. In 1901 Viscarra (1901:57, 70–72) published a document he claimed was an inventory concerning "contributions" of gold and silver objects made by different communities of the Copacabana Peninsula and of the islands toward the construction of the basilica (Table 3.1). This inventory is said to date to 1617 and to be signed by two senior justices. According to this document, the Island of the Sun provided 33 gold objects weighing more than nine pounds, while the Island of the Moon provided 180 gold objects with a total weight of almost 12 pounds. The 78 "shrine houses" on the Copacabana Peninsula furnished 84 gold objects with a total weight of nearly 12 pounds. Silver objects were even more plentiful. The sixteen largest islands of the lake and various sites on the peninsula contributed a total of 367 objects, with a combined weight of over 209 pounds (419 marks).[31]

Table 3.1. Gold and Silver Contributions for the Construction of the Basilica of Our Lady of Copacabana (data from Viscarra 1901:57, 70–72 [1617?])

Corresponding to the Temple of the Sun, its ornaments, and that of the Incas on the Island of Titicaca, as follows:[1]

		Total weight
6	plates of the sun	00 lb. 18 oz. 12 ads.[2]
8	plates of the moon	01 lb. 06 oz. 09 ads.
9	plates of the dawn	01 lb. 06 oz. 06 ads.
5	plates of the beam	01 lb. 04 oz. 11 ads.
3	plates of the coca	02 lb. 08 oz. 08 ads.
2	plates of hills	01 lb. 02 oz. 03 ads.
33	objects all of gold	9 lb. 10 oz. 00 ads.

Pertaining to the Shrines of the Island of Coati:

		Total weight
6	plates of the sun	00 lb. 13 oz. 05 ads.
8	plates of the moon	00 lb. 15 oz. 04 ads.
10	plates of the fire	00 lb. 10 oz. 08 ads.
5	plates of the embers	00 lb. 11 oz. 02 ads.
12	plates of hills	00 lb. 12 oz. 12 ads.
8	plates of small trees	00 lb. 08 oz. 11 ads.
9	plates of the lake	00 lb. 09 oz. 09 ads.
8	plates of river	00 lb. 05 oz. 11 ads.
10	plates of branch	00 lb. 13 oz. 10 ads.
20	plates of star	00 lb. 14 oz. 08 ads.
21	plates of springs	00 lb. 14 oz. 05 ads.
12	plates of fowl	00 lb. 13 oz. 06 ads.
11	plates of fish	00 lb. 12 oz. 05 ads.
20	plates of raft	00 lb. 13 oz. 13 ads.
20	plates of raftsmen	00 lb. 11 oz. 14 ads.
180	gold objects	11 lb. 15 oz. 03 ads.

[1]Correspondientes al Templo del Sol, al de las vestales y al de los Incas, en la isla del Titicaca, como sigue:

[2]The abbreviation "ads." stands for *adarmes;* there are 16 *adarmes* in an ounce.

Pertaining to the Peninsula of Copacabana and Its Principal 78 *Huaka-uyus* (Shrine Houses):

		Total weight
10	figurines of *wiscachas* (Viscacha)	12 oz. 08 ads.
6	figurines of lizards	14 oz. 10 ads.
8	figurines of snakes	09 oz. 11 ads.
15	figurines of rabbits[3]	13 oz. 15 ads.
5	figurines of *phisakas* (?)	12 oz. 08 ads.
3	figurines of *ccombaras* (?)	14 oz. 11 ads.
9	figurines of *thagjawaras* (?)	12 oz. 08 ads.
11	figurines of *achullas* (?)	10 oz. 14 ads.
7	figurines of kyrkis (?)	15 oz. 06 ads.
74	gold objects	11 lb. 15 oz. 11 ads.

SILVER PIECES

Gathered from the Shrines of the Sixteen Largest Islands and from Those of the Peninsula:

		Total weight
20	various fowl-style plates	25 marks 02 oz.
40	various fish-style plates	20 marks 03 oz.
60	hoops	31 marks 01 oz.
14	links	15 marks 02 oz.
30	sprigs	16 marks 07 oz.
8	rainbows	20 marks 06 oz.
5	small braziers	22 marks 05 oz.
15	pots	32 marks 07 oz.
50	crescents	34 marks 06 oz.
242	objects of silver	219 marks 07 oz.

In addition to these silver pieces, 120 plates were taken from the same islands, which served to form *sactillejos* (?), stalls, and other adornments of the idols.

In all, the 120 pieces have a net weight of 200 marks.

[3] Guinea pigs.

The islands were seen as sources of funds for other projects as well. For example, it is reported that an additional 252 gold objects collected from the large islands of the lake were sent to Lima between 1610 and 1619 to adorn the coffin of Father Francisco Solano. Of these, 24 pieces are said to have been found on the Island of the Moon and 15 on the Island of the Sun (Viscarra 1901:151). In addition, the Spaniards may have removed more than metal from the islands. Salas, as reported by Viscarra (1901:151), indicates that the Basilica of Copacabana was constructed of stones taken from the islands, and Bandelier (1910:262) suggests that stones were taken from the Island of the Moon for churches in Juli.

Summary and Discussion

According to Cieza de León (1553), Ramos Gavilán (1621), and Cobo (1653), the shrine of the Sun on the Island of Titicaca was of great antiquity. Cobo (1990:92 [1653: Bk. 13, Ch. 18]) is very direct on this point: "Whatever the origin of this shrine may have been, it was very ancient and highly venerated by the people of the Collao before they were subjugated by the Inca kings."[32] When the Inca expanded to the islands, perhaps under Pachacuti, they constructed a series of state installations on the islands. Each successive ruler, including Topa Inca and Huayna Capac, enlarged these facilities. If we can believe the early colonial writers, the islands were of such importance that following their incorporation into the empire they were visited by all subsequent Inca rulers. Even Huascar, who lost the empire to his half brother Atahualpa in a civil war on the eve of European contact, is reported to have made a trip to the Island of the Sun (Santa Cruz Pachacuti Yamqui Salcamayhua 1950:267 [1613]). Successive visits to the island sanctuaries by generations of Inca rulers may have been a necessary political act. Such official pilgrimages served to reinforce Inca authority in the Collao, as well as to enhance each Inca's own ideological authority in Cuzco as the legitimate protector of the state religion.

The Early Colonial Period must have been a perplexing time for the inhabitants of the Lake Titicaca area. Augustinians, Dominicans, Franciscans, Jesuits, Mercedarians, and secular priests were all active, and a series of cults to the Virgin were established in different towns of the region, including Pucarani, Pomata, and Copacabana (Sallnow 1987:66).[33] Meanwhile, the Islands of the

Sun and the Moon continued to be worshipped as sacred places by segments of the indigenous populations, and individuals, perhaps representing communities, continued to make offerings on them.[34] Yet at the same time that these offerings were being buried in the sanctuary areas, the Spaniards were conducting expeditions to the islands to extract metals and other objects of value from them.

4 | THE ISLANDS OF
THE SUN AND THE MOON TODAY

Geography, People, and Research

HISTORICAL DATA suggest that most of the islands of Lake Titicaca were considered sacred to varying degrees. Salas (1901:31 [1618]) notes that in the time of the Inca, pilgrimages were made to *huacas* (shrines) on the fourteen or sixteen largest islands of the lake. Various inventories of gold and silver objects collected from these islands, published by Viscarra (1901:57, 70–72), indicate that the Inca did indeed leave elaborate offerings on most them. Furthermore, archaeological research has identified a number of Inca offerings, occupations, and impressive structures on many of the islands (Solc 1966; Niles 1988; Ponce Sanginés et al. 1992; Reinhard 1992b). Nevertheless, there is no doubt that the two most important islands of the lake were those of the Sun and the Moon.

In the first half of this chapter, we offer an introduction to the geography and the people of the Islands of the Sun and the Moon. Particular attention is given to the fact that maize agriculture is possible on the Island of the Sun, and we describe several of the rituals that its inhabitants continue to practice. In the second half of the chapter, we discuss the history of scientific research on the islands. We begin by describing the early-nineteenth-century expeditions to the islands and then summarize the more recent archaeological work that has been conducted on them. We conclude the chapter by outlining the course of our research program on the islands from 1994 to 1996.

Geography and People of the Islands

The Island of the Sun is the largest inhabited island in Lake Titicaca. In contrast, the Island of the Moon is one of the smallest. The lake between the mainland and these two islands is very deep, with official maps recording soundings of at least 50 meters, and possibly as deep as 100 meters. Paleoclimatic reconstructions of the region indicate that the lake was never less than 50 meters deep during the Holocene Period (Wirrmann et al. 1991), which means that the Islands of the Sun and the Moon have been isolated from the mainland throughout the entire sequence of human occupation in the Lake Titicaca region. It is possible that four thousand years ago the separation between the mainland and the present island was a marshy lowland, but even in this period, watercraft would have been required to reach the island.

The Island of the Sun

The Island of the Sun is located on the southern side of the lake, northwest of the Copacabana Peninsula in Bolivia (Map 4.1). The island is about 21 kilometers long and only about 8 kilometers at its widest part (Map 4.2). It comprises about 20 square kilometers of land and takes the form of an elongated H. The island is a geological extension of the Copacabana Peninsula, but sep-

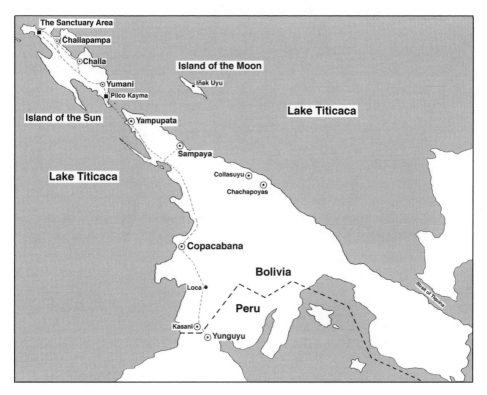

MAP 4.1. The Islands of the Sun and the Moon are located off the Copacabana Peninsula on the south side of Lake Titicaca.

MAP 4.2. View of the Island of the Sun from the south. Note horizontal exaggeration in the south. (Original art by K. Wirt.)

arated from it by 1 kilometer of water. The entire eastern side of the island is a single long ridge that rises out of the lake in the south and continues to the northern end. The Sanctuary area, which includes the Sacred Rock (also called the Titikala) as well as several other impressive archaeological sites, is located at the northern end of the island. The highest peak is Cerro Palla Khasa, with an altitude of about 4,065 m.a.s.l., or approximately 255 meters above the lake.

We classify the Island of the Sun into a number of distinct ecological zones (Map 4.2). The richest zone is near the lake edges and is generally associated with active springs, such as those found in the areas of the Fountain of the

Inca, eastern Yumani, the Challa Bay, northern Challa, Challapampa, and Kasapata. This zone is particularly fertile because it combines well-watered fields with locations near the lake. The soils are generally deep and are kept in place by well-constructed terrace systems. The ambient temperatures in this zone are elevated by the proximity to the lake, resulting in an extended growing season and higher crop yields. This is the ecological zone where most of the maize is grown and, not surprisingly, where most of the modern population is located.

The next richest ecological zone includes the hill slopes immediately above the lake edge (Photo 4.1). These slopes are covered with rain-fed terraces that produce much of the island's quinoa, beans, and potatoes. The principal areas of terraced, hill-slope fields include Cerro Pucara, Apachinacapata, Kea Kollu, Titinhuayani, as well as the Kalabaya Peninsula, the Chucaripupata hillside, and the extreme western side of the island on the Kona Peninsula.

The third most important ecological zone consists of low pampas, found near Challa, North Kona Bay, and South Kona Bay (Map 4.2). These pampas are fed by springs that maintain a rich pasture grass. Each of these pampa areas

PHOTO 4.1. Cerro Kea Kollu is covered with terraces, which is typical of hill slopes immediately above the lake.

has vestiges of former raised-field agriculture that left distinctive patterns on the landscape (Photo 4.2). Most raised-field systems are characterized by long ridges that form waffle-like patterns in lower, seasonally inundated areas. The remains of canals can also be found in Challa and near South Kona Bay. In both cases, the canals connect small streams in nearby ravines with reservoirs and are associated with elaborate Inca sites with niches.

The highest areas of the island are dry and dusty even in the rainy season. There are a few areas of relict agricultural terracing in these high parts, but most of the higher zones of the island were probably used, as they are today, to pasture animals. There is currently little settlement on the higher areas of the island, except for some isolated houses on the southern side of Yumani. On the other hand, a large trail, paved in sections, runs along the summit of the major ridge of the island. So although the ridge tops on the island were not cultivated, they were used as convenient roadways as well as grazing areas to support camelid herds (Map 4.3).

PHOTO 4.2. Raised fields in Challa. Most raised-field systems are characterized by long, low ridges that form waffle-like patterns in lower, seasonally inundated areas.

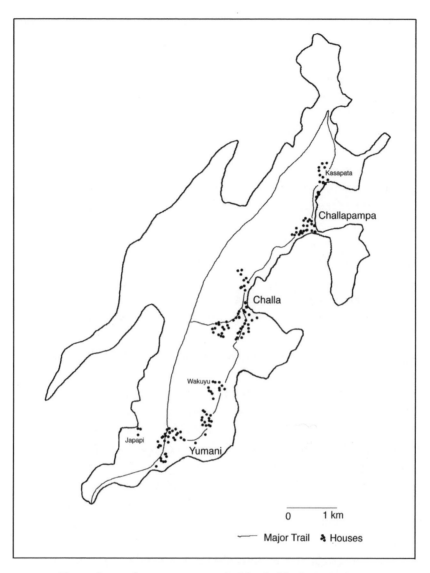

MAP 4.3. The modern settlement pattern on the Island of the Sun. (Adapted from topographic maps based on air photographs from 1956 and 1963.)

The extreme western side of the island represents a special ecological zone and remains something of a mystery for us. It is much warmer than other areas of the island due to its peculiar topography that protects much of this zone from cold winds. Ferns and bracken can be found in protected pockets, and in some cases the vegetation can almost be described as lush, with moist stands of moss occurring near caves. Not surprisingly, we found the remains of agricultural terracing throughout much of the extreme west side. Yet, there is no human occupation in the area today, and we found no evidence of prehispanic habitation.

The rest of the island is composed of marginal agricultural land. The higher and unwatered areas are dry most of the year, and the summer rains are insufficient to maintain crops in most areas of the island without some irrigation from springs. Eucalyptus stands have been planted in some of these marginal areas. This nonnative tree is a successful transplant to the island and provides the bulk of the wood products used by the inhabitants today. As in the rest of the Lake Titicaca region, eucalyptus is pushing out the slower-growing indigenous trees on the island and is the favored tree for the contemporary peoples.

Modern Settlements. For years, two haciendas controlled the island. In the 1950s, the revolutionary land-reform movement that swept across Bolivia redistributed land to the individuals who actually lived on and worked the farms. Now, all land on the island is either privately owned or is held by one of the three communities. The people who live on the island are Aymara speakers (Photo 4.3). Although the island is famous as a major Inca shrine, the people who live on it today are not direct descendants of the Quechua-speaking Inca peoples, but are most likely related to the aboriginal Aymara inhabitants of the region who lived there prior to the Inca Conquest. In fact, the Aymara peoples resisted Inca domination, and early documents are full of references to rebellions in the Lake Titicaca region during the fifteenth century.

Today, the Island of the Sun is divided into three communities: Yumani, Challa, and Challapampa. It is difficult to know precisely how many people live full-time on the island.[1] The latest census indicates that a few thousand people live or own property there, but the population varies because many families maintain two or more homes, one on the island and another in La Paz or Copacabana. The principal economic activities of the islanders involve farming and fishing, a lifestyle that has predominated throughout much of the island's occupation.

PHOTO 4.3. Aymara people in traditional festival dress from the Island of the Sun. The festival was to commemorate the construction of a new community center.

The modern villages cluster near the most productive agricultural land. Map 4.3 shows the settlement pattern as derived from the official 1964 topographic maps of the island (Carta Nacional, Bolivia 1:50,000; Hoja 5746 I and II), as well as recent aerial photographs (Map 4.3). The three major settlement clusters are spread more or less equidistantly along the northeast shore of the island. Interspersed between these villages are hamlets that are located near springs and areas of agricultural land. The southwest side is virtually uninhabited, but it is utilized for grazing, limited terrace agriculture, and eucalyptus tree groves.

The Island of the Moon

The Island of the Moon, also called Coati (or Koati), lies 8 kilometers east of the Island of the Sun and approximately 4 kilometers north of the mainland (Map 4.1). Although the island is a political annex of the community of Yumani, its inhabitants also maintain close relationships with several communities on the northern shore of the Copacabana Peninsula, particularly that of Sampaya.[2] The Island of the Moon, with just over 1 square kilometer of land, is much smaller than the Island of the Sun. It is formed by a single, 3-kilometer-long ridge that rises 115 meters above the lake level. At its maximum width, the island is only 1.2 kilometers wide. The northwest end of the island is defined by a very distinctive steep red cliff, the middle section bulges slightly, and the southeast end tapers to a fine point of sand.

The Island of the Moon has a limited amount of agricultural land, the best of which lies on its north slopes. A notable shortage of fresh water also limits human occupation. During the Colonial and Early Republican Periods, the island was held as a single hacienda; more recently, it was used as a prison for political prisoners.[3] Today, portions of the island are owned by the local villagers and other parts by the national government. The islanders rely largely on a combination of subsistence farming and lake fishing. In the past few years, tourism has become an important economic activity as well.

The population on the Island of the Moon is currently between thirty and forty individuals. Squier (1877:359) states that in 1864 the island housed three to four families. Bandelier (1910:50) reports a permanent population of twelve to fifteen individuals in 1894. In Inca times its population was much greater, perhaps in the hundreds (Salas 1901:48 [1618]). It is therefore doubtful that the inhabitants during Inca times could have supported themselves fully on the limited natural resources of the island.

Agriculture on the Islands

Interpreting the prehispanic settlement patterns on the Islands of the Sun and the Moon requires an understanding of the ecology of the Titicaca Basin, as the islands represent unusual ecological features in the region. Specifically, the overall higher ambient temperatures on the islands provide a longer growing season and permit the cultivation of maize and other agricultural products at a scale not achievable elsewhere in the basin. This is especially true for the production of maize on the Island of the Sun. Although maize is grown in selected areas of the mainland, it is produced in larger quantities and with greater success on the Island of the Sun than at any other place in the lake region (Photo 4.4). Early colonial writers even suggest that the microclimates of the Islands of the Sun and the Moon tempted the Inca to grow coca (Ramos Gavilán 1988:44, 45 [1621: Bk. 1, Ch. 5]; Salas 1901:32 [1628]; Cobo 1990:94 [1653: Bk. 13, Ch. 18]). However, because coca is a subtropical plant that is unable to grow in the altiplano, we discount the possibility that coca actually grew on the island. Nevertheless, these references serve to emphasize the fact that the Island of the Sun is notably warmer than the mainland.

PHOTO 4.4. Maize from the Island of the Sun. During Inca times, maize from the island was considered sacred.

It is important to note that the Sacred Rock area, near the northwest end of the island, is a zone of minimal agricultural potential relative to the island as a whole. Today, it is uninhabited and it was also uninhabited in the late nineteenth century (Bandelier 1910). Nevertheless, we know that during the Inca Period it housed one of the most important shrine complexes of the Andean world. Because there are no strong economic incentives to inhabit this part of the island, we can rule out these factors as primary settlement determinants. Given the ritual significance of the area and its low agricultural potential, major sites near the Sacred Rock can be assumed to have had noneconomic, ritual functions.

Maize and the Island of the Sun

The unusual fact that maize can be successfully grown on the Island of the Sun may be important for understanding the unique role that the island held in prehispanic times. Maize was a major source of nutrition and the base for the maize beer (*chicha*) that was consumed during all Inca rituals. Maize production and consumption in the Inca Empire occurred at all social levels. It was a basic food crop for many peasant communities and a major tribute item to the state. Grown on state-controlled fields with the use of corvée labor, maize was stored in massive granaries established around the empire in Inca regional administrative centers. The major deities of the Inca—the Sun, the Moon, the Stars, and Thunder and Lightning—were assigned large tracts of maize land. The produce from these fields was used to support the cults of these deities.

Maize was also closely associated with the ruling elite. The first maize seeds are said to have been brought to Cuzco by the first mythical Inca and his sister/wife (Betanzos 1987:20 [1557]: Ch. 4]; Hernández Príncipe 1986:466 [1621]; Cobo 1979:104 [1653: Bk. 12, Ch. 3]), and these legendary figures are also credited with the invention of agriculture. Furthermore, two of the most important events in the Inca calendar were the maize planting and harvest celebrations. Both of these festivals were orchestrated by the ruling elite in Cuzco in carefully scripted ritual activities (Bauer 1996).

The Inca considered the maize that grew on the Island of Titicaca, the birthplace of the Sun, to be special. Garcilaso de la Vega describes the unique importance this island-grown maize held for the people of Tawantinsuyu:

> Apart from the temple and its decorations, the Inca kings greatly honored the
> island as being the first place trodden by their forebears when they came down
> from the sky, as they said. They flattened the island as much as possible, remov-
> ing the rocks, and made terraces which they covered with good fertile soil
> brought from a distance so as to bear maize, for the whole of that region is too
> cold for growing maize. On these terraces they sowed the seeds and by dint of
> great care grew a few cobs, which were sent to the Inca as sacred objects. He
> took them to the temple of the Sun and sent them to the chosen virgins in
> Cuzco, and ordered them to be taken to other temples and convents through-
> out the Kingdom, in some years to some and in other years to others, so that all
> might enjoy the grain sent from heaven. It was sown in the gardens of the tem-
> ples of the Sun and houses of the virgins where these existed and the crop was
> divided among the peoples of the provinces. A few grains were cast in the gran-
> aries of the Sun and of the king and in the municipal barns, so that its divine
> power would protect, increase, and preserve from corruption the grain gath-
> ered there for the general subsistence. Any Indian who could get a grain of that
> maize or any seed to cast in this barn thought he would never want for bread
> for his whole life, so great was their superstition in any matter relating to the
> Incas. (Garcilaso de la Vega 1966:191 [1609: Pt. 1, Bk. 3, Ch. 25])[4]

Like relics from a holy place, the grains of maize from the Island of the Sun were distributed across the empire as physical manifestations of its divine nature and as a symbol to the subjugated peoples that the Inca state controlled the production of this sacred crop. In other words, maize was one natural product that lay at the heart of Inca religion. The Island of the Sun's unusual capacity to produce high-quality maize in a cold and high environment most likely contributed to its status as a sacred place.

Modern Rituals on the Island of the Sun

The Aymara peoples of the Lake Titicaca Basin have a rich and varied religious life. As outsiders, we were only able to glimpse the surface of these rituals, but our ability to observe some of them offers insight into the nature of Andean pilgrimages and shrine worship. In spite of the fact that, as in all cultures, Andean rituals perpetually change as people negotiate and renegotiate their relationships with natural, social, and supernatural forces, there appear to be some enduring aspects of these religious behaviors that can be used to help interpret the archaeological record.

In the introductory section of this book, we outlined the distinctions between the Turnerian and Durkheimian theoretical views of pilgrimages and shrines. The Turnerian approach emphasizes shrines as examples of ritual institutions created in class societies as a means of resisting the power of social elites, while in the Durkheimian perspective, shrines are used in the maintenance of state ideologies. Although we have already stated our theoretical position that the Inca occupation of the Islands of the Sun and the Moon is best understood within a Durkheimian approach, we also recognized that concurrent with all such sanctuaries were nonstate- or non-elite-controlled rituals that are best understood within the Turnerian approach. Furthermore, and most significantly, many state religions have their roots in local traditions. These state or "great traditions" evolve from a particular class of folk or domestic rituals that have implications for reinforcing social class and status quo. This class of rituals is public and is laden with politically and socially charged content. It is a reasonable proposition that much of Inca state ritual had relatively recent roots in peasant folk culture of the Central Andes.

The Aymara people living on the Island of the Sun today guard many of their ritual secrets from outsiders. However, they did permit us to participate in some ritual events. We observed the syncretism of Christianity and folk beliefs in the periodic pilgrimages to mountaintops during which the Stations of the Cross are intermixed with Andean mountain worship. Such treks are important village events that occur with some frequency, usually coinciding with Catholic sacred days and national holidays.

Another class of rituals known generically as *pagos* are regularly conducted in Aymara villages. A *pago,* or "payment," to the earth involves a series of prescribed ritual acts. It may be as simple as choosing a few near-perfect coca leaves and then burying them in a few inches of soil after a quick prayer, or as elaborate as a major offering that is orchestrated by an entire community and directed by a *yatiri,* or ritual specialist (Photo 4.5).[5]

One type of *pago* that is of particular importance involves a propitiation ritual prior to breaking soil. These *pagos* are conducted, for example, before plowing, house foundation building, well digging, and archaeological excavations. They involve a prescribed series of acts, including the drinking and tossing of alcohol in the directions of mountain gods, the smoking of tobacco, the selection of coca leaves, and the collection of miniature objects and llama fetuses (Photo 4.6). The miniature objects and coca leaves are placed first on a cloth and then bundled in paper. After the appropriate prayers are said, the bundle is burned (Photo 4.7). A "good" burn is important. If the entire offering is carbonized, usually helped by a good wind and an experienced *yatiri,* then the groundbreaking can proceed. If the burning is not complete, then the *yatiri* has to make a decision: either a second *pago* is to be performed or the work is not to proceed.

PHOTO 4.5. A simple *pago* consisting of coca, alcohol, and cigarettes on a cloth *manta.*

PHOTO 4.6. *Yatiris,* or ritual specialists, conducting a *pago* prior to archaeological work near Juli, Peru, in 1991.

PHOTO 4.7. *Yatiris* conducting a *pago* prior to archaeological excavations on the Island of the Sun in 1994. The offering is directly in front of the *yatiri* in the center of the photograph.

A fascinating aspect of this ritual is that although the *yatiri* is "leading" the ritual, it is actually the community that is deciding the outcome. More appropriately put, the selection of the *yatiri* and the conditions under which the *pago* is performed can predetermine the outcome. If the community consensus is positive for the proposed activity then the *pago* is inevitably successful. The investiture of ritual as the "decision maker" provides a means for the entire community, and not one individual or group of individuals, to control what goes on in that community. If the consensus is against a decision, a *pago* generally is unsuccessful. An unsuccessful *pago* requires a renegotiation of the terms of the agreement, but no particular group of individuals has to publicly make the negative decision.

Such a ritual practice has profound sociopolitical implications. It acts as a means of community resistance and control over outsiders, all masked in ideological sanctions that remove any individual responsibility for a negative outcome. It gives particular power to the *yatiri* chosen to perform the ceremony, while at the same time vesting ultimate power in the community to choose the *yatiri*—a *yatiri* who fails to carry out the will of the community has little chance of officiating future *pagos*. A successful *yatiri* is one who carries out the will of the community without having a public or formal roll call at community meetings at which individual or family opinions are officially recorded in the village logbooks. Likewise, these rituals serve to isolate and marginalize individuals who are not part of the consensus while avoiding the difficulties and political instability of having community "leaders" publicly disagree with them. At their base, *pagos* are a powerful way for a community both to exert control over decisions while maintaining political unity and to maintain some degree of unity while enforcing that control.

Research on the Islands of the Sun and the Moon

In August of 1825, Bolivia (formerly called Alto Peru [Upper Peru]) successfully fought for and won its independence from Spain. With the end of the South American wars of independence, the arrival of American and European explorers, and the development of Bolivian research institutions, the Islands of the Sun and the Moon became objects of frequent visits and scientific study. Joseph Barclay Pentland, an Englishman who traveled in Bolivia for about seven months between 1826 and 1827, wrote the first extensive report on the sacred islands. The primary goal of his work was to report on the commercial prospects of this newly established country for the British government. Nevertheless, Pentland was intrigued by the Islands of the Sun and the Moon, and he wrote a vivid description of what he saw on them (Pentland 1827; Fifer 1974:176–181). His little-known work also contains the first maps of two important sites: Pilco Kayma on the Island of the Sun and Iñak Uyu on the Island of the Moon (Terry and Bauer n.d.).

In June of 1833 the French explorer Alcide Dessaline d'Orbigny (1835) also made drawings of Pilco Kayma and Iñak Uyu.[6] Some twenty years later, these two sites were mentioned again by Rivero and Tschudi, first in Spanish in 1851 and then in English in 1854.[7] Unfortunately, their descriptions are extremely brief and not wholly accurate. For example, Rivero and Tschudi write that the remains on the Island of the Moon were in a poorer state of preservation than those on the Island of the Sun. The errors are not surprising, since the authors do not seem to have visited the Island of the Moon.

Ephraim George Squier, perhaps the most celebrated nineteenth-century explorer of the Andes, also visited the Islands of the Sun and the Moon. He traveled to Peru as part of a special negotiating commission appointed by President Lincoln to settle a variety of issues with the Peruvian government. After completing his official work in Lima, Squier spent two years (1864–1865) exploring the Andes. On his return from South America, Squier wrote his classic study *Peru: Incidents of Travel and Exploration in the Land of the Incas,* which is filled with detailed discussions of the places he saw, maps of many of the sites he visited, and numerous engravings of the lands, ruins, and peoples he encountered. In all, Squier provides no less than fifteen engravings as well as four site maps related to the Islands of the Sun and the Moon.

An equally significant contribution by Squier, although largely unpublished, is a collection of photographs that he took during his travels.[8] His pictures of the coast are of extremely high quality and contain the earliest photographs of many important coastal sites. Unfortunately, Squier's photographer died as soon as they arrived in the Bolivian highlands, so he was forced to take his own pictures during the later months of his trip. Squier had little photographic experience, and thus his pictures of the Island of the Moon as well as those of Tiwanaku and Cuzco are of poor quality. Nevertheless, they preserve important architectural information.

Charles Wiener was commissioned by the French government to travel through and report on Peru and Bolivia in 1877. As he traveled, Wiener took numerous photographs, some of which were later published in 1880 in the form of accurate wood engravings (McElroy 1986:120). Among his many engravings are images of the Fountain of the Inca, Pilco Kayma, the Chincana, and an area of carved rocks said to be on the Island of the Sun. He also provides two details of Iñak Uyu on the Island of the Moon (Wiener 1880:440–442, 473, 489). Copies of many of his photographs from the Islands of the Sun and the Moon are in the Peabody Museum at Harvard University.[9]

Local researchers were also active during this time. Among the most important was Rafael Sans, a resident of La Paz. In 1860, this Franciscan priest edited and published Ramos Gavilán's *Historia de Copacabana*. Sans did not, however, possess the original first three chapters of the work, so he added his own view of Andean prehistory in his edition (Bandelier 1910:327). Later, in 1885, Sans visited the sacred islands and left a report (1913) describing many of the ruins.

Ernst Middendorf (1973:318–329 [1893]) journeyed to the Island of the Sun in 1887. He traveled there with Miguel Garcés, the Challapampa hacienda owner who some eight years later would sell his spectacular private collection of artifacts to Adolph Bandelier. Using Sans's edition of Ramos Gavilán's work as a guide, Middendorf provides a brief description of the Sacred Rock area as well as photographs of Copacabana, the Fountain of the Inca, Pilco Kayma, Yampupata, and Miguel Garcés.

Max Uhle, one of the "fathers" of Andean archaeology, conducted active fieldwork in Peru for several decades after his first visit in 1892.[10] Early in his South American experience Uhle was drawn to the altiplano, and he met with Bandelier on a number of occasions in La Paz (Rowe 1954:5). Between September and December of 1894, while collecting samples for the Museum für Völkerkunde (Berlin), Uhle made two trips to the Lake Titicaca area, visiting the Islands of the Sun and the Moon each time. Eisleb and Strelow (1980) illustrate many of the items gathered by Uhle from the islands. In a letter detailing his journeys, Uhle notes that he also made plans of the major sites on the islands (Rowe 1954). Unfortunately, these maps remain unpublished.

From 1911 to 1915 Hiram Bingham led three expeditions to Peru. During the second trip (1912) a member of his team, Herbert Gregory, traveled to Copacabana and visited the Island of the Sun. He produced two articles describing his observations in the lake region (Gregory 1913a, 1913b). During the third expedition (1915), Bingham visited both the islands. He seems to have been especially impressed with the ruins on the Island of the Moon, as he took more than twenty photographs of its temple.[11] Bingham also took photographs on the Island of the Sun, including Mama Ojlia, the sandstone footprints, the Sacred Rock, the Chincana, and Pilco Kayma.[12]

Bandelier conducted the first extensive archaeological research on the sacred islands in 1895. In his book *The Islands of Titicaca and Koati,* Bandelier provides detailed discussions of his research. After visiting the ruins of Tiwanaku as well as villages on the mountain of Illimani, Bandelier and his wife, Fanny Ritter Bandelier, set out for the Island of the Sun in late December 1894. They arrived at Challapampa on January 1, 1895, and spent more than four months on the islands. Then, after a short stay in Puno, they returned to the islands in late May for an additional six weeks of fieldwork.

During his research, Bandelier excavated at more than twenty sites, concentrating largely on cemeteries. Throughout his work, he recovered a large number of ceramic, stone, and metal objects. We are especially intrigued by two bronze pendants, shaped like two joined crescents, that he found, since they are identical to those drawn by the early colonial writer Guaman Poma de Ayala on individuals from the Lake Titicaca region (Photo 4.8, Figure 4.1).[13] As Bandelier (1910:165) states, he made no systematic attempt to record all the

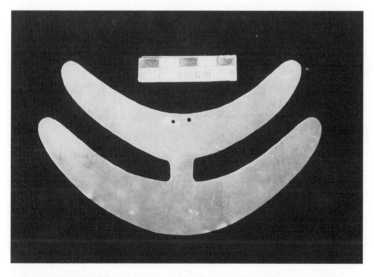

PHOTO 4.8. A double-crescent pendant found by Bandelier is identical to those shown by Guaman Poma de Ayala on individuals from the Lake Titicaca region.

FIGURE 4.1. Throughout his chronicle, the indigenous writer Guaman Poma de Ayala depicts people from the Lake Titicaca region as wearing double crescent-like adornments on their chests. Similar adornments were found by Bandelier on the Island of the Sun. The title of this figure reads "Idols and Shrines of the Collasuyus." Near the cave we find the shrine name "Villca Nota," the llama to be sacrificed is labeled "black sheep," and at the bottom of the drawing is noted "in the Collao."

prehispanic sites on the islands, but visited only those that interested him. Nevertheless, these are small islands, and it is clear that he explored them both and visited all the major sites.

During his work on the island, Bandelier sent many of the objects that he found in his excavations to the American Museum of Natural History, which had sponsored his research.[14] Others were given to the Bolivian government and are now in the National Institute of Archaeology in La Paz. Bandelier's work demonstrated that there was a substantial Inca presence on both islands, as well as an extensive pre-Inca component that he simply called Chullpa.

Before leaving the highlands, Bandelier purchased a large collection of objects from Miguel Garcés. The "Garcés collection," now housed in the American Museum of Natural History, represents one of the finest collections of Inca materials outside of Peru. This is not surprising, since many of its objects were offerings made by the Inca on the Island of the Sun. According to Bandelier (1910:220, 225), who spoke with Garcés as well as some of the locals who had dug for the hacienda owner, most of the metal objects of the collection came from the area in front of the Sacred Rock and from the nearby site of Chucaripupata.[15]

Among the best-known objects in the Garcés collection are six beautiful tunics (*uncus*), most of which appear to be Colonial in date (A. Rowe 1978; J. Rowe 1979). Although the original locations of most of the tunics are not known, Bandelier specifically states that one was found in an andesite box in the Sanctuary area.[16] Equally famous items within the Garcés collection are a large silver llama and a silver alpaca, both of which may have come from in front of the Sacred Rock (Bandelier 1910:220).

Although Bandelier was not as informed about the highland cultures as some of his contemporaries, his book represents a major contribution to Andean studies. We cannot excuse nor ignore his racist attitude toward the Aymara and must conclude that it was extreme even for its time, but we must acknowledge his contributions as well. He conducted extensive archival research in Lima, La Paz, and New York, and his book includes chapters on the local inhabitants and the myths of the islands as well as descriptions of their prehispanic remains. He made the first maps of both islands and dozens of site plans. The book also includes numerous photographs taken on the islands in late July of 1895. In many ways, Bandelier's work represents the beginning of modern archaeological scholarship in the altiplano as it shifted from the "natural history" paradigm of the nineteenth century to the emerging "space-time systematics" of the early twentieth century.

Modern Research on the Islands of the Sun and the Moon

Since Bandelier's time, there has been a steady increase in research interest in the Islands of the Sun and the Moon.[17] Although most researchers have been drawn to the architectural remains on the islands, some limited excavations and surface collections have also been done. Among the most important modern works that discuss the Islands of the Sun and the Moon are Posnansky (1912, 1933), Bennett (1933), Perrín Pando (1957), Portugal Ortiz and Ibarra

Grasso (1957), Mesa and Gisbert (1966, 1972, 1973), Trimborn (1967), Gasparini and Margolies (1980), Rivera Sundt (1984a), and Hyslop (1990). The ruins of Pilco Kayma and Iñak Uyu were also the subject of an intensive architectural study by Mary Anne McArthur (1980). Although most of the recent investigations have been conducted on the islands themselves, there has also been important underwater research in Lake Titicaca near the Island of the Sun. Ponce Sanginés et al. (1992) and Reinhard (1992a, 1992b) led these expeditions and have described their work in unprecedented detail. Most intriguingly, these investigators recovered elaborate Tiwanaku and Inca artifacts in stone containers on a shallow ridge near the island.[18] Items included gold, silver, and shell figurines as well as ceramic *incensarios*. The recovery of these offerings emphasized the sacred nature of the islands during both Tiwanaku and Inca times and set the stage for our research on them.

Proyecto Tiksi Kjarka. In 1994, we began a three-phase research program on the Islands of the Sun and the Moon. Our work included a systematic surface survey of the two islands designed to locate all archaeological sites, a series of test excavations at selected sites to further develop the ceramic chronology of the islands, and a set of more intensive test excavations at several of the largest sites to answer questions concerning site function.

During the 1994 season, we surveyed the northern two-thirds of the Island of the Sun, using a survey methodology that was similar to that employed both in the Juli-Pomata region on the western side of Lake Titicaca (Stanish et al. 1997) and in the Paruro area near Cuzco (Bauer 1992). Three-to-four-person crews composed of archaeologists and local informants walked 10–25 meters apart over the landscape locating sites. All sites were then located on topographic maps and enlarged air photographs. Detailed data were recorded on standardized field forms. These included the size of the site, the location relative to natural and cultural features, the presence or absence of architecture, the presence or absence of cemeteries, and a preliminary dating based upon the collected materials. A sketch map was generally made of each site location, and a Global Positioning System was used to record the location of a number of the sites. Surface artifacts were collected utilizing a "grab-bag" methodology with a conscious attempt to gather a representative sample. With a few exceptions, the survey of the Island of the Sun was intensive and systematic. By this we mean that close to 100 percent coverage was achieved, with the crew walking over the entire island recording all archaeological remains (Map 4.4).[19]

In the 1995 season, we finished the survey of the Island of the Sun and surveyed the Island of the Moon. We also conducted a series of test excavations at sites in the Sanctuary area and near the community of Challa. During the following field season, 1996, we continued excavations in the Sanctuary area and near the community of Challa, and expanded our research to include excavations at the site of Kasapata and on the Island of the Moon. We also mapped several sites with complex standing architecture and revisited various sites discovered during the survey (Map 4.5). Furthermore, we were able to spend additional time at certain problematic sites, recollecting diagnostic ceramics from the surface and checking site-size estimates.

The definition of what precisely constitutes a site is an important methodological consideration that must be explicitly described. We are methodological "splitters" who try to isolate the smallest conceivable surface area as a site. A site by our definition is any contiguous aggregation of related cultural features or artifacts. It may be as large as an urban center or as small as a single tomb. On the Islands of the Sun and the Moon, most sites consisted of light surface scatters of pottery and stone artifacts.

In general, the definition of a site on the islands was relatively unambiguous, but problems did occur. For example, the hill of Kea Kollu contains several large scatters of surface artifacts around its base and also has a large number of tombs and probably collapsed structures on its summit. Instead of considering the entire hill as one site, we considered each large scatter as a separate site, even though the evidence indicates that many were contemporary. We believe that this is the most appropriate methodology for survey work on the islands. Our splitting of sites helped us to "reduce" the number of multi-component occupations and enabled us to better define the total habitation area occupied per period on the islands. Careful definition of habitation areas is especially important, since our population calculations are based on total area. In addition, by splitting sites, we can better characterize the actual area occupied during any one time period. Furthermore, ethnographic analogies suggest that rural populations in the altiplano tend to live in a household for two or three generations and then move a few hundred meters away to construct a new household. By controlling for total population (total occupation area in narrowly defined sites) and then calibrating the data for length of time period, we are able to model population changes through time.

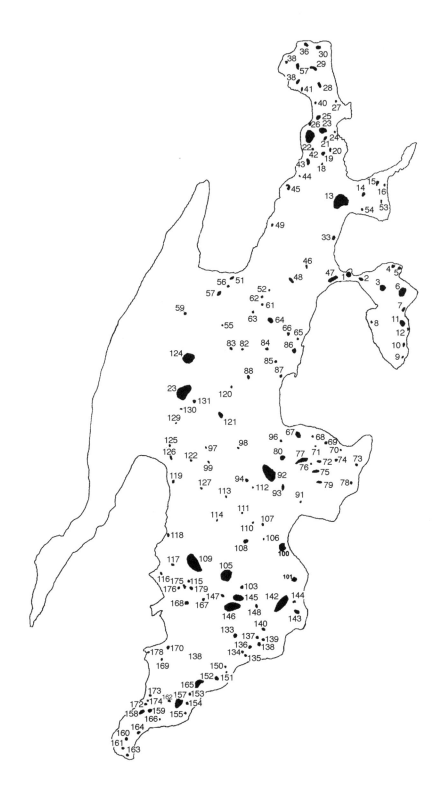

Facing page

MAP 4.4. Distribution of archaeological sites on the Island of the Sun.

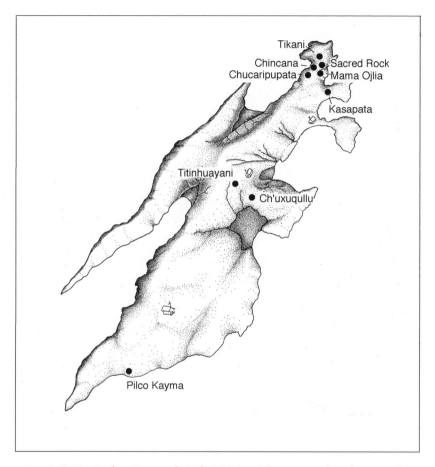

MAP 4.5. In 1995 and 1996 we conducted intensive studies at a number of sites on the Island of the Sun, including the pre-Inca sites of Ch'uxuqullu, Titinhuayani, and Chucaripupata. We also worked at the Inca sites of Mama Ojlia, the Chincana, the ridge of Tikani, the Sacred Rock, Kasapata, and Pilco Kayma.

Diagnostic Ceramic Types

The primary purpose of the survey was to locate, describe, and date all archaeological sites on the sacred islands. Such survey data are inherently important in and of themselves as a means to characterize the settlement history of a research area. They also serve as a database for additional stages of research. That is, once a settlement history was defined, we could then strategically choose certain sites for intensive excavations based on the anthropological and historical problems that we considered most important.

A successful settlement survey requires a secure ceramic chronology to date the sites. Fortunately, prior research conducted elsewhere in the Lake Titicaca region had established a basic ceramic chronology applicable to the islands (Bennett 1934; Tschopik 1946; Rydén 1947, 1957; Hyslop 1976; Ponce Sanginés 1981; Chávez 1988; Albarracin-Jordan and Mathews 1990; Stanish and Steadman 1994; Stanish et al. 1997). To categorize the pottery, and therefore date the sites, we used a modified type-variety "system." While we recognize the problems in type-variety classificatory systems, we still feel that it is the best method to define chronologically sensitive diagnostics from surface surveys.

As settlement archaeologists, our primary goal for pottery classification is largely chronological. To this end, we defined ceramic types that meet the principal goal of chronology building but can also be used for regional comparisons. The typology that was defined is based upon surface decoration, vessel form, and tempering materials. In other words, our ceramic types reflect coherent groups of attributes that would most probably be recognized, both etically and emically, as a "style."

The diagnostic pottery for the Early Formative Period is a distinct type called Pasiri, and it was defined in the Juli region during a previous project (Stanish et al. 1997). Pasiri pottery is defined at the assemblage level. Excavations at the site of Ch'uxuqullu near the community of Challa corroborated this ceramic type for the Island of the Sun (Stanish et al. 1998). About 90 percent of the Pasiri pottery from this site is characterized by heavy grit- and fiber-tempered inclusions, low firing temperatures, and an unslipped surface (Figure 4.2). About 10 percent is composed of sand-tempered, red-slipped pottery that may have been used as serving vessels. Pasiri pottery seems to be characteristic of the Early Formative throughout the southern Lake Titicaca Basin (Stanish et al. 1997). The earliest ceramics appear on the island around 1000–900 BC, based on excavations in a stratified midden at the site of Ch'uxuqullu (Stanish et al. 1998). This date is later than the earliest pottery on the mainland, as indicated by the work of Browman (1980), Ponce Sanginés (1981), Chávez (1988), and Steadman (1995, 1999).[20]

The Middle Formative Period pottery on the islands is related to the fiber-tempered traditions of the Chiripa culture on the mainland. All types seem to be locally manufactured, although intensive analysis of the pottery might uncover imports. We relied on three principal diagnostic types (Early Titinhuayani Plain, Early Titinhuayani Incised, and Early Titinhuayani Polychrome) to define the settlement pattern of the island during this period. Early Titinhuayani Plain is the most common type of Middle Formative pottery. The diagnostic form is red slipped, better fired than Pasiri pottery, and has a finer grit temper. This type is similar to the red-slipped Chiripa pottery from the mainland and to those types described by Steadman for the Juli area as Early Sillumocco plainwares (Stanish and Steadman 1994). Early Titinhuayani Polychromes were occasionally recovered (Figure 4.3). They are related to the Incised and Polychrome types of the Chiripa and Sillumocco pottery traditions as described by Steadman (1994).

FIGURE 4.2. Pasiri ceramics. (Courtesy of the Field Museum of Natural History, Neg. A112880. Photograph by Diane Alexander White.)

FIGURE 4.3. Early Titinhuayani Chiripa Polychrome bowl. (Catalog number B/2605, courtesy Division of Anthropology, American Museum of Natural History. Photograph by Dennis Finnin.)

FIGURE 4.4. Late Titinhuayani Qeya *incensario*. (Catalog number B/2197, courtesy Division of Anthropology, American Museum of Natural History. Photograph by Dennis Finnin.)

The two most common Upper Formative diagnostics on the Islands of the Sun and the Moon include Late Titinhuayani Qeya *incensarios* (Figures 4.4 and 4.5) and Late Titinhuayani Qeya bottles (Figure 4.6). The *incensarios* are easily identifiable by form and paste, particularly the scallops (Wallace 1957: plate 1a, b, c). Paste color tends to be buff, with fine sand and mica temper. Late Titinhuayani plainware diagnostics have considerable amounts of gold-colored mica temper. They are usually characterized by light red slips or are unslipped. The surface has a distinct vertical burnish. Rims tend to be flat or thickened on the side, and the necks on jars tend to be slightly elongated. The moderately

FIGURE 4.5. Late Titinhuayani Qeya *incensario.*
(Catalog number B/2375, courtesy Division of Anthropology, American Museum of Natural History. Photograph by Dennis Finnin.)

FIGURE 4.6. Late Titinhuayani Qeya bottle.
(Catalog number B/2372, courtesy Division of Anthropology, American Museum of Natural History. Photograph by Dennis Finnin.)

well fired micaceous clay is a good diagnostic for these Upper Formative plain-wares. The pastes at least are similar to the Late Sillumocco plainwares de-scribed by Steadman for the Juli region of Peru (Steadman 1994).

Another much rarer Late Titinhuayani diagnostic is the Qeya Polychrome (Bennett 1934; Wallace 1957: plate 1d; Bermann 1990). Qeya Polychromes in this area, as described by Steadman (1994, 1995), are decorated with diagonal lines, triangles, and triangle bands in black and red on a cream (white, light brown, or light orange) background or on an unslipped light brown back-ground. Exterior surfaces are generally burnished, and interiors wiped. Vessel shapes include bottles and slightly flared bowls and cups. Curiously, Qeya frag-ments are rare in the surface collections we made on the island.[21]

Another probable Late Titinhuayani diagnostic is an unslipped shallow bowl with incised opposing nubs (Figures 4.7 and 4.8). The paste is very similar to other Late Titinhuayani pieces. An incised nub from a bottle or jar (not a bowl) was found by Steadman in a Pukara 2 context at the site of Camata near Chucuito (Steadman 1995:606, figure 67d, e). Likewise, reconnaissance in the northern Lake Titicaca Basin indicates that this bowl form is found in Upper Formative sites.

The Middle Horizon Tiwanaku diagnostics represent a highly distinctive pottery style defined largely by surface decoration and vessel form (Figures

FIGURE 4.7. Late Titinhuayani bowl. (Catalog number B/2365, cour-tesy Division of Anthropology, American Museum of Natural History. Pho-tograph by Dennis Finnin.)

FIGURE 4.8. Late Titinhuayani bowl. (Catalog number B/2438, courtesy Division of Anthropology, American Museum of Natural History. Photograph by Dennis Finnin.)

FIGURE 4.9. Tiwanaku *kero*.
(Catalog number B/2212, courtesy Division of Anthropology, American Museum of Natural History. Photograph by Dennis Finnin.)

FIGURE 4.10. Tiwanaku *kero.*
(Catalog number B/2207, courtesy Division of Anthropology, American Museum of Natural History. Photograph by Dennis Finnin.)

FIGURE 4.11. Tiwanaku *kero.*
(Catalog number B/2166, courtesy Division of Anthropology, American Museum of Natural History. Photograph by Dennis Finnin.)

4.9–4.11; Bennett 1934; Alconini 1993; Bermann 1994; Janusek 1994; Stanish and Steadman 1994; de la Vega 1997; Stanish et al. 1997). They are characterized by predominantly black-on-red or black-on-orange decorations. We also discovered Tiwanaku Polychromes on red or orange slips. The most common shapes are *keros* (tumblers) and *tazones* (shorter, *kero*-like bowls). *Keros* are found with and without bands around the body. Tiwanaku blackwares are more common on the Islands of the Sun and the Moon than they are in the Juli-Pomata area.

The Late Intermediate Period diagnostics of the islands fit well into the ceramic styles of the western and southern side of the lake. Based on examples from the Bandelier collection and from our own work, we see two distinct decorated styles (Figures 4.12–4.14). One fits into the black-and-white-on-red style of the Pucarani tradition as described by de la Vega (1990) and Stanish et al. (1997). These vessels are similar to what Tschopik called the Allita Amaya style. They are characterized by black vertical lines with fugitive white outlining on red and reddish orange slips. The paste is often tempered with white cal-

FIGURE 4.12. Altiplano Period small jar or olla. (Catalog number B/2621, courtesy Division of Anthropology, American Museum of Natural History. Photograph by Dennis Finnin.)

FIGURE 4.13. Altiplano Period small jar.

(Catalog number B/2610, courtesy Division of Anthropology, American Museum of Natural History. Photograph by Dennis Finnin.)

FIGURE 4.14. Altiplano Period small jar.

(Catalog number B2172, courtesy Division of Anthropology, American Museum of Natural History. Photograph by Dennis Finnin.)

careous inclusions. The second Late Intermediate Period style is similar to what Tschopik (1946) first defined as the Collao style. Several of the whole vessels from the Island of the Sun collected by Bandelier fit into this style. These vessels are also characterized by pastes with calcareous inclusions.

Decoration is largely black-on-red or black-on-reddish orange slips. Designs include the "butterfly" motif and circles with dots (Figure 4.14). Apart from these decorated styles, Late Intermediate Period pastes are also fairly distinctive. De la Vega (1990) has defined a number of Juli-area, Late Intermediate Period pastes, several of which are chronological markers.

Finally, the Late Horizon, or Inca, ceramic diagnostics are easily recognizable by paste, form, surface treatment, and decoration. Although most of the pottery was locally manufactured, it still conformed to the canons of imperial Inca ceramics that have been documented throughout the former realm of Tawantinsuyu. There are a few unusual Inca types on the Island of the Sun that were recovered from the site of Kasapata by Bandelier and are described by Julien (1993). We also encountered these types in our survey and excavations.

Using the definitions of the site offered above, we identified around 180 sites on the two islands (Map 4.5).[22] The result of this regional survey means that we are able to model settlement dynamics through time, derive population estimates from total habitation area, and define the relationships between large and small sites. Most importantly, we can trace the occupation of the Islands of the Sun and the Moon through time and explore how they came to be recognized as two of the most sacred places in all of the Andes.

We are fortunate that the archaeological remains on the Islands of the Sun and the Moon are relatively intact and that the early colonial documentary information about them is excellent. As we study these islands and their temples, we learn about the nature of Inca religion and statecraft and gain insights into the roles that pilgrimage centers played in the development of the Inca Empire. As we then compare this great pilgrimage center with others from the ancient world, we will learn about the role that such religious shrine complexes played in the development of the great preindustrial empires of antiquity.

5 | THE ISLAND
OF THE MOON

IN THIS CHAPTER we turn our attention to the Island of the Moon (Map 5.1). The most important site on the island is Iñak Uyu. Representing one of the best-preserved prehispanic architectural complexes in the Andean highlands, Iñak Uyu contains an elaborate U-shaped structure (with multiple inner chambers and eleven enormous exterior niches), as well as a series of terraces. We know from early writers that the site was an Inca temple dedicated to the Moon and that it was staffed largely by females. Our surface collections and test excavations at Iñak Uyu also yielded evidence of extensive Tiwanaku, Upper Formative, and Middle Formative Period occupations. These remains suggest that the island was a sacred place long before the arrival of the Inca in the Lake Titicaca Basin.

Colonial References to the Island of the Moon

Although two sacred islands are mentioned by the first Europeans to arrive on the shores of Lake Titicaca in 1534, the Island of the Moon is not specifically featured in the various recorded Inca origin myths concerning the lake. Nor was it specifically described for nearly one hundred years after initial European contact. Ramos Gavilán's relatively late (1621) chronicle offers one of the first detailed descriptions of Inca activities on the Island of the Moon. Since it is known that Ramos Gavilán personally visited the Island of the Sun during his years of missionary work in Copacabana, it is possible that he also visited the Island of the Moon. Suggesting that the name Coati stems from the Quechua term *coya*, or "queen," Ramos Gavilán states that Topa Inca established a shrine with a gold figure in the form of a woman on the Island of Coati (i.e., the Island of the Moon) soon after he founded the shrine on the Island of the Sun.

> [Topa Inca] found comfort on an island more than a league from Titicaca, toward the east, of good climate and some trees although without nearby water. He dedicated this island to the Moon, and he made there an altar on which he

98

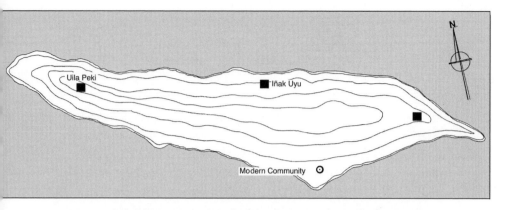

MAP 5.1. The Island of the Moon is about 3 kilometers long and 1.2 kilometers wide. The temple of Iñak Uyu lies near its north shore, and the site of Uila Peki is found at its west end. A single structure of unknown age is located near the east end of the island.

placed a gold figure in the form of a Coya, that represented the wife of the Sun. He called it Coata or Coyata, which is like Queen. This was the second place on the pilgrimage to see after arriving at the island, and was very famous. (Ramos Gavilán 1988:170 [1621: Bk. 1, Ch. 28]; authors' translation)[1]

Elsewhere in his book, Ramos Gavilán suggests that Topa Inca's son Huayna Capac visited and enlarged the Sanctuary, adding a House of Chosen Women to care for the shrine:

There are large buildings on the Island of Coata, because Huayna Capac wanted to surpass his father, and thus attempted new things to distinguish himself. He built a house, as living quarters for the virgins devoted to the Sun, so that they would care for the adornment of his temple and of his wife the Moon whose house he had founded on this same island . . . Speaking of this island . . . there were found [on it] many figures of various animals carved in stone, almost the same as those which the Spaniards found in Mexico, when they arrived at that land . . .

They called the monastery, or house, where the virgins were Acllaquasi (which means House of the Chosen). Each of these houses had its Vicar or Governor, called Apu Panaca, who did not live far away. (Ramos Gavilán 1988:120 [1621: Bk. 1, Ch. 18]; authors' translation)[2]

Perhaps the most unique information contained in Ramos Gavilán's chronicle is his description of the Inca activities that took place between the Islands of the Sun and the Moon. Ramos Gavilán suggests that there was nearly constant communication between these two islands as officials of the shrine complex shuttled back and forth:

> There were many and very frequent missions from one island to the other, and large returns, initiated by the ministers of one temple and the other. The Coya, wife of the Sun, being at the same time the Moon, sent to him [the Sun] her gifts, and the Sun returned them with caresses of equal affection. They came and visited frequently and took time to drink to one another. Moreover, to represent these figures as living beings, they picked from each of the shrines a chief minister and a mamacona to be the personages of the Sun and the Moon, the one that represented the Sun covered with sheets of gold and the one of the Moon with plates of silver. Drinking to the health of the other, the Coya regaled the Sun, begging him for a fertile and peaceful time, and [praying] that the Inca should have a luxurious life, and to the others [she pleaded] that they should dedicate themselves with much faith and devotion in their service [to their lord]. (Ramos Gavilán 1988:171 [1621: Bk. 1, Ch. 28]; authors' translation)[3]

Although we do not know how Ramos Gavilán came by this information, the activities described in the account are not unlike those mentioned by other writers as having taken place within the Coricancha in Cuzco as well as between the mummified kings and their attendants (e.g., Pizarro 1921 [1571]).

Ramos Gavilán's chronicle was published in Lima more than thirty years before Cobo's work was completed. Cobo copied sections of Ramos Gavilán's accounts into his *Historia del Nuevo Mundo,* adding and subtracting information as he apparently felt was necessary. For example, Cobo elaborates on Ramos Gavilán's description of the visits that occurred between the priests and priestesses of the two sacred islands:

> There was constant communication between the priests and attendants of this shrine [on the Island of Titicaca] and those of Coata, and there were frequently missions from one island to the other with large groups returning the visits. The attendants of both sanctuaries pretended that the Sun's wife [the Moon] sent him messages, however this might have been done by the Moon in the Indian's estimation. The Sun answered these messages with caresses of tender fondness and mutual love, and this took up a great deal of time. For the pur-

pose a great many rafts were used that went back and forth from one island to the other. And in order to show a live representation of this, the chief attendant at the site of the shrine took the part of representing the person of the Sun, and at the site of the other one, an Indian woman took the part of the person of the Moon. They would drink to each other's health, and the lady who represented the Moon caressed the man who had the part of the Sun. She would beg him with her caresses to shine brightly every day, never hiding his rays, so that they would make the fields fruitful until the time when the rains were necessary. In addition to this she would ask him to keep the Inca alive, in good health, and rested. She also asked the same for the others who with so much faith and devotion took care of the services and rites of the Sun. And the person who pretended to be the Sun would respond with enough flowery words to fit the occasion. (Cobo 1990:98 [1653: Bk. 13, Ch. 18])[4]

Cobo also tells of the arrival of Topa Inca in the lake region and the nearly simultaneous construction of temples on the Islands of the Sun and the Moon.

But the Inca was not content with what had been done to decorate and enhance this sanctuary. He felt that he still had not entirely fulfilled his obligation and that he was not responding with prudence to the service of the Sun if he did not designate a woman or even women for the use and service of the Sun. Therefore, he decided to do it, and while he had this on his mind, he found a convenient way to carry it out. It was the Island of Coata, which he dedicated to the Moon, giving it the name Coata or Coyata, which means "of the Coya," that is to say "queen," and he constructed a magnificent temple on it. In the temple he placed a statue of a woman; this statue was gold from the waist up and silver from the waist down. The statue was the size of a woman, and it appeared to be an image of the Moon. Thus, along with the living women who were dedicated to the service of the Sun on the Island of Titicaca, there was this idol; it was a representation of the Moon and had the name of the Inca's first wife. Nevertheless, some hold that this statue was called Titicaca, and they say that it represented the mother of the Incas. Be that as it may, the statue was carried to the city of Cuzco on the orders of the Marques Francisco Pizarro, who sent three Spaniards for it. (Cobo 1990:95 [1653: Bk. 13, Ch. 18])[5]

These descriptions are largely based on information supplied by Ramos Gavilán, but Cobo did add his own observations and thoughts to them. For example, Cobo indicates that the statue of the Moon was life-size. This may not be an exaggeration, since Fernández de Alfaro (1904 [1534]) lists several life-size statues among the objects collected for Atahualpa's ransom, and Sancho de la Hoz (1917:129 [1534: Ch. 14]) and Estete (1924 [ca. 1535]) both describe a group of life-size gold and silver female figures found on the outskirts of Cuzco. Furthermore, rather than being made of only gold, as suggested by Ramos Gavilán, Cobo writes that the statue was made of gold from the waist up and of silver from the waist down.[6] In addition, he indicates that it was removed from the island and taken to Cuzco on the orders of Francisco Pizarro, who sent three men for it.

Bandelier (1910:63) uses the above passage from Cobo to suggest that a second expedition (composed of three men) went to Lake Titicaca, sometime between 1534 and 1538, to extract the wealth of the islands. It seems more likely, however, that the three-man expedition referred to by Cobo was the initial one sent by Pizarro to explore Cuzco in 1532 while the rest of the Spanish forces were entrenched in Cajamarca. If this is the case, then the statue of the Moon may have formed part of Atahualpa's ransom.

Pedro Pizarro, writing in 1571, provides the only other description we have of the statue of the Moon: "In this lake there is an island that is called Titicaca, where they had a female idol, from the waist up gold and from the waist down silver, the size of a medium woman" (Pizarro 1986:46 [1571]; authors' translation).[7] It is intriguing that within the list of objects carried back to Spain for the inspection of the king after the death of Atahualpa there are various references to large female statues (Fernández de Alfaro 1904 [1534]). Perhaps one of these statues represented the Moon.

The Early Colonial History of the Island of the Moon

It is difficult to determine when the first Spaniards arrived on the Island of the Moon. Since the first two Europeans to visit the region give no details of this island but simply state that there were two sacred islands in the lake, we cannot presume that they actually arrived at the Island of the Moon. According to Salas, who is, unfortunately, an untrustworthy observer, the island still had not been visited in 1536, when Copacabana was established as a *doctrina*. He writes that "when the captains Alzures [*sic*] and Illescas came to the peninsula with the Franciscan Fathers in 1536, although they intended, they could not get to it [Island of the Moon] because of lack of time and because they thought it was like that of the Sun, deserted and abandoned" (Salas 1901:33 [1618]; authors' translation).[8] Given the Europeans' desire for gold and silver, and the well-known importance of the island in Inca ritual activities, it seems probable that the Island of the Moon was visited early on, certainly by the time Hernando Pizarro and Paullu Inca passed through the area in 1538, and most likely well before.

The first reference to a trip to the Island of the Moon by the Spaniards is provided by Cobo, who reports: "While I was in this province in the year 1616, I heard the report that there is a great deal of wealth on Coata [Coati] Island, and at that time certain Spaniards went there on a boat, but they were unable to find anything" (Cobo 1990:99 [1653: Bk. 13, Ch. 18).[9] A second trip to the island may have occurred soon afterward. The source document for this journey is the poorly drafted manuscript by Salas, which has been extensively edited and altered by Viscarra. The account was composed on the Island of the Moon itself, on June 3, 1618, at the conclusion of Salas's trip. As proof of its authenticity, Viscarra (1901:30–54) indicates that the report carried three ecclesiastical seals and twelve signatures. Nevertheless, because both the original author and the editor of the narrative have taken considerable liberties in describing the journey, the information presented in the account should be considered tentative at best.

According to Salas, the trip to the island began on May 13, 1618, when he and his companions left Copacabana. They traveled to the small village of Sampaya on the upper peninsula, where for many months several boat builders had been working under the direction of community leaders (see Map 4.1).[10] In the end, no less than sixty reed and two wooden boats made the three-hour voyage across the lake to the Island of the Moon.[11] Although there had been some kind of communication between the island and the mainland eight years before, during which Salas had concluded that the Island of the Moon was inhabited by three to four families with ten to twelve youths, he was surprised to find on his arrival a group of elderly individuals as well.[12]

Salas's descriptions of the architectural remains on the Island of the Moon are largely fanciful, and as noted by Bandelier (1910:132–133), they are rendered even worse by the changes and additions of Viscarra. Nevertheless, Salas does note that there were three sets of two-story buildings with extensive terraces on the island. Salas (1901:48 [1618]) also states that formerly there were two hundred individuals dedicated to maintaining the complex, although we cannot be sure of the accuracy of this figure.

Most of Salas's activities on the Island of the Moon went unrecorded. However, he does suggest that the expedition found a stone chest somewhere in Iñak Uyu.[13] It seems that within this chest was a second box of tin (probably a silver alloy), and within that, a third box (or cylinder) of silver. Inside the third container was a mummified arm, eight gold discs, and perhaps several other objects (Salas 1901:46, 51, 54 [1618]). Although we do not know what happened to most of the items collected during this trip to the island, the eight gold discs were sent by Salas (1901:20 [1618]) to Lima in a letter to Don Francisco de Borja two weeks after leaving the island.

Other objects said to be from the Island of the Moon are scattered across the world in museums and private collections. The Museum für Völkerkunde in Berlin contains an extensive collection of materials from the Island of the Moon gathered by several individuals between 1880 and 1910 (Eisleb and Strelow 1980:86, 89, 94–95). These items include a carved stone head, two small stone figures, and a carved stone cylinder, all of which date to the Upper Formative or Tiwanaku times. In addition, the museum owns four metal pumas, one etched on silver sheet and three on gold sheet, from the Island of the Moon. These pumas are nearly identical to those recovered by Bandelier during his excavations on the island.

Important postconquest objects have also been found on the island. Posnansky (1957:70–71, plates XLVc, XLVIa, c) illustrates three Colonial era wooden *keros* from the Island of the Moon at the Tiwanaku Institute of Anthropology in La Paz (now the National Institute of Archaeology). However, the most remarkable artifacts said to be from the island are two Colonial era ponchos (Posnansky 1957:136–138, plates XCVIIa, XCIX). The first is in a private collection, and the second is owned by the Museum of the American Indian (Photo 5.1).

The Site of Iñak Uyu

The most important site on the Island of the Moon is that of Iñak Uyu (Aymara: *iñak* = women, *uyu* = enclosure), and it is the only site to be discussed by the early colonial writers (Photo 5.2).[14] The site is located about 150 meters from the lake and stands at about 3,840 m.a.s.l. (Map 5.2). The principal building at Iñak Uyu is composed of three units, what we call the south component and the east and west wings, and is built around a plaza that measures 56 by 26 meters (Map 5.3). The structure also contains eleven immense exter-

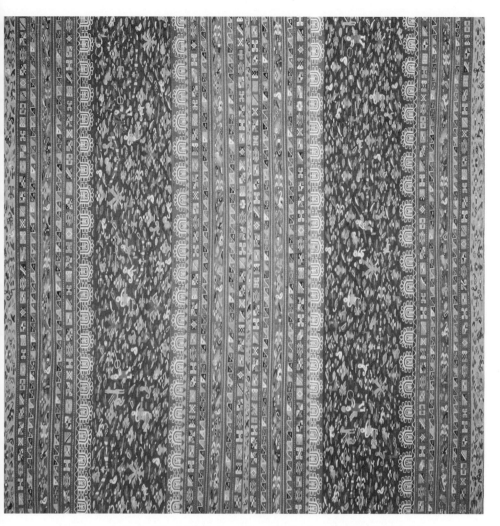

PHOTO 5.1. An Early Colonial Period poncho said to be from the Island of the Moon. (Courtesy of the Museum of the American Indian, Smithsonian Institute.)

nal niches that measure 3 meters in width, over 4 meters in height, and are 1.5 meters deep. These niches are set into the walls of the plaza with quadruple jambs (Photo 5.3).

At first glance the principal building appears to be symmetrical, but closer examination reveals numerous architectural irregularities. The south component of the principal building is about twice as long as its east or west wings.[15]

PHOTO 5.2. Overview of Iñak Uyu.

It is made up of a single line of chambers that face approximately twenty degrees east of north. Two of the rooms contain immense entryways, and there are five large external niches. The eastern and western wings of the principal building each contain three large external niches. The east wing is longer than the west wing, although the west wing is larger than the eastern, as it contains a double row of rooms and a large space defined by a curving wall.

The chambers of the south component were cut into the steep hill slope of the island, and parts are now buried as a result of centuries of erosion. Nevertheless, sections of five-meter-high walls, capped with cornices, still surround the plaza.[16] Iñak Uyu remains, even in its rapidly deteriorating state, one of the most impressive Inca sites south of Cuzco and perhaps the best-preserved Inca temple anywhere in the empire.

Previous Research at the Site

The archaeological remains on the Island of the Moon can be considered an extension of those on the Island of the Sun. Nevertheless, they are visited far

PHOTO 5.3. Large niche on east wing at Iñak Uyu. Compare this photograph with the etching shown in figure 5.4. (Photograph by Wiener in 1877. Courtesy of the Peabody Museum, Harvard University [catalog number H9607].)

less frequently than the sites on the other island. The first modern reference to Iñak Uyu comes from Pentland's 1827 report (1827: f.93–93v). He completed the first site plan, and he wrote a detailed account with descriptions of its well-preserved staircases and adobe gables. Pentland also mentions that he found "the head of a male figure bound round with the band or fill which distinguished the Inca . . ." (Pentland 1827: f.93–93v). It seems unlikely that this

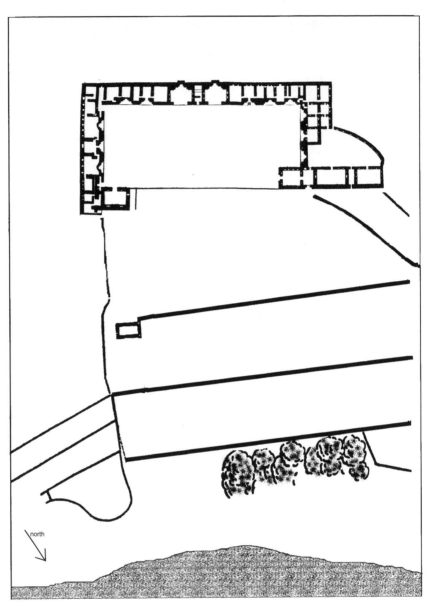

north

Lake Titicaca

MAP 5.2. Several large terraces lead from the lakeshore to the temple of Iñak Uyu.

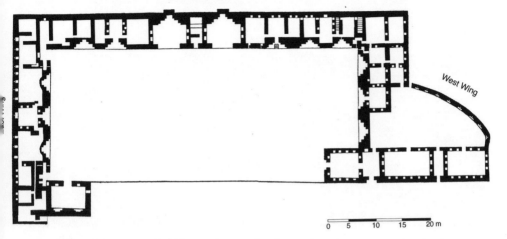

South Component

West Wing

0 5 10 15 20 m

MAP 5.3. The principal building at the site of Iñak Uyu. (Based on Squier and updated with 1996 measurements.)

head was of an Inca, since similar figures are unknown in the Inca realm. However, statues with headbands are remarkably common features of Tiwanaku sites, suggesting that Pentland may have found a pre-Inca carving during his brief stay on the island, perhaps the carved head that was later taken to Germany (Eisleb and Strelow 1980:86).

Many of the late-nineteenth-century travelers who journeyed to the Island of the Sun also came to the Island of the Moon. D'Orbigny (1835) visited the island in 1833 and provides a short description of the site of Iñak Uyu as well as a reasonably accurate watercolor of it (Figure 5.1). Two decades later, Rivero and Tschudi (1851, 1854) mentioned the site. They furnish a view of the front of Iñak Uyu that shows its final terraces, three wings, elaborate niche entranceways, and stepped diamond motifs. They also furnish a reasonable, although somewhat flawed, ground plan and an imaginative reconstruction.

Squier, during his 1864 tour of the Lake Titicaca region, spent three days on the Island of the Moon, most of which was spent mapping the site of Iñak Uyu. At the time of his visit, the site was still well preserved. Squier (1877:360–366) provides a detailed account of Iñak Uyu and an etching of the central courtyard (Figure 5.2). Although not included in his book, four of his original photographs of the site have also survived. These are the earliest known photographs of Iñak Uyu (Photo 5.4).[17]

FIGURE 5.1. Alcide Dessaline d'Orbigny's watercolor of Iñak Uyu (1835).

FIGURE 5.2. The central courtyard of Iñak Uyu in 1864 (Squier 1877:360–366). Compare this etching with Photo 5.4.

Thirteen years later, Wiener arrived in the Lake Titicaca region. In 1877 Wiener was near the end of a two-year trip to Peru and Bolivia, and he covered much of the area visited by Squier. Although his narrative gives little information on the Island of the Moon, Wiener (1880:473, 489) does include two excellent drawings, one of the fine Inca terrace wall (Figure 5.3) and the other of a large exterior niche (Figure 5.4). Both of these drawings are based on photographs that he took at the site.

Bandelier's Research on the Island of the Moon. Bandelier spent approximately twenty days on the island in 1895, noting that many of the details recorded by Squier some thirty years earlier had already disappeared (Bandelier 1910:263). Like Squier, Bandelier carefully inspected the site and provided a detailed discussion of the remains as well as a series of maps and illustrations (Map 5.4). He also had permission from the hacienda owner to conduct exca-

PHOTO 5.4. The east and south facades of Iñak Uyu. Compare this photograph of the site with the etching shown in figure 5.2. (Photograph by Squier in 1864. Courtesy of the Latin American Library, Tulane University.)

FIGURE 5.3. Classic Inca-style wall at Iñak Uyu (Wiener 1880: 473). Compare this etching with Photo 5.11.

vations on the island. Bandelier was told that the buildings of Iñak Uyu had been extensively looted, so he dug on the terraces. He chose to work on the first terrace because the others were covered with ripening maize (Bandelier 1910: 269–272).

Soon after starting work, Bandelier found two likely burials near the center of the terrace. The first, a stone cist, was found 42 inches below ground. It was polygonal in shape and measured about 33 inches across and 32 inches deep. This cist is similar in shape, depth, and size to those found during our excavations in the complex. Bandelier reports that the cist was intact, but empty. Based on our excavations, which revealed several intact cists, it is very likely that the cist once contained a burial, but that it had completely dissolved as a result of the high humidity of the soil. The second burial found by Bandelier was different from anything we found at the site. It was rectangular, with in-

FIGURE 5.4. Large niche on east wing at Iñak Uyu (Wiener 1880:489). Compare this etching with Photo 5.3.

ternal measurements of 36 by 21 inches. First encountered 40 inches below the ground, the burial extended down for an additional five and one-half feet and contained five pre-Inca vessels.

Bandelier (1910:270) states that he excavated an area of about 200 square feet on the terrace to a depth of two feet (Map 5.4). However, the area he marks on his map as being excavated is considerably larger than this, perhaps covering 6,000 square feet. Not surprisingly, this immense excavation yielded a number of objects. Among the most elegant of the ceramic vessels was a pair of Inca-style, puma-handled bowls (Bandelier 1910, plate LXXVI; Morris and von Hagen 1993:169, fig. 156).[18] Bandelier (1910:270–272, plates LXXVII, LXXXIa) also found a carved human head of andesite that appears to be Upper Formative Period in date, as well as various smaller stone objects. In addition, he recovered several metal items in the excavations, the most important being

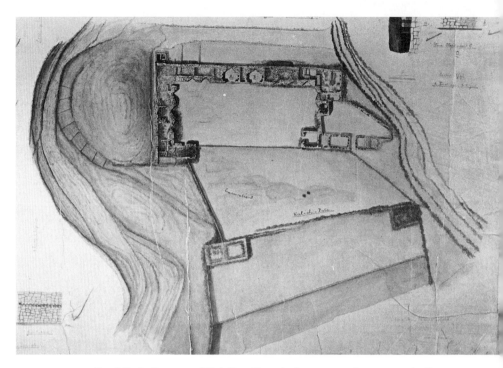

MAP 5.4. Bandelier's 1895 map of Iñak Uyu. Note the large excavation area on the first terrace. (Courtesy of the Division of Anthropology, American Museum of Natural History.)

six Inca-style female silver figurines, a set of three Tiwanaku-style pumas inscribed on sheet gold (Bandelier 1910, plate LXXVIII),[19] and numerous fragments of silver.

Encouraged by Bandelier's discoveries, the local inhabitants began their own excavations. The resulting confusion, and the sudden concern of the hacienda owner over the discovery of precious metals at the site, forced Bandelier to end his investigations on the island. Afterward, he learned that the locals recovered various objects made of gold or silver sheet, and that additional excavations by the hacienda owner provided several more gold and silver items as well as a limited number of ceramic and stone artifacts.

Research Results from the Island of the Moon

Over the past century, the Island of the Moon and its prehispanic remains have been mentioned in various works. Among the most important of these are Posnansky (1912, 1933), Bennett (1933), Mesa and Gisbert (1966, 1972,

1973), Trimborn (1967), Gasparini and Margolies (1980), Hyslop (1990), and Ponce Sanginés et al. (1992). Portugal Ortiz and Ibarra Grasso (1957) recovered three lithic objects from the island during one of their visits. Although these authors do not include illustrations of their finds, they do describe one of them: "The principal is a sculpture in the form of a nail, which represents a zoomorphic figure in the form of a face, with drooping ears, and that ends in the form of a point at the other extreme (with a height of 41 cm. and a head thickness of 26 cm.)" (Portugal Ortiz and Ibarra Grasso 1957:38; authors' translation).[20] Based on similar figures found elsewhere in Bolivia, especially in Oruro, they suggest that the stone is of pre-Tiwanaku date. The site of Iñak Uyu was also the subject of a study by McArthur (1980), who supplies information on its internal organization and compares it with the site of Pilco Kayma on the Island of the Sun.

We have incorporated the most recent data from the Island of the Moon into this section, but we also rely on information provided by Pentland (1827) and Squier (1877) and, to a lesser extent, Bandelier (1910). Each of these earlier researchers saw the site in a better state of preservation than it is today. Pentland and Squier produced outstanding maps of the principal building at Iñak Uyu that show many details that have since been lost to erosion, looting, and vandalism. In all, only about 40 percent of the principal building shown on these early maps is visible today. We made a new map of the remains, but this new map has been supplemented with many details provided by Pentland and Squier for the areas that have been destroyed or buried over the past century (Map 5.3). The areas of greatest losses include the back walls of most of the rooms of the south component, the back walls of the east wing, the cluster of rooms in the west wing, and much of the curved wall. Though this is not the place for a lengthy discussion of the architecture of the complex, several features demand commentary, including two rooms with large entrances in the south component, the unusual exterior facade of the building, and the series of terraces that lead from the principal structure down to the lakeshore.

The Two Rooms with Large Entrances. The south side of the principal building at Iñak Uyu is formed by a single line of rooms (Photo 5.5). Its plaza facade includes five large niches, as well as two rooms with large entrances. These two rooms are among the most impressive features of the site. Their slightly trapezoidal entrances are about 4.1 meters wide at their base and more than 4 meters tall (Photo 5.6). Since these enormous entryways are too large to have

PHOTO 5.5. Section of the south component of Iñak Uyu showing the two central rooms with large entrances.

PHOTO 5.6. One of the two rooms with large entrances at Iñak Uyu. Note the slightly trapezoidal entrance and the large interior niche. Excavations in this room found evidence of an Inca floor.

held doors, it is clear that the Inca architects intended visitors to view into the rooms from the plaza.

Each of the two rooms contains a large quadruple jamb niche countersunk into its back wall. Standing nearly five meters high and more than four meters wide, these are perhaps the largest interior niches found in Inca architecture. The side walls of the rooms have two small niches each. Squier (1877:363) indicates that the floors of these rooms are raised approximately four feet above the plaza, an observation that was supported by our test excavations. Squier also states that these rooms were reached by short flights of stone steps, although he did not include these in his plan. The ceilings loomed some five meters above the floors, lending an almost cathedral-like atmosphere to their interiors. The central locations of these rooms, as well as their stairways, elaborate niches, large doorways, and high ceilings strongly suggest that they served special purposes.

The Exterior Facade. The exterior facade of the principal building at Iñak Uyu is decorated with a number of ornaments. A linear motif with horizontal bars runs the length of the buildings and is broken in places with stepped diamonds (Photos 5.7–5.9).[21] The central rectangle of many, but not all, of these stepped diamonds forms a small passage and provides light to the attached chamber. The smaller panels between the niches on the east and west side held a single stepped diamond, and pairs of stepped diamonds were placed in the larger panels of the south component.

The buildings of Iñak Uyu are made of fieldstones laid with mud mortar and covered with a thick coat of stucco. The plaster, which in places exceeds 20–30 cm in thickness, was used to shape the step motifs on the large niches, the curved tops of keyhole-shaped niches found in the east wing, and the rectangular elements for the stepped diamonds that decorate the exterior facade of the principal building. The stucco contains a large amount of locally grown *ichu* grass, and in many areas the builders added a rope matrix to help support the plaster (Photo 5.10). Although only a few minute patches of painted stucco have survived, we know from earlier researchers that the outside of the temple was painted yellow and that the niches were painted a variety of colors including red, yellow, and white (Squier 1877:362; Posnansky 1912:69). All of these pigments can be produced from mineral deposits found on the Islands of the Sun and the Moon.

PHOTO 5.7. The east wing of Iñak Uyu. (Photograph by Wiener in 1877. Courtesy of the Peabody Museum, Harvard University [catalog number H9613].)

PHOTO 5.8. Stepped diamonds and linear motif on the facade of Iñak Uyu.

The Terraces. A series of broad terraces led from the temple toward the lake-shore. These terraces decrease in size as they descend the slope of the island (Map 5.2). The first and largest of the terraces is called Kalich Pata, and this is where Bandelier conducted his excavations. The south wall of the second terrace presents the best example of Inca stonework on the two islands (Photo 5.11), and it is among the finest in all of Bolivia (Mesa and Gisbert 1966:61; 1972:134; 1973:23). This terrace wall was more than seventy meters long and stood at least three meters high. It is now in a poor state of preservation, with only a few sections of the original stonework still intact.

Recent Excavations at the Site of Iñak Uyu

In 1996, we conducted a series of test excavations at Iñak Uyu to understand the Inca use of the site and to test for evidence of pre-Inca remains. Test excavations were placed along the east, west, and south sides of the plaza, and one unit was positioned near its center. The lower levels of these excavations contained Middle Formative, Upper Formative, and Tiwanaku Period materials, most of which had been disturbed by Inca construction activities at the site. The levels immediately above these remains contained few cultural materials

PHOTO 5.9. Detail of a stepped diamond at Iñak Uyu.

PHOTO 5.10. The plaster on the walls of Iñak Uyu is 20 to 30 cm thick. It contains *ichu* grass, and in many areas the builders added a rope matrix to help support the stucco.

PHOTO 5.11. The wall of the second terrace in 1877. Compare this photograph with the etching shown in figure 5.3. (Photograph by Wiener. Courtesy of the Peabody Museum, Harvard University [catalog number H9609].)

and were frequently composed of cobblestones or sand.[22] These strata appeared to be construction fill placed there by the Inca architects to create a level plaza.

Although our excavations were limited, they yielded several important Tiwanaku-style objects, including an intact *kero* (Figure 5.5) with a front-face god motif and fragments of a large incense burner. The Upper Formative materials included puma-head incense burners (Figure 5.6), a llama foot from an incense burner, as well as various other vessel fragments.[23] The Middle Formative collections from these test units contained only domestic materials.

FIGURE 5.5. Tiwanaku kero with a front-face god motif recovered in the central court of Iñak Uyu.

FIGURE 5.6. Upper Formative puma-head incense burner recovered in the central court of Iñak Uyu.

Excavations in the plaza of the site also exposed five cist burials that were polygonal in shape and located one-half meter to one meter below the modern ground surface. Four had been looted or disturbed by postburial activities, and one was intact but devoid of artifacts. The shattered remains of two incense burners were found just outside one of the disturbed cists. Because the soil at the site is extremely humid, the only human skeletal remains preserved were fragments of teeth.

Three test excavations were placed in the semicircular area behind the west wing of the principal building. These units uncovered an intact cist burial. However, the levels just above the burial contained various Upper Formative and Tiwanaku pottery fragments as well as a carbon sample that yielded a date of 1310 ± 80 BP (AD 640 ± 80).[24] Excavations in this area also exposed an Inca terrace with a canal running beside it, as well as fragments of high-quality Inca ceramics.

A test excavation was placed within the eastern room with a large entrance in the south component. Because the site had been extensively looted, we began this unit with little hope of finding intact cultural remains. Nevertheless, after removing a meter of wall fall, we found a well-preserved floor with a large amount of carbon and several pieces of Inca pottery on its surface. Carbon from the southeast corner of the building yielded a date of 410 ± 80 BP (AD 1540 ± 80).[25] Further excavations indicated that there were no earlier materials beneath this floor and that it rested directly upon sterile subsoil.

A series of test units were also placed on the first terrace level of the site. Bandelier found two burials and many elaborate offerings during his massive excavations of this terrace. Although we found the terrace to be extremely disturbed, we identified the remains of three canals and recovered fragments of Middle Formative, Upper Formative, Tiwanaku, and Inca pottery. Among the more notable ceramic artifacts were various fragments of Upper Formative and Tiwanaku incense burners and fragments of a large Inca plate with an approximate diameter of 35 cm. We also found various fragments of miniature Inca vessels that the Inca frequently included in burials and offerings. Despite the fact that the terrace has been extensively looted, three of the units contained small metal fragments. One unit had a small piece of gold sheet, and a second unit yielded three additional minute fragments. The largest number of metal items was discovered in a test unit on the west side of the terrace that provided the remains of three miniature silver *tupus* (pins), two miniature copper *tupus*, various small fragments of silver sheet, and the shattered remains of several miniature Inca vessels.

Dating the Principal Building of Iñak Uyu

The earliest researchers on the island simply accepted the chroniclers' statements that the principal structure at Iñak Uyu was built by Topa Inca and then later expanded by Huayna Capac. More recent investigators, however, have struggled with the fact that Iñak Uyu displays a mixture of classic Inca as well as regional Lake Titicaca architectural elements. The same is true for the site of Pilco Kayma at the southern end of the Island of the Sun. For example, the trapezoidal entranceways, large niches, and gabled windows that are found in Iñak Uyu are common elements of Inca structures. On the other hand, the stepped-diamond motifs found on the facade of the central court are similar to those carved in stone at the site of Tiwanaku (Photo 5.12) and are not widely found in the Cuzco region.

PHOTO 5.12. Stepped-diamond motifs carved in stone at the site of Tiwanaku are similar to those found at Iñak Uyu on the Island of the Moon and at Pilco Kayma on the Island of the Sun.

Based on the fact that stepped-diamond motifs are rarely found in Inca state buildings, Portugal Ortiz and Ibarra Grasso (1957) and McArthur (1980) propose that the principal building at Iñak Uyu was constructed during either the Tiwanaku Period (AD 400–1100) or the Altiplano Period (AD 1100–1400). Other researchers, such as Gasparini and Margolies (1980:264), argue that the Inca built the principal building, but included Tiwanaku-influenced decorative elements within the plaster work. The results of our investigations lend support to the latter of these views. Most important, while mapping the principal structure, we documented door-bars identical to those in Inca buildings of the Cuzco region in both the east and west wings (Photo 5.13), and excavations within the principal structure identified an Inca floor with no evidence of pre-Inca materials before it.

Furthermore, two carbon samples taken from grass contained within the plaster of the principal building yielded AMS dates of BP 445 ± 45 (AD 1505 ± 45)[26] and BP 470 ± 50 (AD 1480 ± 50).[27]

The use of Tiwanaku-influenced motifs during the construction of the principal building at Iñak Uyu should not be surprising, since the Inca relied

PHOTO 5.13. One of the internal door-bars of the north-facing entrance. Similar door-bars are commonly found at Inca state installations.

on local populations to provide much of the workforce for their projects. Cieza de León (1976:277 [1553: Pt. 1, Ch. 101]) suggests the Inca drew upon the Colla to build the temple on the Island of the Sun. It is likely that they would have drawn on the same labor to construct the buildings on the Island of the Moon.

The cut-stone masonry of the second terrace wall demands special attention in any discussion of the site. The interlocking masonry of this terrace wall stands in sharp contrast to the earth and fieldstone edifices of the temple. One must ask why this wall, apart from all others on the two islands, was built using this extremely labor-intensive and clearly Inca building style. McArthur (1980:343), who suggests a pre-Inca date for the principal structure of Iñak Uyu, feels that this terrace wall represents the only Inca architectural component of the site. In contrast, we suggest that the architectural differences between this wall and the rest of the complex reflect separate construction phases during the Inca Period. Such phases of construction are hinted at in the chronicles. As we discussed above, Ramos Gavilán (1988:120 [1621: Bk. 1, Ch. 18]) states that although the temple on the Island of the Moon was established by one Inca, his son and heir felt a great need to enlarge and improve it.

The Archaeological Survey of the Island of the Moon

The only other habitation site on the Island of the Moon is located at its west end in an area known as Uila Peki (Red Head). This site contains the faint remains of structures and extensive surface ceramics (Photo 5.14). Squier (1877:335) reports that the site had two buildings so close together that they formed a portal. Bandelier (1910:274, plate LXXX) mentions the scattered remains of buildings and a few burials.[28] He also notes that the site was heavily looted and that his excavations there recovered very little. Our surface collections indicate that the site of Uila Peki was first settled during the Middle Formative Period and that it was continuously occupied until the fall of the Inca Empire.

There are also several smaller prehispanic sites on the island. The most notable one is a series of stone cists on the crest of the island. Bandelier (1910:259) excavated a number of these cists. According to him, most had been looted, although a few contained pre-Inca vessels. However, in one cist, Bandelier (1910:272) recovered one of the largest Inca-style female figurines discovered to date in the Andes (Photo 5.15).

PHOTO 5.14. The west end of the Island of the Moon contains a large, multicomponent site called Uila Peki.

PHOTO 5.15. Bandelier (1910:272) found this large silver female figurine on the Island of the Moon.
(Neg. No. 323437. [Photo by Lee Boltin.] Courtesy American Museum of Natural History Library.)

At the east end of the island, near its summit, are the poorly preserved remains of a single structure. At the time of our study, the structure was so disturbed that its original shape could not be determined and there were no surface artifacts surrounding it. Bandelier (1910:260) reports that this spot once held the vestiges of a rectangular building. The age of the structure remains unknown.[29]

Summary and Discussion

The chronicles suggest that the Inca constructed a temple on the Island of the Moon that was staffed by women.[30] The site of Iñak Uyu is most certainly that temple (Photo 5.16). On the basis of data recovered during our work on the island, and on the materials recovered by earlier researchers, we present a series of conclusions concerning the long-term occupation and use of this island by highland Andean cultures across several millennia.

PHOTO 5.16. Aerial photograph of Iñak Uyu. (Photograph courtesy of Johan Reinhard.)

Unlike the results of research on the Island of the Sun, surface collections and excavations found no evidence of Late Archaic or Early Formative remains on the Island of the Moon. This is not surprising given the limited resources of the island. We did, however, recover Middle Formative materials at the sites of Iñak Uyu and Uila Peki. The Middle Formative materials were, however, largely domestic, and no ritual or elite artifacts were present. In contrast, the Bandelier collection at the American Museum of Natural History contains a number of elaborately carved stone objects dating to the Middle Formative said to be from the Island of the Moon. Unfortunately, the original field provenience of these objects is in doubt. Although they were sent to the museum by Bandelier, and are catalogued as being from the Island of the Moon, Bandelier does not mention them in his book. This is strange, since Bandelier provides extensive notes on the other objects he found during the course of his research on the island, many of which are far less noteworthy. Accordingly, although these stone artifacts are clearly Middle Formative in date and come from the Lake Titicaca region, we cannot be certain that they were actually found on the Island of the Moon.

The nature of the Upper Formative activities that occurred on the island is much clearer. Bandelier (1910) and Portugal Ortiz and Ibarra Grasso (1957) found stone objects on the Island of the Moon dating to this period, and several others are illustrated in Eisleb and Strelow (1980). During our stay on the island, we were shown a small stone figure that may date to the Upper Formative Period. Furthermore, our excavations recovered a large number of Upper Formative incense burners at Iñak Uyu. Bandelier (1910:275) states that the Island of the Moon was of little importance in pre-Inca times and that it was only after the conquest of the Lake Titicaca region by the Inca that a shrine was established on it. Our investigations suggest a very different view of the history of this island. The recovery of numerous Upper Formative, ritually significant artifacts at Iñak Uyu indicates that the special nature of the site was already present or being established during this period.

Elite artifacts were used and offered at Iñak Uyu during Tiwanaku times. Our test excavations in the plaza recovered high-quality Tiwanaku ceramics, including an intact *kero* with a front-face god motif and fragments of large incense burners. At least six gold Tiwanaku pumas and one silver one have also been recovered on the island (Bandelier 1910; Eisleb and Strelow 1980:94–95).[31] These artifacts indicate that the Island of the Moon was held in high regard during Tiwanaku times, and that the Tiwanaku state may have been support-ing ritual activities on it.

The Altiplano Period occupation on the island remains obscure. Excavations at Iñak Uyu and surface collections at Uila Peki yielded only a few Altiplano Pe-riod pottery fragments. There appears to have been a population decline on the Island of the Moon during this period, although the magnitude of this decline and the nature of the activities on the island during it require further research.

Excavations indicate that the earlier occupations at Iñak Uyu were sub-sequently disturbed by the Inca. What had been a hill slope during pre-Inca times was filled with cobblestones and sand to form a level plaza.[32] The Incas then constructed the elaborate architectural complex that still dominates the site today. The forms of the structures were influenced by Lake Titicaca tradi-tions as well as by those of Cuzco. The recovery of high-quality artifacts, in-cluding large serving plates, fragments of copper, silver, and gold items, as well as numerous miniature vessel fragments, stresses the special nature of the site for the Inca.

Extensive wealth was extracted from the island after the arrival of the Span-iards. Some of the gold and silver objects may have been taken for Atahualpa's ransom, and it is documented that numerous gold and silver objects were ex-tracted in the early seventeenth century to help defray construction costs of the basilica in Copacabana. The religious importance of the Island of the Moon did not, however, end with the Spanish Conquest or with the looting of the island in subsequent decades. Elaborate Colonial era materials have been recovered from the island, including two spectacular ponchos. The existence of these textiles, like those purchased by Bandelier from a hacienda owner on the Island of the Sun, indicates that the Island of the Moon continued to be ritu-ally important even after the Inca Empire had collapsed and the Spanish ad-ministration was in control of the Lake Titicaca region.

Iñak Uyu, Maukallaqta (Pacariqtambo), and the Architecture of Origin Places

Iñak Uyu was a major Inca temple dedicated to the worship of the Moon. The plaza of Iñak Uyu is surrounded on three sides by small, cell-like rooms. Such plazas and cellular structures are rare components of Inca installations. There is, however, one site, called Maukallaqta, that contains architectural features that are strikingly similar to those of Iñak Uyu (McArthur 1980:319; Bauer

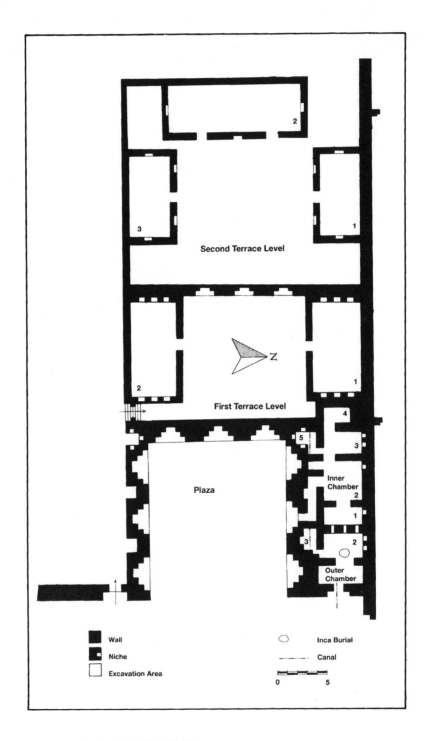

1992b). This impressive Inca complex, composed of more than two hundred structures, is built on a slightly curving mountain shelf, some thirty-five kilometers south of Cuzco. The most outstanding feature of Maukallaqta is its plaza (Map 5.5), which is made of Inca stone masonry and measures approximately 13.5 meters across. Each of its three sides contains three large triple-jamb niches, all measuring approximately 1.80 meters at the base and more than 1 meter deep. Their height is difficult to determine because of poor preservation, but the niches probably measured more than 3 meters high.

Although each of the nine niches is striking, the central one on the north wall deserves special attention. Unlike the other eight niches in the plaza, this one provides access to a passageway leading into an inner chamber of the court. In contrast to the rest of the single-room structures at Maukallaqta and to Inca architecture in general, this inner chamber comprises four adjacent rooms in a line with a smaller connecting room off the southwest corner.

The plaza of Iñak Uyu is much larger than the plaza at Maukallaqta. Nevertheless, the two plazas resemble each other in a number of interesting ways. For example, both are outlined by a series of large, multiple-jamb niches. In addition, the plaza at Iñak Uyu is surrounded on three sides by a series of single rooms that are reminiscent of the rooms on the northern end of Maukallaqta's plaza. Furthermore, access to the rooms at Iñak Uyu is gained through the back of several large niche-entrances. A similar niche-entrance is present in Maukallaqta's plaza.

The site of Maukallaqta has long been associated with the Pacariqtambo Origin Myth of the Inca. This myth tells of the emergence of the first Inca (Manco Capac) and his three brothers and their four sisters from a cave called Tambo Tocco. From this origin place these royal siblings are said to have walked north to the Cuzco Valley, where they established the imperial city. Various archaeologists (Muelle 1945; Pardo 1946, 1957; Bauer 1991, 1992a, 1992b) suggest that Maukallaqta represents the remains of a temple complex built by the Inca to commemorate the emergence of the first Inca in this area. The shared similarities of the plazas within Iñak Uyu and Maukallaqta suggest that the Inca may have developed a specific architectural style to mark locations associated with major origin myths.

Facing page

MAP 5.5. The central court of Maukallaqta shares many similarities with the central court of Iñak Uyu.

6 | THE PRE-INCA OCCUPATIONS ON THE ISLAND OF THE SUN

IN THIS CHAPTER, we present the results of our research at the pre-Inca sites on the Island of the Sun. A summary of our excavation data from three important pre-Inca sites is presented in the first part of the chapter. In the second part, we examine the settlement history of the Island of the Sun from the arrival of the first people to the conquest of the Lake Titicaca Basin by the Inca. The results of our excavations and surveys significantly improved our understanding of the history of the sacred islands, and our research indicates that the Inca were the last of several complex polities to occupy them. Perhaps most important, new excavation and survey data suggest that the Islands of the Sun and the Moon emerged as a major focus of religious beliefs and activities long before the Inca arrived in the Lake Titicaca region.

Excavations at Pre-Inca Sites

To gain a more thorough understanding of the early history of the Island of the Sun, we conducted test excavations at three pre-Inca sites (see Map 4.5). We were especially interested in establishing the dates of the earliest occupations on the island and refining our ceramic sequence. We also wanted to know more about the Challa area, since this region appears to have supported some of the first inhabitants of the island and held the largest population levels throughout history. With this goal in mind, we directed excavations at the sites of Ch'uxuqullu and Titinhuayani, both of which are in the Challa area. These sites were selected for test excavations because surface artifacts indicated that together they spanned most of the pre-Inca occupational history of the island. Surface collections at Ch'uxuqullu, for instance, yielded several Late Archaic projectile points as well as examples of Early to Middle Formative pottery. Titinhuayani had Formative and Tiwanaku pottery along with some post-Tiwanaku ceramics.

We also wanted to better understand the pre-Inca occupations in the Sanctuary area. Associated with our project was that of Matthew Seddon, who conducted excavations at the Tiwanaku site of Chucaripupata near the Sacred Rock. His work, summarized below, is presented in his dissertation (Seddon 1998).

The Site of Ch'uxuqullu

Ch'uxuqullu is an open-air site in the community of Challa. It is located on a low knoll, above several springs, relatively near to the bay (Photo 6.1). The site would have been in one of the most fertile areas of the island during the earliest occupations. The springs, in combination with the low *bofedales* (swampy areas) in the pampa below the site, would have provided an ideal area for animal grazing, hunting, and horticulture.

Ch'uxuqullu is a small site, totaling no more than 0.25 hectares. Diagnostics from the surface included three Late Archaic projectile points, an Early Formative projectile point, and Late Formative ceramics. Based on these sur-

PHOTO 6.1. Ch'uxuqullu is an open-air site in the community of Challa. It is located on the low terraced knoll, above several springs, in the center of this photograph.

face finds, the site was selected as the best place to investigate the earliest peoples of the island as well as the period of lithic-ceramic transition (cf. Santoro and Núñez 1987; Aldenderfer 1988).

We excavated four test units at Ch'uxuqullu. Two of these units uncovered intact and deeply stratified middens. The most informative unit was located at the southern side of the site overlooking the lower valley. The highest strata, near the ground surface, provided ample ceramic and lithic materials, plus carbon and some poorly preserved bone. In contrast, the lowest stratum, which rested above a sterile, undisturbed clay subsoil at 186 cm below the surface, was virtually identical in the archaeological matrix to the levels above it, but was aceramic, yielding only lithics.

Three radiocarbon dates from the Ch'uxuqullu middens indicate that the site was occupied from 3780 ± 170 BP (1830 ± 170 BC) to at least 2110 ± 100 BP (160 ± 100 BC).[1] The lowest pottery-bearing level did not contain sufficient carbon to be dated, but based on the radiocarbon dates from the stratum directly above it, pottery was first used before 900 BC. This unit therefore spanned the preceramic to ceramic period transition on the island.

The second unit was shallower than the first, although it was similar in soil composition and depositional history. Its upper strata also contained the same kind of pottery. The earliest pottery from both of these units is consistent with the earliest pottery from other sites in the Lake Titicaca Basin (Stanish et al. 1997:40–41). Importantly, the lowest pottery-bearing levels at Ch'uxuqullu contain a 9:1 ratio of fiber-tempered to nonfiber-tempered pottery. Through time, the ratio of fiber- and nonfiber-tempered pottery gradually decreased to a ratio of 1:9 around 200 BC. A similar pattern of a progressive shift from fiber tempering to sand tempering is suggested by data from the site of Tumatumani on the mainland (Stanish and Steadman 1994).

Obsidian fragments obtained from the Ch'uxuqullu excavations were sourced by Richard Burger and Michael Glascock (Stanish et al. 1998). Their analysis indicates that all the obsidian samples are from the Colca Valley of southern Peru, more than two hundred kilometers away. These data suggest that, as early as the Late Archaic, the people who occupied the island had access to a wide-ranging lithic exchange network. The fact that the first pottery styles of the island also parallel those of the mainland is further evidence that the early peoples on the Island of the Sun were in contact with the rest of the basin. Although they lived on an island, the people were not culturally isolated, but were integrated within the Lake Titicaca region as a whole.

The Site of Titinhuayani

Titinhuayani is a large site in Challa, located on a hill above Ch'uxuqullu. It was originally excavated by Bandelier (1910:172), who recovered a number of ceramic vessels from tombs at or near it.[2] Esteban Quelima excavated three test units on top of the site in 1995.[3] This area of the site is a large, relatively flat summit between the modern cemetery and the eastern edge of the hill. There is a slight depression on the surface, suggesting a sunken court or another below-ground feature. There are also several shaped blocks of stones on the summit, which are typical of architectural constructions.

We sought potentially stratified contexts so our excavation units were placed outside the depression area. Each of the test units on Titinhuayani reached over 2.5 meters deep, and each exposed undisturbed early middens that were overlaid by later architectural fill episodes. Our test pits indicate that the hill was first occupied in the Late Archaic Period (circa 2000 BC), a date confirmed by the presence of diagnostic projectile points on the surface. Substantial obsidian debris associated with this Late Archaic occupation was also sourced to the Colca Valley (Stanish et al. 1998). The early strata, that is, those prior to the fill episodes, are similar to those at the nearby site of Ch'uxuqullu.

The existence of an Early Formative Period occupation at Titinhuayani is indicated by Pasiri ceramics and intact strata between the Late Archaic and Middle Formative strata. The Middle Formative (or Early Titinhuayani, as the local period is known) occupation was large (about 3.0 hectares based on surface materials) and was identified in all the excavation units. The Early Titinhuayani ceramic assemblage is stylistically similar to Early and Middle Chiripa styles from the mainland.

Large fill layers were directly above the Middle Formative (Early Titinhuayani) middens. These were dated, based on diagnostic ceramics, to the Upper Formative (or Late Titinhuayani) Period. The large, Late Titinhuayani fill episodes were clearly designed to create a flat surface area on the naturally uneven hill. The architects used existing midden to fill in low areas, and they cut into the hill in elevated parts of the site. This created a broad, flat plaza near the center of the site. Evidence suggests that the periphery of the plaza held public architecture and that a sunken court may have been constructed near its center. In other words, we suggest that the Early Titinhuayani Period site was altered in the Late Titinhuayani Period to construct a large public area.[4] This is a pattern evident at the mainland sites of Tumatumani (Stanish and

Steadman 1994) and Sillumocco-Huaquina (de la Vega 1997). Based on the distribution of surface materials, it appears that the site of Titinhuayani reached its maximum size (4.0 hectares) during the Late Titinhuayani Period.

The Tiwanaku occupation at Titinhuayani was much reduced from that of the Late Titinhuayani Period and was concentrated on the terraces, below the hilltop, covering just a few hectares. This pattern contrasts with other parts of the southern Lake Titicaca region where Tiwanaku co-opted existing complex sites and enhanced the architecture in Tiwanaku styles. In the case of the Island of the Sun, populations continued to live in the principal Late Titinhuayani site, but they also chose to enhance other sites on the island.

The Site of Chucaripupata

Chucaripupata is a large pre-Inca site located within the Sanctuary area (Photo 6.2).[5] The site was first noted by Bandelier during his fieldwork, and he accurately describes it as a rectangular platform "lined by walls and surrounded by lower terraces on three sides, whereas in the northeast it abuts against a higher plane" (Bandelier 1910:225). He states that many high-status

PHOTO 6.2. Chucaripupata is a large pre-Inca site within the Sanctuary area. Bandelier found various high-status artifacts at it.

PHOTO 6.3. Bandelier recovered this silver Tiwanaku artifact near Chucaripupata.

artifacts were found near the surface of this site, including gold, silver, bronze, and copper objects (probably figurines) and elaborate metal pins (Bandelier 1910:225–226). He also claims that "a few inches below the surface" a stone chest was found above the site on the southern slope of an outcrop called Murokata (Bandelier 1910:221). These finds suggest that the site served as a center for elites and important ritual activities. They also suggest that the Murokata outcrop, which is actually much higher than the Sacred Rock, may have been a point of ritual activity. Furthermore, Bandelier reports finding a silver "mask" on the hill slope above the site. This is a remarkable Tiwanaku silver artifact with a raised front-faced deity in its center (Photo 6.3).

Chucaripupata is the largest and most important pre-Inca site in the Sanctuary area. It is therefore puzzling that Bandelier does not mention excavating it, especially in light of the fact that elegant objects were found in and around it. Since he describes the site as being badly disturbed, perhaps Bandelier felt that it was not worth his while. Nevertheless, phrases such as a "few inches below the surface" suggest that he was directing at least some digging at the site.

We recorded the site of Chucaripupata during our initial 1994 survey, and the surface collection yielded evidence of Middle Formative, Upper Formative, and Tiwanaku occupations, with a light scatter of Inca pottery as well. During Tiwanaku times, the site reached its maximum size, which we estimate to be over several hectares, making it one of the largest Tiwanaku sites on the island.

At the beginning of the project, we proposed that Chucaripupata was the focus of religious activities on the island during Tiwanaku times. In 1995 and 1996 Seddon conducted extensive excavations at Chucaripupata to test this hypothesis. His work (Seddon 1998) details the rich cultural history of the site and provides critical insights into the political, economic, and ritual dynamics between the people of the island and those of the mainland (see below).

The Early Prehistory of the Island of the Sun (2000 BC–AD 400)

Much of our research on the Island of the Sun concerns documenting and interpreting the distribution of archaeological sites across the landscape. We believe that a systematic documentation of site types, locations, sizes, and ages in a region will yield a data set for modeling the changing social, political, ritual, and economic systems of the region through time. This is based on the well-supported methodological position that the spatial distribution of the sites of a society will reflect certain fundamental organizing features of that society. Combining the information we gain through test excavations at the sites described above with the results of our systematic survey, we are able to model the settlement history on the island from the time of its first occupants to the arrival of the Spaniards on the shores of Lake Titicaca.

The First People on the Island of the Sun (2000–1000 BC)

The earliest evidence of human settlement on the Island of the Sun was found at three sites that yielded Late Archaic projectile points: Titinhuayani, Ch'uxuqullu, and Wakuyu (Map 6.1). As mentioned above, the points are typologically similar to ones from the mainland that date to around 2000–1500 BC, and the site of Ch'uxuqullu provided radiocarbon dates as early as 2000 BC.[6] These diagnostic artifacts indicate that humans migrated from the mainland to the Island of the Sun in the latter part of the Late Archaic, a period prior to the development of fully settled villages and agriculture in the Titicaca region as a whole. They also suggest that these migrants had a boating technology sufficiently sophisticated to reach the island.

The Late Archaic economy in the Lake Titicaca Basin was based on the exploitation of lake resources, as well as on the collection of wild plants, hunting, and perhaps some horticulture (Aldenderfer 1998). The three Late Archaic sites found on the Island of the Sun clustered around Challa Bay. Today the land bordering this bay is the richest agricultural area on the island, and it

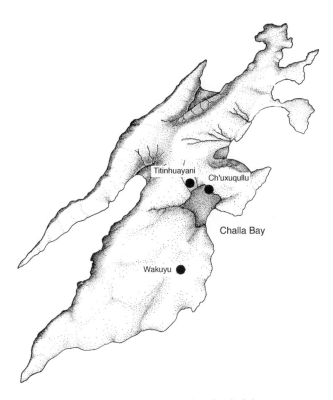

MAP 6.1. Late Archaic settlements on the Island of the Sun.

would have been a prime area for Late Archaic settlement. Assuming that the paleoclimatic reconstructions are correct, the period around 2000 BC was significantly drier than present day. In fact, the Challa area may have been one of the few areas on the island with sufficient fresh water to support a Late Archaic population. Wild animals, particularly camelids, would have grazed in the low swampy areas of Challa Bay, and small plots of land may have been amenable to horticulture.[7] Furthermore, the lake area in front of Challa is rich in both fish and *totora* reeds. In sum, there are clear economic reasons why the earliest sites on the island are clustered around this exceptionally rich area.

The Early Formative Period (2000–1300 BC)

The Early Formative Period in the Titicaca Basin is defined as the time when the first sedentary populations living in largely permanent villages developed out of the earlier, more mobile Late Archaic Period lifeways. The transition from the Late Archaic to the Early Formative was a process, not an event. It is, however, frequently associated with the gradual appearance of ceramics.[8]

The earliest pottery from the Island of the Sun is similar to the type called Pasiri, first defined in the Juli-Pomata region. This pottery is known to date to before 1500 BC (Stanish et al. 1997), a date consistent with the newer data provided by Steadman (in press). The first pottery at Ch'uxuqullu and Titinhuayani occurs over aceramic levels and is 90 percent fiber tempered, with a small percentage tempered with sand and mica.

Ten Early Formative sites were found on the Island of the Sun (Map 6.2). The typical Early Formative site is a small scatter of pottery on the surface of a field with no visible architecture. All of the Early Formative sites are located near springs in areas that were optimal for the exploitation of extensive agriculture and lake resources. The largest cluster of Early Formative sites is in

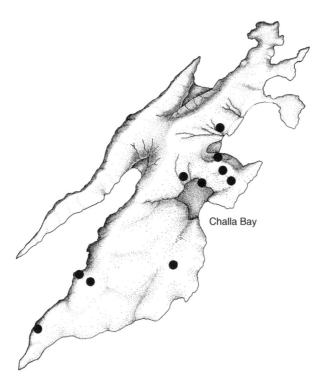

Challa Bay

MAP 6.2. The Early Formative settlement pattern on the Island of the Sun (2000–1300 BC).

Challa, the richest area on the island in terms of water, swampy lands, and access to the lake resources. It is important to note that all of the sites of this period are small, most likely representing small hamlets, and that the population levels were very low. Equally noteworthy is that there are no sites on the resource-poor northern end of the island during the Early Formative Period. In sum, the Early Formative settlement pattern represents an intensification of Late Archaic lifeways. The advent of pottery did not in and of itself represent a major change in the economy of the island, but it does document a slight demographic increase and an expansion of the population across the most fertile zones of the island.

The Middle Formative (Early Titinhuayani) Period (1300–500 BC)

On the mainland, the Early Formative ends with the development of moderately complex polities of the Middle Formative. The cultural development on the Island of the Sun parallels that of the mainland in a number of interesting ways. By at least 800 BC, a relatively complex society developed on the island that was organizationally similar to the Middle Formative societies of the mainland. Around this time, a new set of ceramic diagnostics also appeared on the island. These new diagnostics are related to the generalized elite pottery style known as Chiripa. Chiripa-related pottery is found over the entire southern and southwestern Lake Titicaca Basin, from at least the Ilave and Escoma Rivers in the north, to areas well south of the lake into Bolivia and extreme northern Chile. On the Island of the Sun, we can date these diagnostics with reference to earlier work done on the mainland by Browman (1978), Ponce Sanginés (1981), Chávez (1988), Alconini (1993), Bermann (1994), and Steadman (1994, 1995). Our survey and excavation data indicate that during this period the Island of the Sun was in the general cultural orbit that traditionally has been characterized as "Chiripa."

We name this period, and its associated culture on the island, Early Titinhuayani, after the largest site in the community of Challa (Map 6.3). In other words, Early Titinhuayani represents the local expression of the Middle Formative Period of the Lake Titicaca Basin as a whole. Based on stylistic comparisons to ceramics on the mainland, Early Titinhuayani dates are bracketed between 1300 and 500 BC.

The Early Titinhuayani settlement pattern reflects some major differences from that of the Early Formative Period. There is, for instance, a substantial increase in the number and size of sites, suggestive of a rise in the island's popu-

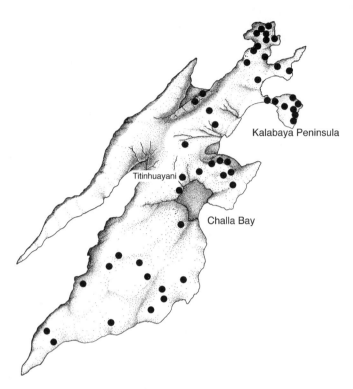

MAP 6.3. The Middle Formative (Early Titinhuayani) Period settlement pattern on the Island of the Sun (1300–500 BC).

lation. Furthermore, as with the Lake Titicaca Basin in general, there is evidence of the development of site-size hierarchies and the emergence of ranked societies. We have defined two basic Early Titinhuayani Period site types on the Island of the Sun: villages and hamlets. The villages range in size from one to three hectares, while the hamlets are less than one hectare in size and may be as small as a single household. The largest site of this time period is Titinhuayani. We calculate that the site was approximately three hectares during the Early Titinhuayani Period.

There are four settlement clusters on the island: the Southern Cluster near modern day Yumani, the Challa Bay Cluster, the Kalabaya Peninsula Cluster, and the Northern Cluster. We interpret the existence of settlement clusters on the Island of the Sun as a reflection of the emergence of modest political ranking and bounded groups centered on the larger villages.[9]

Another major change between the Early Formative Period and the Early Titinhuayani Period is that new sites were established well away from the lake edge in the Early Titinhuayani, although other lake and spring-side sites continued to be occupied. The most logical explanation for this pattern is the adoption of terrace agriculture. This is particularly true for the Kalabaya Peninsula and the northernmost site cluster, where there are large areas of relict or in-use terraces.[10]

The Early Titinhuayani Period settlement pattern offers compelling evidence for the development of terrace agriculture on the island. This shift is entirely consistent with paleoclimatic reconstructions of the Lake Titicaca Basin environment for this time. Recent data indicate the period around 1500 BC was characterized by increased precipitation (Binford et al. 1991; Abbott et al. 1997:169) and that there was "a progressive rise of the lake level" at this time (Wirrmann et al. 1991). Such a climate shift would make terrace agriculture on the Island of the Sun not only feasible but highly productive. We can also hypothesize diminishing wild animal resources through time as a result of human population growth. That is to say, the increasing population, the shrinking of wild resources, and the increase in precipitation provided the context for the emergence of intensive agriculture and the development of settlement clusters, which themselves may have promoted the establishment of social or political boundaries during the Early Titinhuayani Period.

It should be noted that eleven sites with Early Titinhuayani Period diagnostics were discovered on the northern peninsula of the island. Could this be evidence of early ritual use of the Sacred Rock area? Although this question cannot be definitively resolved without intensive excavations, close examination of the archaeological survey data does not provide positive support for such a statement. Most important, the sizes and nature of the sites on the northern peninsula parallel those in the other areas of the island, and no single site stands out as distinctive or unique in the north. Furthermore, the northern sites are all associated with terraced areas or are located near the lake. The settlement distribution of the Early Titinhuayani Period sites on the northern peninsula is, in other words, explainable by economic factors alone, and does not appear to reflect the development of a unique, ritually important area on the island.

In summary, it is most likely that the Early Titinhuayani Period sites were sedentary populations engaged in fishing, agriculture, and economic exchange with the mainland. The general similarities in the ceramic styles between the mainland and the Early Titinhuayani styles on the island indicate strong cultural links. During this time the island was not an isolated area but was linked to, and part of, the general cultural developments of the southern Lake Titicaca Basin. Importantly, no settlement or excavation evidence suggests that the Sacred Rock area was ritually significant during this period. Although there were occupations on the northern end of the island, the sites are not significantly different in surface characteristics and settlement distribution from those of other parts of the island. This settlement pattern contrasts with the Tiwanaku and Inca Periods, in which there were architecturally and functionally distinct sites on the northern end of the island. Future excavations, of course, could alter this conclusion by demonstrating qualitative differences between the Sanctuary area sites and those of the rest of the island during the Early Titinhuayani Period. However, the current evidence suggests that the northern end was not of ritual importance during this time.

The Upper Formative Period (Late Titinhuayani) (500 BC–AD 400).

The Upper Formative Period on the Island of the Sun is represented by the Late Titinhuayani Period (see Table 2.1).[11] Its dates are based on stylistic similarities to ceramic sequences developed on the mainland, such as that from Tumatumani (Steadman 1994). The end of the Late Titinhuayani corresponds to the first control of the island by the Tiwanaku state. Work by Seddon (1998) at the site of Chucaripupata indicates that the Tiwanaku state first controlled the island in the mid-seventh century AD.

The Late Titinhuayani settlement pattern is seen on Map 6.4. There is a reduction in the number of sites from 48 to 31, a decrease of more than one-third between Early Titinhuayani and Late Titinhuayani times. However, mean site size increases, and when the different lengths of the periods are factored in, there does not appear to be a decrease in population as determined by total habitation site size per period. In other words, there seems to have been a nucleation of the existing population into fewer but larger settlements.[12]

The clustering of sites in the Early Titinhuayani Period continues in Late Titinhuayani times. In fact, the clustering intensifies around the larger settlement centers, and the majority of the population is still located near agricultural terraces. Settlement around the raised-field system in the Challa area increases dramatically, although settlement next to the terraced fields was still the dominant site location. Research has shown that raised fields were an integral part of the economy on the mainland during the Upper Formative (Erick-

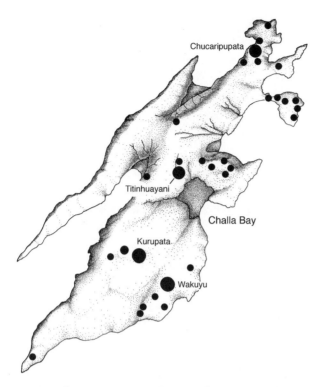

MAP 6.4. The Upper Formative (Late Titinhuayani) Period settlement pattern on the Island of the Sun (500 BC–AD 400).

son 1988; Graffam 1992; Stanish 1994). The location of the large habitation sites around Challa suggests that raised fields were also an important settlement determinant on the Island of the Sun during this same period.[13]

The largest Late Titinhuayani site is the type site of Titinhuayani. The site is large by island standards, about four hectares in this period, including extensive domestic terrace areas around its hilltop. As mentioned above, excavations by Esteban Quelima indicate the site was founded in the Late Archaic and that the top of the hill was rebuilt several times prior to the Tiwanaku Period. Excavations also suggest that the hill area was intentionally filled with soil and midden during Late Titinhuayani times. The intent seems to have been to create a large flat area with some sort of corporate architecture made with cut stones.

Three other large sites, each approximately three hectares in size, were occupied in the Late Titinhuayani Period: Wakuyu, Kurupata, and Chucaripupata.

Wakuyu is on the southeast side of the island near present-day Yumani (Map 6.4). It is a typical Upper Formative site (Stanish et al. 1997:35–36) in that it is built on a low hill with domestic terraces around its base. Abundant surface pottery, including large quantities of decorated pieces, indicates that Wakuyu was an important secondary center in the settlement system of the island. The second site, Kurupata, has Late Titinhuayani pottery scattered over a series of domestic terraces on the side of a hill. The site does not have corporate architecture characteristic of a secondary regional center, thus it most likely functioned as a large non-elite settlement. Chucaripupata, the third site, is especially important because it is located in the Sanctuary area within view of the Sacred Rock. This would be the first time in the settlement history of the island that a site with nondomestic architecture was constructed in the Sacred Rock area.

The settlement shift from the Early Titinhuayani Period to the Late Titinhuayani Period at the northern end of the island is intriguing. One minor Early Titinhuayani occupation exists at Chucaripupata, although there is no evidence that it was anything more than a small village or hamlet, and a few other small Early Titinhuayani Period sites occur on the northern peninsula. However, during the Late Titinhuayani Period six sites were abandoned, and the total population in the area, adjusted for length of time and calculated by total site size, decreased. Simultaneously, Chucaripupata emerged as the largest site on the northern half of the island, and it ranked among the four largest Late Titinhuayani Period sites of the entire island. In short, the total population in the Sacred Rock area decreased, but the people who remained concentrated themselves in Chucaripupata.

The nature of the political organization on the Island of the Sun during the Late Titinhuayani Period is unclear. Based on analogies to the mainland, we would expect to see a unified political entity on the island during this period. This would be evident by a breakdown in the settlement clustering and a distribution of sites for optimal economic maximization in a context of political unification of the island. Furthermore, we would anticipate the rise of a single, quantitatively larger site that represented the paramount village of an emergent ruling lineage. But these expectations are not met by the Late Titinhuayani Period settlement data. Surface evidence suggests that the four sites of Titinhuayani, Wakuyu, Kurupata, and Chucaripupata were of roughly similar size.[14] Titinhuayani, Wakuyu, and Chucaripupata have evidence of corporate architecture. In contrast, Kurupata does not. Rather than reflecting the settlement pattern of a single overarching political unity centered in a disproportionately large site, the data suggest that there were three polities, each composed of a large site and its satellite occupations.

Building on these observations, we propose that an emergent elite was developing in the economically important Challa and Yumani areas during the Upper Formative. We also suggest that during the Late Titinhuayani Period, the northern part of the island was taking on slightly different cultural functions, becoming more of a ritual center according to the work of Seddon (1998) described below. In the northern part of the island, the main center was the site of Chucaripupata. Seddon's (1998) research indicates that a substantial Late Titinhuayani Period occupation existed at Chucaripupata that was characterized by elite and ceremonial objects. That is to say, ritually significant objects dating to the Late Titinhuayani Period were recovered in the area known to be part of a sacred precinct during the later Inca Period. We believe that these data support the hypothesis that a local *huaca* of island-wide importance was established on the island during this period.[15]

The Tiwanaku Occupation (AD 400–1100)

Sometime in the middle of the first millennium AD, the peoples of Tiwanaku began to expand from their homeland in the Tiwanaku Valley to create the first altiplano state. At its height, the Tiwanaku state controlled parts of southern Peru and much of Bolivia (see Map 2.2). The Islands of the Sun and Moon were among the first areas to be controlled by this expanding polity.

Evidence of Tiwanaku occupation on the Islands of the Sun and the Moon was found more than one hundred years ago. Both Uhle and Bandelier recovered Tiwanaku ceramic vessels as well as various gold and silver objects from the islands and the nearby Copacabana mainland. The high quality of many of the ceramic and metal items and their strict adherence to Tiwanaku stylistic canons suggest that they were manufactured in Tiwanaku itself.

Our survey and excavation work offers additional information on the Tiwanaku occupations on the sacred islands. The survey located twenty-eight Tiwanaku sites on the Island of the Sun and two on the Island of the Moon (Map 6.5). The total number of sites decreased from the Late Titinhuayani Period, but again, the mean site size increased through time, with Tiwanaku settlements averaging over one hectare in size. The Tiwanaku state continued the process of settlement nucleation first noted in the Late Titinhuayani Period.

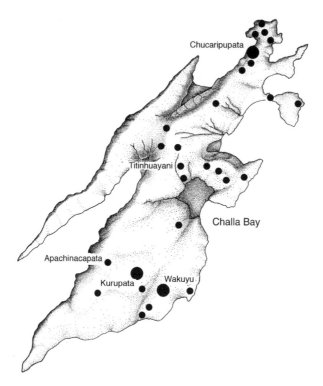

MAP 6.5. The Tiwanaku Period settlement pattern on the Island of the Sun (circa AD 400–1100).

This consolidation process created the highest average site size in the history of the island.

In contrast to the Late Titinhuayani Period, distinct settlement clustering broke down on the Island of the Sun during the Tiwanaku Period. The site of Titinhuayani decreased in size, while Chucaripupata, Wakuyu, and Kurupata increased in size. Kurupata continued to be a domestic habitation site without evidence of corporate architecture. The earlier areas favored by the Late Titinhuayani Period polities were still favored by Tiwanaku peoples, but new sites were established between the clusters.

In the Tiwanaku Period, the evidence for a centralized political organization is strong. The settlement pattern suggests that the entire island was a single political entity. Late Titinhuayani sites were abandoned in a context of population growth. These populations aggregated in larger sites but did not cluster into separate areas. Rather, the population shift was to larger villages and political centers.

From the survey data we can see that the islands were a fundamental part of the expanding Tiwanaku polity (ca. 650 AD), and we suggest that they were incorporated into the Tiwanaku state at this time. During this period, Titinhuayani ceased to be a political center and two sites emerged as the dominant settlements on the Island of the Sun: Wakuyu and Chucaripupata. The site of Wakuyu is extensively damaged by modern construction; nevertheless, it is clear that it was a major Tiwanaku site and that it may have contained elaborate architecture, although any such structures are no longer visible. The site is on a low hill, surrounded by terraces. The terraces have a high density of surface pottery, indicating that they were domestic terraces used at one point as floor surfaces for houses. This pattern is typical of other Upper Formative and Tiwanaku sites in the Lake Titicaca region (Stanish et al. 1997). The hill above the domestic terraces was modified to create a large, flat surface. Since excavations in other Tiwanaku sites have revealed wall enclosures and a small sunken court in similar flat areas, we believe that this site may contain elaborate structures beneath the modern ground surface.[16]

During Tiwanaku times, the site of Chucaripupata was about the same size as Wakuyu. Although there is currently no surface evidence of corporate architecture at the site, excavations by Seddon (1998) revealed substantial Tiwanaku architectural constructions. Seddon documented a series of large walls, domestic areas, and terraces. Furthermore, Seddon's excavations, like Bandelier's work at the site, recovered a large number of elite ceramic vessels not typical of simple villages.

With the growth of Chucaripupata in the Tiwanaku Period, we see the construction and maintenance of the first state installation on the Island of the Sun. Its location in the Sanctuary area, and within sight of the Sacred Rock, suggests that what was a local *huaca* in earlier times was becoming a site of great importance to the mainland populations. Indeed, the fact that Chucaripupata is so large and that many of its artifacts appear to be direct imports from the mainland, if not from Tiwanaku itself, indicates to us that some of its inhabitants may have been retainers who were moved to the island to help support what was becoming a major ritual center within the Tiwanaku polity. In sum, we hypothesize that Chucaripupata was a major ritual center during the Tiwanaku Period and that Wakuyu was simultaneously the principal elite political center on the island.

The First Pilgrimage Center on the Island of the Sun

Although there is evidence to suggest that the Sacred Rock was worshipped as a local *huaca* as early as the Late Titinhuayani Period, we believe that it became a shrine of regional importance in the Tiwanaku Period. It was also during this period that pilgrimages were first conducted from the mainland to the Island of the Sun. The survey data reveal several Tiwanaku sites along the road between Apachinacapata, near the southern end of the island, and Chucaripupata in the north. This road indicates a route that led directly across the island to the Sanctuary area. This is the pattern seen in the Inca Period as well, when we know from documents that the area was a pilgrimage destination. It is also during the Tiwanaku Period that we see the first construction of a major site with large quantities of elite materials in the Sacred Rock area. In short, these data suggest a formalized pilgrimage route from the mainland to the Sacred Rock area.[17]

Excavations on the Island of the Moon indicate its ceremonial center, the temple site of Iñak Uyu, was occupied in the Tiwanaku Period as well. The fact that substantial numbers of ritually significant objects dating to the Tiwanaku Period, including finely made ceramic vessels and gold and silver objects, were recovered at Iñak Uyu supports the hypothesis that a ritual pilgrimage complex was established on the islands by the Tiwanaku state.

Furthermore, underwater research by Ponce Sanginés et al. (1992) and Reinhard (1992a, 1992b) on a submerged ridge just off the Island of the Sun has revealed a Tiwanaku and Inca offering place in the lake. Their project recovered the remains of numerous Tiwanaku metal objects, including a gold pendant with an engraving similar to the "Gateway God" (Photo 6.4), a gold beaker, and an incised puma, as well as various Tiwanaku incense burners. These spectacular finds reinforce the conclusion that the islands and their surrounding waters were considered sacred places by the Tiwanaku polity.

Chucaripupata and the Pilgrimage Route

According to Seddon's (1998) reconstruction, Chucaripupata began as a small domestic occupation in the Early Titinhuayani. There may have been some small houses on the site, but there was no reworking of the hill. The pottery demonstrates some general stylistic links to Chiripa pottery on the mainland, but the percentage of ritually significant or fineware fragments is quite low (Seddon 1998:463).

PHOTO 6.4. Gold disk with an engraving similar to the "Gateway God" recovered in Lake Titicaca near the Island of the Sun by Ponce Sanginés and Reinhard.

Substantial changes in the Late Titinhuayani and Early Tiwanaku IV Periods were noted by Seddon, who writes, "The area [of Chucaripupata] began to be used for feasting and redistribution. Formal, stone-lined structures were sunk into the surface of the hill to store goods for these ritual events. Then, a small canal to drain ritual offerings or ritually manipulate rainwater was placed through the area" (1998:463). Until this point Chucaripupata was still not architecturally modified to any substantial degree, with no evidence of human modification, apart from the small pits and offerings that were conducted at the site (Seddon 1998:298). This all changed around the mid-seventh century AD, when strong contacts with the expanding Tiwanaku polity were first evident at the site (Seddon 1998, Appendix A).

First contact with Tiwanaku occurred in late Tiwanaku IV times, as indicated by pottery styles and radiocarbon dates. Significantly, both imported and locally made Tiwanaku pottery was discovered in these levels. As occurred at other sites in the Lake Titicaca Basin that were incorporated into the Tiwanaku state, Tiwanaku pottery canons were adopted by non-Tiwanaku peoples and were manufactured locally. Such a process indicates that the expansion of Tiwanaku involved more than the mere dispersal of an art style. The spread of these artistic canons represented the adoption of the Tiwanaku ritual, political, and cultural ideologies, and it was an important part of the state expansion process.

At this time, ritual feasting was a major, if not the principal, activity of Chucaripupata. Seddon reports finding trash pits containing the remains of feasting activities with high quantities of Tiwanaku *keros*, the principal vessel form used in such events. Tiwanaku influence is evident in mortuary practices as well, for a small number of tombs were built in a local style but contained imported Tiwanaku pottery (Seddon 1998:464). Likewise, imported materials such as turquoise and precious metals suggest that the political ties to Tiwanaku permitted access to high-status resources well beyond the island borders (Seddon 1998:359).

During this period, Chucaripupata, and presumably the island society in general, underwent another major transformation. As Seddon writes, "It appears that the local structure of power relations was sufficiently changed to enable the Tiwanaku polity to effectively take over the site and remodel it to their own form and to suit their own uses" (1998:465). The excavation evidence shows no signs of conflict, including fire or other types of intentional destruction. Yet, the site was completely remodeled in a way that was unparalleled in the history of the Sacred Rock area. Storage bins were emptied and tombs were capped with sand. This new period witnessed the construction of large walls with cut stones that enclosed the previously open central area. According to Seddon (1998:465), the "form and construction of this temple indicate that it is a model or copy of the Kalasasaya temple at Tiwanaku itself. There are no local precursors for this temple on the island; the temple is a Tiwanaku state imposition." He further notes that "previously very independent local people were now behaving like Tiwanaqueños. The site had been absorbed into the Tiwanaku polity" (Seddon 1998:466).

It was during the Tiwanaku Period that the Sacred Rock area first achieved a ritual status of regional importance. "The moment at which Tiwanaku reconstructed Chucaripupata seems to be the first moment that the island achieved status as a sacred area off of its own shores" (Seddon 1998:473). Seddon feels that this status as a regional power was restricted to the immediate southern lake region and that Chucaripupata was not a pilgrimage destination for the general populace of the basin. He bases this interpretation on several facts: first, no non–Titicaca Basin pottery fragments (with one insignificant exception) were found at the site, and second, the area was "private," that is, enclosed by a high wall and sealed off from public view. Finally, he argues that, unlike the later Sacred Rock area and other pilgrimage shrines, there was a domestic component at Chucaripupata. Chucaripupata functioned, in Seddon's model, "as one of a series of important shrines for a restricted set of Tiwanaku elite" (1998:473).

We are in fundamental agreement with Seddon's interpretations. We would, however, expand his argument and suggest that Chucaripupata was a pilgrimage center of regional significance characteristic of an archaic state. The Tiwanaku state was not a miniature version of the Inca state. Rather, it was a "first-generation" state with a less complex organization and reach. The entire area directly controlled by Tiwanaku is smaller than some scholars have previously suggested (e.g., Ponce Sanginés 1981; Kolata 1986, 1993). The directly and contiguously controlled Tiwanaku territory in the Lake Titicaca Basin reaches no farther north than the Ilave River on the west side of the lake and the Escoma River to the east (see Map 2.2). Tiwanaku also established enclaves in several far-flung regions—Moquegua, Cochabamba, Juliaca, and Larecaja— but these incorporated relatively small geographical areas into the state. In short, we do not expect pan-Andean pilgrimage sites the size and complexity of Coricancha, Pachacamac, or Titikala to have existed under Tiwanaku rule. However, we do expect smaller, more modest ones that reflected the nature and complexities of the state in which they developed and were maintained.

Similarly, we do not expect pottery from outside the area of Tiwanaku control at a pilgrimage center such as Chucaripupata. Indeed, extensive excavations in the Inca Period Sanctuary area reveal that there was no "non-Inca" pottery in the Sacred Rock area even when it functioned as a pilgrimage shrine for the whole empire. Furthermore, the "private" nature of Chucaripupata does not preclude its use as a pilgrimage center, albeit one on a smaller scale than Inca pilgrimage sites. In fact, the distinctive features of the site, most notably the lack of a sunken court, argue that it did function differently, if not uniquely, in the Tiwanaku cultural orbit.

It is true that there is no domestic component in the small plaza area immediately attached to the Sacred Rock during the Inca Period. But taken together, the sites of Kasapata, Challapampa, and even the Chincana and Mama Ojlia constitute domestic and support areas of the shrine. The geographical extent of the Inca state was a magnitude larger than that controlled by the Tiwanaku state, thus the scale of the Inca shrine was correspondingly larger. We argue that all state pilgrimage shrines will have nearby domestic components that serve as the habitation sites where the caretakers lived.

In Tiwanaku times, the domestic component of Chucaripupata was adjacent to the ritual area; in comparison, the domestic component of the Inca shrine was larger, more varied, and more dispersed, but still within a thirty-minute walking radius. We feel that Chucaripupata functioned not only as a center of regional ritual importance, bringing elites to the island as Seddon argues, but also as an early pilgrimage center for many peoples of the Lake Titicaca Basin living within the political orbit of Tiwanaku.

In summary, the Islands of the Sun and the Moon were incorporated into the Tiwanaku state around the middle of the first millennium AD. During the period of Tiwanaku control, there were two principal population centers on the Island of the Sun. The first was the site of Wakuyu in the Challa area, and it is best interpreted as the political and economic center of the island. The second was the site of Chucaripupata, situated near the Sacred Rock, which served as the focus of religious rituals. The area of Chucaripupata had been an important ritual area in the Late Titinhuayani Period, and evidence of offerings dating to that period have been found at the site. However, there is nothing to distinguish this ritual use from that at other such sites throughout the region during this period. It was only in Tiwanaku times that a transformation occurred. The site of Chucaripupata, we argue, then became a destination point for people who were politically linked to the Tiwanaku elite.

The first formalized pilgrimage route to the Sacred Rock area coincides with Tiwanaku control of the island. Prior to this time, the Sacred Rock area and the Island of the Moon may have been important local *huacas,* but there is no evidence that they were regionally significant. In the Tiwanaku Period, ritual complexes, complete with architectural constructions and elaborate, imported offering materials, were established on both islands. The incorporation of local shrines on the Islands of the Sun and the Moon, their promotion through the creation of a pilgrimage route to them, and the presentation of elite objects at them were integral parts of the process of Tiwanaku imperialism as this early state expanded throughout the Lake Titicaca region and beyond.

The Altiplano Period Settlements (AD 1100–1400)

The time immediately prior to Inca expansion into the Lake Titicaca Basin is referred to as the Altiplano Period by Hyslop (1976) and Lumbreras (1974a). It is defined as the time after the collapse of the Tiwanaku state (circa AD 1100) and prior to the control of the area by the Inca sometime in the early fifteenth century.[18] The collapse of Tiwanaku led to a period of conflict in the Lake Titicaca Basin during which the political organization shifted from a centralized state to a series of smaller polities, and the region witnessed the development of the Aymara kingdoms referred to in historical texts as *señoríos*. Map 2.3 shows the general political boundaries of the Lake Titicaca region during this period as reconstructed from sixteenth-century historical texts.

The two largest polities of the lake region during the Altiplano Period were the Lupaqa and the Colla. Cieza de León suggests that the Island of the Sun was conquered by one of these polities, but he does not specifically state which one.[19] There is, however, some indirect evidence that suggests that the Island of the Sun may have been part of the Lupaqa polity. First of all, the island is located close to the core Lupaqa territory. Second, although the Altiplano Period pottery diagnostics found on the island fit into the general southern tradition of the Lake Titicaca Basin as a whole, they are extremely similar to the pottery of the Lupaqa area sites along the southwest side of the lake (de la Vega 1990; Stanish et al. 1997). Furthermore, the Inca may have continued the tradition of a Lupaqa presence in the Copacabana area by sending representatives of the Lupaqa in their *mitimaes* program (Diez de San Miguel 1964:81 [1567]); Ramos Gavilán 1988:84–85 [1621: Bk. 1, Ch. 20].

During the Altiplano Period, people built fortified hilltop sites, or *pucaras,* in the Lake Titicaca Basin. On the Island of the Sun, the earlier site of Kurupata developed into a *pucara.* It is a very typical fortified hilltop site similar to hundreds of others built in the region during this period. This site grew in importance in the Altiplano Period and became the principal fortified site on the island.

The Altiplano Period sites on the Island of the Sun are small and dispersed over the island. The total number of habitation sites drops to a mere twenty-four. There is some clustering in the richest agricultural areas such as the Kalabaya Peninsula and the northern side of the Kea Kollu hill (Map 6.6). The settlement pattern conforms to the model proposed in Stanish et al. (1997:66, figure 37) of a major fortified hilltop site surrounded by smaller, undifferentiated settlements. It is suggestive of very moderate political ranking.

The settlement pattern of the island also indicates a population size substantially lower than that of the Inca Period, and even lower than the earlier Tiwanaku Period. Average site sizes on the island revert to pre-Tiwanaku levels. These data conform to the Altiplano Period pattern in the Juli-Pomata region as well (Stanish 1994; Stanish et al. 1997).

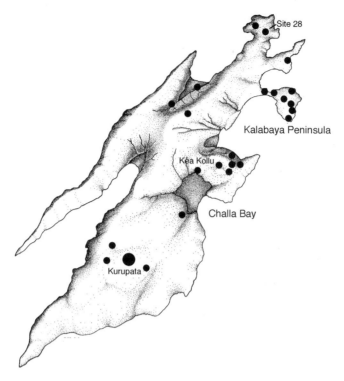

MAP 6.6. The Altiplano (Late Intermediate) Period settlement pattern on the Island of the Sun (AD 1100–1400).

Settlement on the northern end of the island during the Altiplano Period was concentrated in only two sites. These sites do not have complex architecture, and there is no evidence for any special constructions or elite/ceremonial artifacts. It is nevertheless significant that people continued to live in this agriculturally poor but ritually rich area. The main occupation on the northern end of the island during this period is Site 28, a moderate-sized (1.5 ha.) site located some distance from the Sacred Rock. A series of excavations conducted within the Sanctuary area, including some beside the Sacred Rock as well as in the Inca sites of the Chincana and Mama Ojlia, provided no evidence of Altiplano Period occupations. Furthermore, extensive research at Chucaripupata indicates that it was abandoned with the collapse of the Tiwanaku and remained unoccupied during the Altiplano Period (Seddon 1998). The lack of large sites, special structures, support facilities, elite materials, and offerings suggests that the Sacred Rock area was not of regional importance during the Altiplano Period. It seems that what had been a major shrine in the Tiwanaku Period, and what would again be a place of profound religious importance for the Inca, was reduced to the status of a local *huaca* of the polity on the island or was not even venerated at all.

7 | THE ISLAND OF THE SUN UNDER INCA RULE

THIS CHAPTER examines the Inca remains on the Island of the Sun. Our systematic survey recorded seventy-seven Inca sites on the island, ranging from isolated platforms along the pilgrimage road to large villages.[1] We visited each of the Inca sites during the survey phase of the project and collected surface remains at them. We also conducted intensive mapping and test excavations at several Inca sites during the later phases of our research program. Because the island has long been considered the birthplace of the Sun by the native populations, we also completed an astronomical investigation of its standing ruins to determine if there was any relationship between the Inca architecture and astronomical phenomena.

We begin by examining the Inca settlement pattern on the Island of the Sun, paying particular attention to how the Inca Empire administrated control over the island as well as the roads and raised fields that the Inca built on it. In the second section of the chapter, we present the results of our excavations at some of the most important Inca sites on the island, including three sites within the Sanctuary area. In the third section, we describe a pair of towers found on the island, which were used by the Inca to mark the June solstice sunset. In the next chapter, we combine the survey and excavation data presented in this chapter with historical information gathered from a variety of sources to reconstruct the course by which the Inca pilgrims arrived and worshipped on the Island of the Sun.

The Incas on the Island of the Sun

Recent archaeological research documents a significant Inca presence on the Island of the Sun (Map 7.1). Nevertheless, most of the sites were small, nondescript scatters of Inca pottery on domestic terraces near good agricultural land. These habitation sites did not contain architectural remains apart from an occasional wall foundation. The small sites (less than one hectare in size) are widely scattered across the island, and each most likely represents the remains of one or two households. The sites that approach one hectare in size probably represent a cluster of three to seven households. The island also has several large village sites and a range of special function sites, including ports, tombs, and, of course, the Sacred Rock area. We also recorded the road system used by the Inca pilgrims.

The Inca Roads

The Inca roads on the Island of the Sun were built on earlier roads that had crossed the island for millennia (Map 7.1). The Inca were adept at formalizing

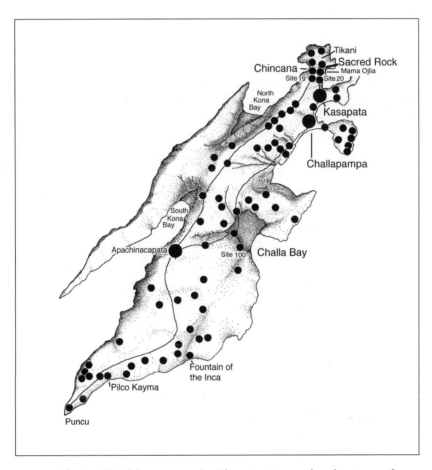

MAP 7.1. The Inca Period (AD 1400–1532) settlement pattern and road system on the Island of the Sun.

earlier road systems throughout the Andes, and they did the same in the Lake Titicaca Basin. There were two principal Inca roads that led from the southern end of the island to the Sacred Rock area. The first begins near Yumani and leads north along the summit of the island to the site of Apachinacapata. It then continues on the high ridge, passing several small platforms, and then descends to the Sanctuary area. The second road drops from Apachinacapata to the densely populated northeast shore of the island. It passes though the settlements of Challa, Challapampa, and Kasapata, before reaching the Sacred Rock.

The Inca Settlement Pattern

One of the most striking characteristics of the Inca settlement pattern on the Island of the Sun is the plethora of small sites. More than sixty of the Inca sites on the island are less than one hectare in size, and even the largest sites are only between three and five hectares in size. This settlement pattern, a bimodal distribution of a few medium-sized centers with a large number of hamlets surrounding them, has also been documented on the mainland in the Juli-Pomata region (Stanish et al. 1997). In the case of the Island of the Sun, the centers were the sites of Apachinacapata, Challapampa, and Kasapata. These sites are, however, small by mainland standards. The town of Juli, for instance, was at least 20 hectares in size during the Inca Period (Stanish et al. 1997), and Chucuito was at least 50 hectares. Hatuncolla, located on the northern side of the lake, could have been as large as 80 hectares. There is absolutely nothing comparable to these sites on the Island of the Sun. It is therefore likely that the Inca settlement at Copacabana was the administrative center responsible for the islands during the time of Inca rule. We do not know the exact size of Copacabana during the Inca occupation, but our examination of the streets, exposed middens, and road cuts in the town indicates that it was at least three times the size of the largest Inca site on the Island of the Sun. In other words, the site-size data suggest that the island was not an independent administrative district of the Inca state but was directly tied to the mainland via Copacabana. These findings corroborate historical accounts that describe the settlement of Copacabana as an important node of Inca administration in the southern Lake Titicaca Basin.[2]

It is also important to note that the bulk of the small Inca settlements on the Island of the Sun are situated in areas of primary agricultural land.[3] The Island of the Sun was indeed a major ritual and pilgrimage center, but the settlement data indicate that the Inca organized the populations to provide for the island's subsistence. The density of Inca settlement is approximately seven times higher on the Island of the Sun than it is in the Juli-Pomata survey area (Stanish et al. 1997).[4] This suggests that much of the agricultural produce that sustained the people on the island, including the priests, Mamacona, and other ritual specialists, was produced on it. This contrasts with the pattern on the Island of the Moon, which has notably poor agricultural lands. It is unlikely that the meager resources of the Island of the Moon could have supported its inhabitants, so food and other supplies must have been brought to it from the mainland.

The number of sites and the total size of the habitation area during the Inca Period on the Island of the Sun is extremely high relative to the earlier periods. This increase cannot be accounted for by natural population growth alone. Rather, even accounting for some minor methodological biases, there is little doubt that people were brought into the area from elsewhere.[5] It is also important to note that the three largest Inca sites on the island contain no surface evidence of Altiplano Period remains. This suggests that the Inca specifically built these villages after the incorporation of the Island of the Sun into their empire. These findings concur with the documentary sources that indicate that the Inca imported colonists to help maintain the island sanctuaries.

Inca Raised Fields

Our survey work on the Island of the Sun identified an important Inca site in close association with unusual agricultural features in the southern Kona Bay area that deserve description (Photo 7.1). The Inca site is composed of a walled platform with several large niches. The platform is located on the lower slope of the island between two streams. The water flow of both streams was directed by walls built within the separate gullies. These walls narrowed downslope and funneled the water into a large oval depression located on the pampa. This depression most certainly functioned as a reservoir. Below the oval depression is a series of relict raised fields. Although these fields do not cover an extensive area, due to the microclimate of the Kona Bay, they would have been exceptionally productive. The presence of this Inca site with its adjacent raised fields is all the more noteworthy, given the fact that the southern Kona Bay contains no other prehispanic remains.

A similar clustering of Inca sites around raised fields can be found in the Challa area. There one finds the Inca occupation that Bandelier calls Pucara, as

PHOTO 7.1. The southern Kona Bay area.

well as a set of elaborate niches in the adjacent valley slope. In the low-lying area adjacent to these Inca remains is a set of causeways and the remnants of raised fields (see Photo 4.2). The Challa area fields are surrounded by both Inca and pre-Inca sites. The dates of these fields cannot be determined by settlement proximity. Using the methodology developed for the Juli-Pomata area (Stanish 1994), the Challa fields could have been used by people from every time period represented on the island. That is, sites from all time periods are found within a kilometer of the fields.

In the southern Kona Bay, however, there are only Inca sites. The use of raised fields during the Inca Period is extremely rare (Kolata 1986; Graffam 1992; Stanish 1994). Studies indicate that most raised fields were abandoned at the time the Inca expanded into the Lake Titicaca region. Nevertheless, given the settlement distribution and architecture associated with the raised fields on the Island of the Sun, there is little doubt that these fields were used by the Inca.

The land near the lake edge, particularly in the small protected areas of Kona and Challa Bays, is appreciably warmer than the Lake Titicaca Basin in general. Also, the stream valleys and, in the case of the southern Kona Bay, the reservoir would have provided sufficient fresh water for these fields, a necessary condition for successful raised-field production. In other words, an unusual set of environmental conditions encouraged the Inca to construct raised fields on the Island of the Sun, even though the use of this agricultural technology was no longer widespread on the mainland. Furthermore, the association of raised fields on the Island of the Sun with Inca sites with large niched walls suggests that the produce from the fields was considered special. We propose that the Kona Bay raised fields, and perhaps those of Challa Bay, were agricultural areas designed to grow maize and possibly other plants for the support of the pilgrimage center.

Research at the Sites of Pilco Kayma and Kasapata

In 1996 we conducted research at two Inca sites outside the Sanctuary area. We mapped the site of Pilco Kayma near the southern end of the island and dug a series of test excavations at the site of Kasapata, a large Inca occupation on the road to the Sanctuary. Below, we outline our research findings at these two important Inca sites.

The Site of Pilco Kayma

Pilco Kayma is the best-preserved prehispanic site on the Island of the Sun. The site rests on a cliff more than twenty meters above the lake in a crescent-shaped bay. It is composed of a nearly square principal building, a set of small outlying buildings to its north, and a suite of surrounding terraces (Map 7.2). Looking east from the site one can see the Island of the Moon eight kilometers away and the Cordillera Blanca in the far distance (Photo 7.2).

The principal building at Pilco Kayma is two stories high and built into the slope of the island. As a result, access to the second floor is gained by walking up the hill slope and entering at ground level. This exceptional building is best known for its closely spaced interior chambers, its high corbeled vaults, and its large doorways.

Research at Pilco Kayma. Because Pilco Kayma is relatively close to the mainland and contains standing stone architecture, it is today the most visited archaeological site on the island. Strangely, Pilco Kayma is not specifically mentioned in any of the early colonial accounts of the island. Pentland visited

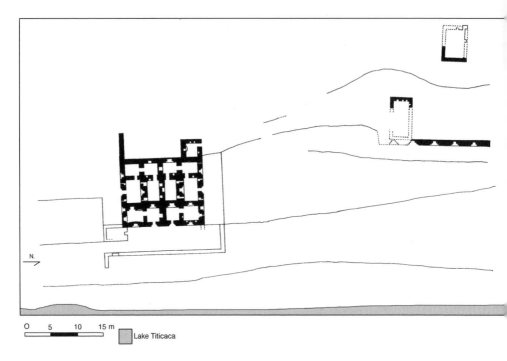

MAP 7.2. The site of Pilco Kayma (drawn by Bauer and Dearborn, 1996).

PHOTO 7.2. The Island of the Moon can be seen from Pilco Kayma.

the island in 1827 and offers the earliest description of Pilco Kayma as well as the first map (Terry and Bauer n.d.). A few years later, d'Orbigny (1835) journeyed from Copacabana to the Island of the Sun. He recorded his 1833 visit to Pilco Kayma in a watercolor (Figure 7.1). His figure shows the east face of the principal building, complete with its two central doorways flanked by large niches, as well as a row of high smaller niches. The watercolor also illustrates a small annex room off the building's southeast corner and a glimpse of the north facade. Although somewhat simplistic, it is a reasonably accurate drawing of the building.[6] A far less precise rendering of Pilco Kayma is provided by Rivero and Tschudi (1851:185).

Squier also documented the site during his stay in the Lake Titicaca region in 1864. He visited Pilco Kayma at least two times. He provides detailed floor plans (Map 7.3), a description of the remains, and two engravings.[7] Squier's engraving of the exterior of the site shows the south facade of the principal building with its central doorway and large flanking niches (Figure 7.2). Above these is a row of smaller niches. The engraving also records various features of the second floor, including several interior walls, niches, and doorways that

FIGURE 7.1. D'Orbigny recorded his visit to Pilco Kayma in this watercolor. Note that the east face of the building (facing viewer) was still intact at the time of his trip.

FIGURE 7.2. Squier's (1877:342) illustration of the south facade of the principal building at Pilco Kayma. Patches of plaster on the wall as well as the stepped motif above the trapezoidal doors and niches are clearly depicted.

FIGURE 7.3. Squier's (1877:342) illustration of the interior of one of the east-facing chambers at Pilco Kayma.

are now largely destroyed. Squier's second engraving illustrates the interior of one of the east-facing chambers (Figure 7.3). The figure is extremely accurate, showing the chamber's triple-jamb niche, its slightly trapezoidal interior doorway, and its corbeled ceiling.

Only thirteen years later, in 1877, Wiener visited the Islands of the Sun and the Moon. He recorded his visit in a series of photographs, some of which were later made into engravings and published. We have identified two of the pictures that he took of Pilco Kayma. The first is a view of the north face of the principal building (see Photo 8.4). The second photograph, which was later made into an engraving (Figure 7.4), views the building from approximately the same position as d'Orbigny did in his watercolor. This photograph reveals that a major section on the east facade collapsed in the thirteen years between Squier's and Wiener's visits (Photo 7.3).

Bandelier spent several days exploring Pilco Kayma. He made a variety of large- and small-scale maps of the complex, several of which remain unpublished. Bandelier (1910:191–196) also includes a comprehensive description of the site and illustrates many of the architectural details. Other early visits to Pilco Kayma were made by Sans (1913) in 1885, Middendorf (1973:318–329) in

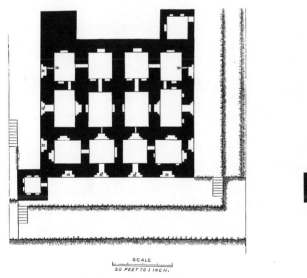
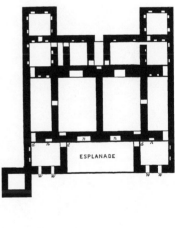

ESPLANADE

SCALE
20 FEET TO 1 INCH.

MAP 7.3. Squier's (1877:344–345) plan of the principal buildings at Pilco Kayma.

FIGURE 7.4. Wiener's (1880:441) engraving of the northeast corner of Pilco Kayma.

PHOTO 7.3. The northeast corner of Pilco Kayma in 1877. Note the collapsed east face of the building at the far left edge of this photograph. (Photograph by Wiener. Courtesy of the Peabody Museum, Harvard University [catalog number H9830].)

1895, and Bingham (1922) in 1915. The site of Pilco Kayma has also drawn the attention of various modern researchers working in the Lake Titicaca region, as well as scholars interested in Inca architecture. Among the most noteworthy are Mesa and Gisbert (1972), Hyslop (1990), Ponce Sanginés et al. (1992), and Escalante Moscoso (1994).

Site Description. The principal structure of Pilco Kayma is a densely constructed building that is difficult to summarize succinctly because of its many internal chambers, niches, and doorways (Map 7.4, Photo 7.4). The lakeside, east-facing facade contains two large entryways, which lead into nearly symmetrical double chambers. The south and north sides of the principal building have single entryways, framed by large niches, which lead into chambers composed of four interconnected rooms. Perhaps the most notable features of the interior are the well-preserved corbeled vaults that support the second floor (Photo 7.5). The interior of the building is impressive, but it is worth mention-

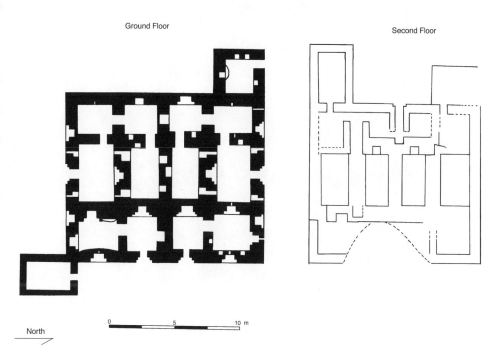

MAP 7.4. Plan of the principal building at Pilco Kayma (drawn by Bauer and Dearborn, 1996).

PHOTO 7.4. An interior niche at Pilco Kayma.

PHOTO 7.5. A corbeled vault at Pilco Kayma.

ing that there is a casualness of construction at Pilco Kayma that has left doorways and niches of varying shapes, ranging from rectangular to trapezoidal, and of differing dimensions.

Nevertheless, the exterior is remarkable for its trapezoidal triple-jamb doors and its large trapezoidal double-jamb niches. These are classic hallmarks of imperial Inca architecture as seen in monumental structures across the empire. However, the exterior doorways and niches of Pilco Kayma are unique in that they are capped with a stepped motif that is typical of Lake Titicaca cultures, and particularly of formal Tiwanaku-style doorways.

The remains of the second story are poorly preserved, and little of the original layout can be seen (compare Maps 7.3 and 7.4). Close examination of the second level during our work on the island did, however, reveal patches of crushed greenstone. These remains suggest that the second level of Pilco Kayma once contained a greenstone floor, not unlike that found during our excavations in the plaza of the Sacred Rock.

It is apparent from the older descriptions and etchings that Pilco Kayma was once covered with a painted stucco. Squier's engraving (Figure 7.2) shows large patches of plaster clinging to the south face of the building, and he notes, "Some patches of this stucco still remain, and indicate that the building was originally yellow, while the inner parts and moldings of the door-ways and niches were of different shades of red" (1877:345). In contrast, Pentland suggests that the outside was painted mostly red, and that there were figures in some places: "The walls were plastered with mud the surface of which was painted of a brick red colour, on which figures representing men and animals were traced" (1827: f. 86).[8] Today, only minute fragments of plaster are still preserved in the corners of a few of the niches, and there is no evidence of paint.

The Outlying Buildings. A set of small buildings is located to the north of the principal structure. Bandelier describes three outlying buildings: two on either end of a large terrace wall and one structure further upslope. Only two of these buildings are currently visible, and the terrace wall is in poor condition (see Map 7.2). Bandelier, who saw the wall in a better state of preservation, describes it in the following:

> The rear wall of the [terrace] . . . is of very fair construction and has eight
> trapezoidal niches. . . . Between every two of the large niches is a smaller one
> in the shape of a lozenge, the deep middle recess of which is lined by four thin

plates of stone set on edge, and as many small pebbles forming the corners. This wall presents, therefore, quite an ornamental appearance. Its height is eight feet [2.5 m]. (Bandelier 1910:191)

Although the terrace wall is now largely destroyed, it is still possible to see that it once had a set of large niches and a series of diamond-shaped motifs (Photos 7.6 and 7.7).

PHOTO 7.6. An elaborate terrace wall at Pilco Kayma.

PHOTO 7.7. A diamond-shaped motif at Pilco Kayma.

Dating the Site. The date of Pilco Kayma has been the topic of some discussion. Portugal Ortiz and Ibarra Grasso (1957), followed by McArthur (1980), suggest on the basis of the stepped motifs around the outer doorways and niches of the principal structure and the diamond-shaped motifs of the terrace wall that the complex was built during Tiwanaku times or perhaps in the Altiplano Period. Other researchers, however, stress that the trapezoidal shape of the exterior doors and niches indicates an Inca Period construction date, although they also see the influence of "Tiwanaku" decorative elements at the site. For example, Gasparini and Margolies (1980:13) write that Pilco Kayma contains "the most illustrative example of the Tiwanaku-Inca combination. The typical Tiwanaku double-jamb rectangular doorway takes on the Inca trapezoidal shape retaining on both ends of the lintel the stepped sign which so frequently decorates the doors, windows, and niches of Tiwanaku monuments."

We concur with the latter group of researchers and believe that the complex was built by the Inca. Two samples of grass taken from the plaster at Pilco Kayma were submitted for AMS dating. One sample provided a date of 470 ± 50 BP (AD 1480 ± 50),[9] and the other yielded a date of 420 ± 60 BP (AD 1530 ± 60).[10] Both of these dates fall within the period of Inca control of the sacred islands. Nevertheless, we recognize that many of the decorative motifs at Pilco Kayma, like those at the site of Iñak Uyu, reflect local traditions. This may be the result of the Inca's extensive use of local *mitima* labor to construct the state facilities on the sacred islands (Gasparini and Margolies 1980:154).

The Site of Kasapata

Approximately halfway between the community of Challapampa and the Sanctuary area lies the site of Kasapata. This site covers an area of more than five hectares between two large hills at the beginning of an isthmus (Photo 7.8). The road that leads from Challapampa to the Sacred Rock divides the site in half. On the south side of the road stands a large Inca structure with five doorways (Photos 7.9 and 7.10). The building measures 40 meters by 10 meters (Figure 7.5). Along its north face are the remains of five trapezoidal doorways. In between these doorways, at a considerable height, are pairs of windows. The east and west interior ends of the building contained four niches each. The back wall is largely destroyed, and only one of the many niches that once adorned its interior has survived.

PHOTO 7.8. The site of Kasapata covers the area between two large hills at the beginning of an isthmus.

PHOTO 7.9. An Inca building with five doors stands near the center of Kasapata.

PHOTO 7.10. One of the five doorways in the principal building of Kasapata.

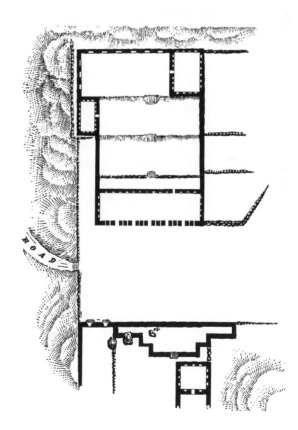

FIGURE 7.5. Squier's (1877:368) plan of Kasapata. Few of these remains are still visible at the site.

To the north of the central road are various foundations and a carved stone (Photo 7.11). Cut andesite, basalt, and sandstone blocks dot the landscape, suggesting that other public structures once stood in the area. Kasapata is also associated with an expansive zone of well-made terraces that in the past served as domestic house platforms. Surface artifacts at the site are exclusively Inca in date.[11]

Pentland offers the earliest description of this site. He visited the area while the remains of adobe gables could still be seen at the ends of the building with five doorways. Squier also visited the site of Kasapata. He was frustrated after visiting the Sacred Rock area, since he saw no structure near it that resembled a Temple of the Sun. Squier later returned to the island to look for such a temple, and it was during this second trip that he arrived at Kasapata. Squier (1877: 369) completed a fine description of the site as well as a detailed drawing (Figure 7.6). He concluded that the building with five doorways at Kasapata was the Temple of the Sun mentioned by the chroniclers.

The site has deteriorated since Squier's visit. Squier notes that the principal building was once stuccoed and painted, but none of the plaster remains today. Furthermore, few of the elaborate terraces, stairs, walls, or buildings shown surrounding the main building on his plan are visible now.

Bandelier (1910:203–214) began his excavations on the Island of the Sun at Kasapata. He notes that many features on Squier's plan were no longer visible.[12] The large hall must have also been in poor condition, since Bandelier records only three of its five doors. He also indicates that looters had damaged the site.

Bandelier furnishes a detailed description of his work at Kasapata, which included a variety of trench and broad-area excavations. He concentrated his excavations on the north side of the site as well as on the slopes of the adjacent hill called Llaq'-aylli. His research revealed various burials, an unusual five-meter-long canal that ended in a rectangular tank, and numerous foundations. The work recovered a wide range of cultural materials, including bones, pottery, grinding stones, stone beads, spindle whorls, and some small metal objects. He found various intact vessels, ranging from domestic cooking pots to plates of the finest Inca craftsmanship. Bandelier also recovered several large Inca jars, complete with standing rings, which measured more than one meter high. The Inca used these vessels to ferment and store *chicha*. Examples of the artifacts found at Kasapata are illustrated in his book, along with a general map, two detailed excavation plans, and a photograph of the site (Bandelier 1910, plates II, XLV, XLVI, XLVII, XLIX, L, LI, LIII, LIV).

PHOTO 7.11. A large carved stone at Kasapata.

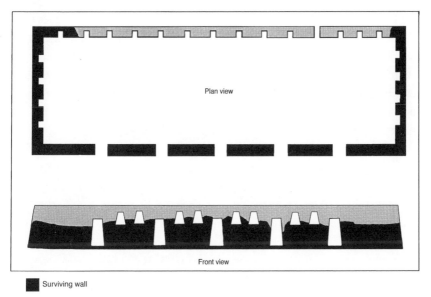

Plan view

Front view

■ Surviving wall

▨ Suggested wall

FIGURE 7.6. The structure with five doorways at Kasapata.

Surface Collections and Test Excavations. Our surface collections at Kasapata yielded a vast amount of Inca ceramics. Further test excavations confirmed the presence of a large Inca settlement and provided no evidence of earlier occupations at the site. We excavated eleven test units at Kasapata, six inside the building with five doorways and five outside. The units inside the building revealed various features, including occupation surfaces and concentrations of ceramic fragments. Many of the pottery shards came from large storage jars that stood along the south wall. Areas of burnt clay, suggestive of ephemeral cooking locations, were also found in the structure. Although all artifacts recovered inside the building are of Inca date, a carbon sample yielded an age of 270 ± 80 BP (AD 1680 ± 80).[13] This sample suggests that the building, and most likely many of its vessels, continued to be in use after the fall of the Inca Empire.

Test excavations outside the principal building exposed additional wall foundations as well as a gutter paralleling the road that cuts across the middle of the site. The exterior units yielded a great quantity of cultural debris, including domestic and finer ceramics, various spindle whorls, copper pins (*tupus*), and many animal bones.

Overview of Kasapata. The large amount and great variety of domestic refuse found by both Bandelier and our research team at Kasapata indicates that the site held a large residential occupation. Nevertheless, the presence of a building with five doorways, a carved rock, and numerous stone foundations suggests that this was no simple settlement. Kasapata may well be the town in which Ramos Gavilán (1988:86 [1621: Bk. 1, Ch. 12]) suggests Topa Inca Yupanqui built a royal palace,[14] and where Cobo (1990:93 [1653: Bk. 13, Ch. 18]) suggests there was "an impressive tambo or inn for the pilgrims to stay in."[15]

Squier, concerned by the fact that there was no single, large building in the Sanctuary area, felt that the principal structure at Kasapata was the Temple of the Sun, as described by the early colonial writers. Bandelier (1910:211–212) dismissed this idea and proposed that the principal building, based on information provided by Ramos Gavilán, was the palace of Topa Inca Yupanqui. Most subsequent researchers have followed Bandelier's classification. We propose, however, that the architecture of the principal building is more suggestive of a structure intended for public use than a building built as a private palace. In fact, long rectangular buildings with multiple doorways are common features of Inca centers (Hyslop 1990; Lee 1998). Garcilaso de la Vega (1966:320

[1609: Pt. 1, Bk. 6, Ch. 4]) states that the largest of these were used to hold festivals during rainy weather.

A close reading of Ramos Gavilán (1988:176 [1621: Bk. 1, Ch. 29]) reveals that this author specifically mentions the principal structure of Kasapata in his description of the June and December solstice celebrations on the island. Ramos Gavilán states that the Inca gathered on a great square near a "temple" with five doors to celebrate the solstices. Based on this account of solstice celebrations taking place at Kasapata and on the recovery of a variety of artifacts—including domestic and fancy ceramics as well as fragments of *chicha* storage jars—within the building with five doors, we suggest that it served as a public gathering place in which ritual feasting and drinking took place.

Archaeological Research in the Sanctuary Area

The Inca, and perhaps earlier peoples of the Lake Titicaca region, believed that the Sun rose for the first time from a large rock near the north end of the Island of the Sun. The Sanctuary area that surrounds the Sacred Rock (or Titikala) is still readily identifiable and has been visited and described by many researchers (Squier 1877; Wiener 1880; Middendorf 1973 [1893]; Bandelier 1910; Hyslop 1990). It is separated from the rest of the island to the east by a wall that runs north-south. Within the Sanctuary area are two separate sets of Inca buildings (the sites of Mama Ojlia and the Chincana) as well as a well-defined plaza near the Sacred Rock. There is also a large Tiwanaku occupation in the Sanctuary area at the site of Chucaripupata (Seddon 1998). A small ridge called Tikani, which looms on the horizon, defines the west end of the Sanctuary. Because the Sanctuary represents one of the most sacred places in the Andes, it demands special consideration and detailed discussions. In the following, we summarize the nineteenth-century research conducted there as well as the results of our archaeological survey and excavation program (Maps 7.5 and 7.6).

The Sanctuary Wall

The east edge of the Sanctuary is defined by a low wall that runs roughly north-south (Photo 7.12). The wall, made with simple fieldstones, rises from the northeast slope of the island, crosses the summit, and drops down to the terraces of Chucaripupata on the other side.[16] The paved road from Kasapata to the Sacred Rock passes through the wall precisely at the point where the site of

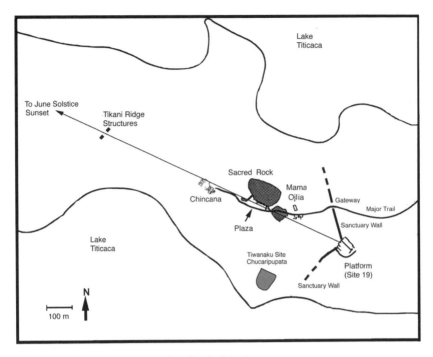

MAP 7.5. The Sanctuary area on the Island of the Sun.

Mama Ojlia and the Sacred Rock are revealed for the first time. This entrance-way into the Sanctuary may have once been called Pumapuncu (Ramos Gavilán 1988:94 [1621: Bk. 1, Ch. 15]).

Along the wall, near the crest of the island, is a roughly rectangular platform defined by terraces and wall foundations. This platform, which we called Site 19, contains a light scatter of Inca pottery. Bandelier (1910:215) also noted archaeological remains in this area: "On the crest, outside of the wall, are faint vestiges of two quadrangular structures." This platform is the only constructed feature adjacent to the wall. Since the platform is located on the outside of the Sanctuary, we presume that it was accessible by all pilgrims.

Facing page

MAP 7.6. The Inca sites in the Sanctuary area are concentrated along the road that leads from the Sanctuary entrance (A) to the large Inca complex of the Chincana (D). Before arriving at the Sacred Rock (C), the pilgrims passed through three separate gateways (1, 2, and 3) and passed by the site of Mama Ojlia (B).

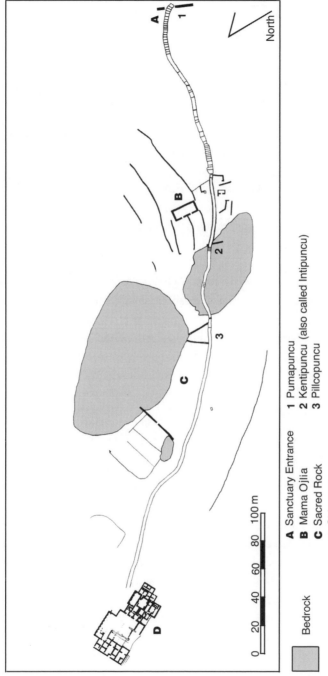

Bedrock

0	20	40	60	80	100 m

North

A Sanctuary Entrance
B Mama Ojlia
C Sacred Rock
D Chincana

1 Pumapuncu
2 Kentipuncu (also called Intipuncu)
3 Pillcopuncu

PHOTO 7.12. A low wall defines the east side of the Sanctuary area.

Near the entranceway, a few meters off the road to the west of the wall, we found another light scatter of Inca pottery at a place we recorded as Site 20. The fact that both Sites 19 and 20 are located on the east side of the wall and that there are no traces of remains tangent to its west side is not surprising. The wall separates the Sanctuary area from the rest of the island. The Sanctuary was kept clean, but the area immediately outside of it witnessed a variety of other activities.

The Site of Mama Ojlia

The site of Mama Ojlia is located in a shallow ravine within the Sanctuary area, halfway between the Sanctuary wall and the Sacred Rock, along the road (Photo 7.13). Above the road are the remains of three small structures, several low terrace walls, and a seasonal spring (Map 7.7). The water from the spring crosses the road in a channel and flows some 250 meters to the lake. Below the road is a series of long, straight terraces that crosscut the natural contour of the hill slope, as well as a single rectangular structure measuring approximately 16.80 × 6.75 m. Ramos Gavilán (1988:94 [1621: Bk. 1, Ch. 15]) suggests that these structures were "the living quarters of the Ministers of the Sanctuary and of the Virgins devoted to the Sun."[17] Similarly, Cobo (1990:98 [1653: Bk. 13, Ch. 18]) states that these remains "were lodgings for the attendants and servants of the temple."[18]

PHOTO 7.13. The site of Mama Ojlia is crossed by the road to the Sacred Rock. Below the road are a set of terraces and a single large structure. Above the road is a group of much smaller buildings and terraces. In the distance, at the top of the hill, is the entrance to the Sanctuary area.

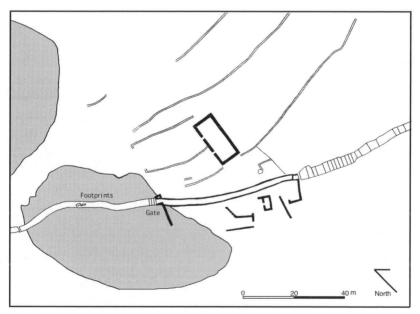

MAP 7.7. The site of Mama Ojlia. The site contains a single large building below the road and a series of small structures above it. Nearby are the remains of a gateway, most likely called Kentipuncu, and the so-called "Footprints of the Sun."

Footprints of the Sun

Squier (1877:338) is the first of the nineteenth-century explorers of the is-land to mention these remains. Likewise, Bandelier describes the archaeologi-cal remains in this area, and he notes that this section of the road retained the name of Kentipuncu. Bandelier also indicates that the ruins were referred to as Mama Ojlia.[19]

> The bottom [of the ravine], which the Indians call Mama-ojlia (we also heard the name Iñak-uyu), lies east of the plateau on which the Sacred Rock stands and slopes gently to the lake.[20] It is mostly terraced and bears the vestiges of at least four small buildings. Three of them stand west of the trail, the largest one is on the east and somewhat lower. To this last building the name Mama-ojlia is more particularly given . . . Beyond them the trail winds along the rocky slopes of Muro-kato for a short distance, and here again are a few well made stone steps, sometimes called by the Indians Kenti-puncu, and said to have been one of the gateways through which the enclosure of the Sacred Rock was entered . . . Above Kenti-puncu large nodules of limonite appear, two of which, each about three feet long [1 m], have the outline of huge moccasins. These marks are called "Tracks of the Sun" or of the Moon . . . (Bandelier 1910:216–217)

Our research at this site included mapping, surface collections, and limited test excavations. This work was especially important, since Mama Ojlia ap-pears to be the only site in the Sanctuary area that is not extensively looted. In-tensive surface collections at the site recovered more than 160 fragments of Inca pottery and a small number of nondiagnostic wares. No pre-Inca ceram-ics were recovered on its surface. The abundance of Inca pottery and the lack of earlier materials indicate that the site was only occupied during Inca times.

Our excavations were restricted to the larger structure below the road. Its stone and mud-mortar walls are poorly preserved, standing in most places less than one meter high (Photo 7.14). The south end of the building, containing the best-preserved wall, is cut into the hill slope. The opposite end has been raised approximately two meters above the natural hill slope to provide a level floor for the building. The pre-excavation cleaning of the structure revealed two doors—a common feature of Inca buildings—on its west side.[21] Because of poor preservation, it is not known if the building had any niches.

In total, we excavated an area of fourteen square meters in the southwest corner of the building.[22] The excavations revealed the remains of a partially preserved floor, the exact date of which is not known, since no diagnostic

PHOTO 7.14. The largest structure at Mama Ojlia.

shards were found on it.[23] A thin stratum of dark sediment below the floor held a large quantity of Inca ceramics as well as carbon. The shards appeared to be *in situ* since they were large and well preserved and many fit together. Most of the Inca ceramics were of a high quality, although some pieces of utilitarian vessels were also found. A carbon sample recovered in the Inca pottery containing sediment gave a radiocarbon age of 370 ± 60 BP (AD 1580 ± 60).[24] A second carbon sample, found in direct association with an Inca bird-head handle from a bowl, furnished a radiocarbon age of 420 ± 60 BP (AD 1530 ± 60).[25]

In summary, surface remains, excavated artifacts, and radiocarbon dates from the site of Mama Ojlia all indicate that its structures were constructed by the Inca in an area of the Sanctuary that had not been used by earlier cultures. Cobo (1990:97 [1653: Bk. 13, Ch. 18]) and Ramos Gavilán (1988:94 [1621: Bk. 1, Ch. 15]) suggest that Mama Ojlia was the living quarters for shrine personnel.[26] This proposed function is consistent with the range of ceramics found at the site, which included an abundance of fine wares and a small percentage of domestic wares. Perhaps these quarters were for the attendants who guarded the gateways into the Sanctuary (see Chapter 8), and the Mama Ojlia area was selected because of its location along the road beside one of the few springs in the Sanctuary area.

The Site of the Chincana

A little more than two hundred meters from the Sacred Rock is a site with elaborate architecture that has been called the Chincana (labyrinth) since at least colonial times. The site offers a spectacular view of a beach below and, in the far distance, the Peruvian lakeshore. Ramos Gavilán correctly places this majestic site on the southern slope of the island, in a gully facing the Peruvian cities of Juli and Pomata, and he indicates that it was already deteriorating when he visited the island:

> Farther ahead from them [the Temple of the Sun and the sky deities], in the ravine in front of the road (between Juli and Pomata) is the storehouse of the Sun which, before time laid it in ruins, presented a delightful sight with its buildings and layout. Its countless rooms formed a kind of labyrinth, which the Indians call Chincana, that means "place where one gets lost." The rooms had a garden in the center with a grove of alders, its constant freshness sustained by a spring of sweet water that emerges there. In the shade of these trees, the Inca fashioned strange baths of stone for the Sun and its cult. (Ramos Gavilán 1988:93 [1621: Bk. 1, Ch. 13]; authors' translation)[27]

Cobo also provides a description of the Chincana, and his account parallels that provided by Ramos Gavilán:

> Near the temple [of the Sun] the ruins of a storehouse of the Sun can be seen, and the chambers of this place look like the labyrinth of Crete. The skillful workmanship that characterized the construction of this superstitious shrine can be seen in the large walls and other traces of it that remain standing today.

In addition, the outline of a garden with its walk lined with alder trees is visible, and under the shadow of these trees there were some very well made baths of stone that were constructed on the Inca's orders. The Inca said that these baths were constructed so that the Sun could bathe there. (Cobo 1990:97 [1653: Bk. 13, Ch. 18])[28]

A little later in his chronicle, Cobo suggests that this "storehouse" also served as a House of the Mamaconas, in other words, a residence for women of the state who were chosen to serve its major shrines. He writes that on the far side of the Sanctuary there was "a large building which was a retreat of the *mamaconas*, women dedicated to the Sun. There women served in making the beverages and finely woven cloth that were used in the services for the shrine. This house for the *mamaconas* was in the best location of the island" (Cobo 1990:98 [1653: Bk. 13, Ch. 18]).[29] The Chincana is relatively well preserved, with walls two to three meters high, although some recent reconstruction obscures a few of the original foundations (Photos 7.15 and 7.16). The spring (bath), mentioned by both Ramos Gavilán and Cobo, still emerges in a courtyard; however, the trees that once shaded it have long since disappeared (Photo 7.17). Below the complex is a series of steep terraces that lead toward the lake, some 150 meters away.

The Chincana is composed of rectangular rooms, plazas, and passageways of varying dimensions.[30] Numerous doorways, niches, stairs, and other interior features are visible. Vestiges of doorways can be seen in the uppermost tiers of a few walls, indicating that some of the buildings once had second stories. The walls are constructed with fieldstones and earth mortar and were once covered with plaster and painted red and yellow (Bandelier 1910:222). Overall, the construction is similar to that of the site of Pilco Kayma, on the other end of the island.

The Chincana has trapezoidal doors and niches typical of Inca architecture. Although these Inca elements are abundant, the overall plan of the complex is distinct from plans found in the Cuzco area. In the Inca heartland, and in most Inca administrative centers elsewhere in the empire, three or four independent structures were constructed around a rectangular courtyard or *cancha*. In contrast to this basic canon of Inca architecture, in the Chincana there are many rooms connected by twisting passageways.

It is also worth noting that though most of the doorways and niches are trapezoidal, some are rectangular. Furthermore, like in Pilco Kayma, there is a

PHOTO 7.15. The Chincana is near the Sacred Rock on the southern slope of the island. The Sacred Rock can be seen in the upper left of this photograph, and the Chincana is in the center.

PHOTO 7.16. The Chincana.

PHOTO 7.17. The spring in the Chincana is mentioned by both Ramos Gavilán and Cobo.

general carelessness of construction that is not found in buildings in Cuzco. Most notable is that the sizes and proportions of the doorways and niches vary greatly in the complex and, in some cases, even within the same room. These irregularities may reflect the construction of the building using large crews of local laborers who worked with only general guidance from state overseers.

The Chincana is composed of two architecturally different sectors (Map 7.8). The east sector is made of small rooms, narrow passageways, and two small central plazas. Several of the passageways still retain their original slab-stone ceilings (Photos 7.18 and 7.19). Although the plan of the east zone is not completely symmetrical, the rooms and passageways lead off both sides of its two adjacent plazas. The multiple passageways and internally connected rooms of this sector lend a mazelike feeling to the complex as a whole.

The western sector is more open than the eastern one. It contains two or three parallel rows of larger interconnecting rooms and a significantly larger plaza. This sector has a massive upper wall with eight interior and eight exterior niches (Photo 7.20), the spring described by both Ramos Gavilán and Cobo, and a carved rock (Photo 7.21).

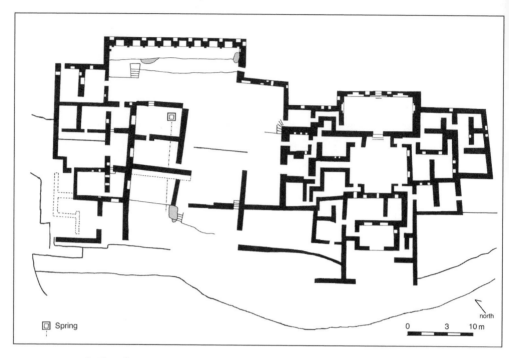

north

0   3   10 m

MAP 7.8. The Chincana is composed of two architecturally different sectors. The east zone contains various small rooms and narrow passageways. The west zone is more open, and it contains parallel rows of rooms and a single large plaza.

PHOTO 7.18. A passageway in the east sector of the Chincana.

PHOTO 7.19. A slab-stone ceiling in one of the passageways in the east sector of the Chincana.

The complex organization of the Chincana has long attracted the attention of researchers. Both Pentland (1827: f. 88v–89v) and Squier (1877:338–339) provide detailed descriptions of the site. The first engravings of the Chincana are furnished by Wiener in 1877 (Figures 7.7 and 7.8). He renders a southwest overview of the site and depicts the interior of one room in the east section (Wiener 1880:441–442).[31]

Although Bandelier did not excavate at the Chincana, he did spend considerable time exploring and documenting its remains (Map 7.9). Bandelier (1910:230) suggests that some of the structures and passages were paved with pebbles or small cobbles. He also produced an early map of the site, two studies of architectural details, and two photographs (Bandelier 1910, plates LVI, LX, LXIII, LXIV, LXV).[32] Other maps of the Chincana have been drawn by Posnansky (1912 [west sector only]) and Escalante Moscoso (1994:361).

Surface Collections and Test Excavations at the Chincana. Surface collections at the Chincana yielded just a few fragments of Inca pottery, most of which were found along the steep, eroding south edge of the site. Seven excavation units were placed in various rooms and open areas of the Chincana to deter-

PHOTO 7.20. The exterior niches of the upper wall in the west sector on the Chincana.

PHOTO 7.21. There is a prominent carved rock in the west sector of the Chincana.

FIGURE 7.7. A southwest view of the Chincana (Wiener 1880:441).

FIGURE 7.8. The interior of one of the rooms in the east sector of the Chincana (Wiener 1880:442).

MAP 7.9. Bandelier's 1895 map of the Chincana complex. (Courtesy of the Division of Anthropology, American Museum of Natural History.)

mine their functions and to test for evidence of earlier occupations. These test pits revealed extensive collapse of the original walls and ceilings as well as evidence of some looting. They also indicated that the interior of the complex was nearly devoid of artifacts. In total, our seven test units within the complex yielded approximately thirty Inca shards, most of which were small, isolated fragments, as well as a lesser number of eroded, culturally unknown fragments.

In the second excavation stage, we excavated several test units on the lower terraces of the Chincana to recover midden materials. The redeposited sediments on these terraces contained a greater number of Inca ceramics than the building interiors, as well as ash concentrations and some faunal remains. The ceramic fragments, which included both domestic and elite Inca wares, indicate that a wide range of functions took place at the site. Two carbon samples from these mix contexts furnished dates of 340 ± 80 BP (AD 1610 ± 80)[33] and 220 ± 80 BP (AD 1730 ± 80).[34]

The Function of the Chincana. Research was conducted at the Chincana to determine the age and function of the east and west sectors of this architecturally complex site and to test for evidence of pre-Inca materials beneath it. We began excavations with two alternative explanations for the contrasting east and west sectors of the site. One theory was that the east sector, with its unusual mazelike construction, was pre-Inca and that the west sector represented an Inca addition to the complex. Alternatively, it was proposed that the two sectors represented areas of distinctly different functions, both built during the Inca Period. The east sector, with its many small rooms, could have been a storage facility, while the more open western sector, with its spring and large plaza, could have served as living quarters for attendants of the shrine.

The idea that the Chincana contained both pre-Inca (east side) and Inca (west side) components was not supported by data recovered during our research at the site. Extensive surface collections at the Chincana recovered only Inca pottery. Furthermore, excavations in both sectors, as well as on the terraces below them, provided no evidence of pre-Inca materials. The absence of earlier ceramics, and the presence of Inca materials across the site, suggests that the complex was built and occupied exclusively during the Inca Period.

The apparent dating of both zones of the Chincana to the Inca Period suggests that the two distinct architectural areas of the site reflect functional rather than temporal differences. Unfortunately, our excavations within the separate rooms and plazas of the Chincana did not yield enough cultural materials to speculate on their functions. Insight into the function of the Chincana can, however, be gained by examining the early colonial descriptions of it. Both Ramos Gavilán and Cobo specifically state that the Chincana served as a storehouse of the Sun. For example, Ramos Gavilán states, "in the gully that falls in front of the road (facing Juli and Pomata) is the storehouse of the Sun, . . . With the countless rooms that it had it was like a labyrinth. So the Indians call it Chincana."[35] And Cobo notes, "Near the temple [of the Sun] the ruins of a storehouse of the Sun can be seen, whose chambers of this place look like the labyrinth of Crete."[36] The suggestion that the Chincana served as a storage facility fits well with the architecture of the multichambered east area of the site.

The complexity of the Chincana, with its two separate architectural sectors, suggests that the site served other functions as well. Cobo notes that a Temple of the Sun was located near the storehouse and that it held a series of "windows, cupboards, or niches along the walls."[37] This could be a reference to the west part of the Chincana, with its impressive wall of large niches. Furthermore, Ramos Gavilán specifically describes the spring of the Chincana as being used for the Sun and its cult. Cobo also suggests that the Chincana held the living quarters for Mamacona who "made beverages and finely woven cloth that were used in the services for the shrine."[38] The fact that such a group of women lived in a structure that was also called a "temple" is not surprising, since we know that a large number of Mamacona lived in the Coricancha in Cuzco to serve its shrines. In sum, given the archaeological and historical data, it is reasonable to suggest the Chincana was a state installation built by the Inca after their conquest of the Lake Titicaca region. It most likely housed some Mamacona and simultaneously served as a temple and storehouse of the Sun.

The Site of Chucaripupata

Seddon's (1998) excavations also provide data on the post-Tiwanaku occupation at Chucaripupata. There is virtually no Altiplano Period occupation at the site. The Inca use of the area, in contrast, is quite significant. In a word, the Inca destroyed any vestige of the remaining Tiwanaku occupation. As Seddon notes, "Upon arriving at the island, the Inka buried the visible remnants of the earlier Tiwanaku shrine" (1998:488). He goes on to point out that "the establishment of the Inka shrine at Santiago Pampa [the Sacred Rock] involved a reconfiguration of the sacred landscape on the barren north end of the island. It appears that the site of Chucaripupata was destroyed, burned, and buried, and that the monumental temple walls, when seen from Santiago Pampa, were deliberately obscured" (Seddon 1998:432). Carbon dates support the destruction of Chucaripupata by the Inca. A split carbon sample recovered from a burned platform at the site yielded ages of 475 ± 35 BP (AD 1475 ± 35)[39] and 540 ± 35 BP (AD 1410 ± 35).[40] The entire site in the Inca Period seems to have been nothing more than an agricultural area.

The Sacred Rock

Near the center of the Sanctuary is the Titikala, the Sacred Rock from which the Sun first rose (Photo 7.22). One side of the rock descends toward the lake (see Photos 1.3 and 8.15), and the other side forms a vertical face near the midline of the island.

A plaza adjoins the rock (Photo 7.23, Map 7.10). The north side of the plaza is formed by the vertical face of the rock that rises nearly 5.5 meters and runs for about 80 meters. The west side of the plaza is about 35 meters long, and is defined by the remains of an Inca wall. The wall runs from the Sacred Rock to a smaller, isolated outcrop. The wall contains a central trapezoidal doorway,

PHOTO 7.22. The Sacred Rock from which the sun rose is a large exposed strata of reddish sandstone.

with a set of eleven small trapezoidal windows (Figure 7.9). An ephemeral terrace defines the east edge of the plaza. The south side of the plaza is open and is crossed by the Inca road that leads from the main entryway of the Sanctuary in the east to the Chincana in the west.

Squier supplies the earliest illustration of the rock (Figure 7.10). This figure is somewhat distorted, since it shows the Inca wall, which runs perpendicular to the rock, directly in front of it and running parallel in his engraving. But other aspects of the etching are insightful. For example, a circular depression recorded in the etching suggests that a large hole once dominated the center of the plaza. Squier also provides an elegant description of the rock and its setting:

> At almost the very northern end of the island, at its most repulsive and unpromising part, where there is neither inhabitant nor trace of culture, where the soil is rocky and bare, and the cliffs ragged and broken high up, where the fret of the waves of the lake is scarcely heard, and where the eye ranges over the broad blue waters from one mountain barrier to the other, from the glittering crests of the Andes to those of the Cordillera, is the spot most celebrated and most sacred of Peru. Here is the rock on which it was believed no bird would

PHOTO 7.23. The Sacred Rock plaza.

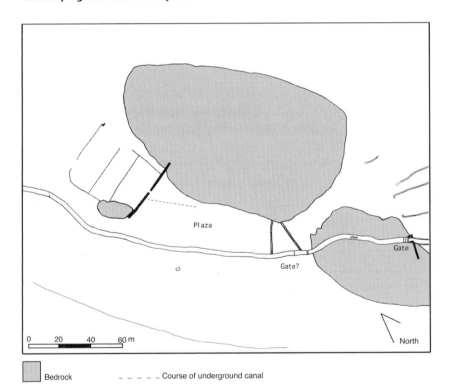

Plaza

Gate?

Gate

0   20   40   60 m

North

Bedrock   _ _ _ _ _ Course of underground canal

MAP 7.10. The area of the Titikala (the Sacred Rock).

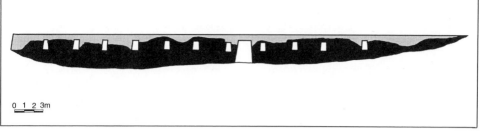

FIGURE 7.9. An Inca wall, about 35 meters long, defines the northwest side of the plaza at the Sacred Rock. The wall contains a central trapezoidal doorway, with a set of eleven small trapezoidal windows.

FIGURE 7.10. Squier's engraving of the Sacred Rock. He writes, "Our guides stopped when it came in view, removed their hats, and bowed low and reverently in its direction, muttering a few words of mystic import" (1877:336–337).

light or animal venture, on which no human being dared to place his foot;
whence the sun rose to dispel the primal vapors and illume the world; which
was plated all over with gold and silver, and covered, except on occasion of the
most solemn festivals, with a veil of cloth of richest color and materials; which
sheltered the favorite children of the Sun, and the pontiff, priests, and king
who founded the Inca empire.

Our guides stopped when it came in view, removed their hats, and bowed
low and reverently in its direction, muttering a few words of mystic import. But
this rock today, alas for the gods dethroned!—is nothing more than a frayed
and weather-worn mass of red sandstone, part of a thick stratum that runs
through the island, and which is here disrupted and standing, with its associated shale and limestone layers, at an angle of forty-five degrees with the horizon. (Squier 1877:336–337)

In 1892, E. Pickering of the Harvard Observatory traveled to the sacred islands and took the earliest photograph of the Sacred Rock (Photos 7.24 and
7.25). These pictures show a barren and eroded plaza, as well as a large irregular depression near its center—in the same area as Squier's etching—suggestive
of a large looters' pit.

PHOTO 7.24. The earliest-known photographs of the Sacred Rock were taken by
E. Pickering in 1892. Here we see the rock from a distance of about 40 meters. (Courtesy
of the Peabody Museum, Harvard University [catalog number H9837].)

PHOTO 7.25. The Inca wall and the Sacred Rock. Note the large irregular depression near the center of the plaza, suggestive of a looters' pit. (Photograph by E. Pickering, 1892. Courtesy of the Peabody Museum, Harvard University [catalog number H9839].)

Bandelier began his research on the island three years after Pickering's visit. Bandelier (1910:217) states specifically that looters had seriously disturbed the area in front of the rock. Elsewhere he notes that some of the most famous Inca objects that he purchased from the hacienda owner came from in front of, or near to, the rock:

> The surroundings of Titi-kala have long ago been searched and rifled. The Garcés collection, now at the [American] Museum [of Natural History], contains gold and silver figurines from this vicinity. The concurrent testimony of the former owners of the collection, as well as of Indians from the Island who excavated for these owners, is that most of the figures of llamas, if not all, came from this neighborhood, as also the small pins of gold and of silver. (Bandelier 1910:220)

Immediately to the northwest of the plaza, on the other side of the Inca wall, is an expanse of terraced land. Most of Bandelier's excavations took place in the northwest corner of this terraced area. There, under a mass of rubble, Bandelier (1910:219, 257) found several wall foundations. He proposed that these remains represented the Temple of the Sun that is described by Ramos Gavilán

(1988:93 [1621: Bk. 1, Ch. 13]) and Cobo (1990:97 [1653: Bk. 13, Ch. 18]) as being thirty to forty steps from the rock. Bandelier's excavations in the terraced area must not have yielded many artifacts, since he does not describe or illustrate any items found in this area.

Surface Collections and Test Excavations at the Sacred Rock. Our research at the Sacred Rock began during the survey of the island. Surface collections recovered a few modern and Inca shards, but no pre-Inca materials. A close inspection of the plaza surface revealed a light scatter of small (1–4 mm) pieces of greenstone. The west and northwest areas of the plaza contained the highest density of greenstone. Subsequent excavations revealed that this material had come from a badly disturbed greenstone floor that once covered the plaza.

Like Squier (1877:338–339) and Bandelier (1910:218), we noted the presence of cut andesite blocks in the area (Photo 7.26). These blocks are intriguing, as there is no source of andesite on the island, so they must have been brought by boat from the mainland. A group of andesite blocks has been placed together, along with a large slab of white sandstone, just south of the plaza (Photo 7.27). Although this cluster of carved stones attracts the attention of tourists and serves as the source of imaginative tales by guides, old photographs of the plaza indicate that it is a recent arrangement.[41] Nevertheless, the presence of cut blocks in the plaza area suggests that an elaborate construction, perhaps an altar or a building, once stood in or near it.

PHOTO 7.26. Carved stone blocks can be found in the Sanctuary area.

PHOTO 7.27. Recently a group of andesite blocks has been placed together, along with a large slab of white sandstone, just south of the Sacred Rock. This "table" attracts the attention of tourists and serves as the source of imaginative tales by guides.

A series of test units were excavated in the plaza. We first dug two parallel lines of 1 × 2 m units across the plaza to systematically test for subsurface remains. These units tended to be relatively shallow, between 30 and 80 cm in depth, and provided only a few artifacts. The most notable artifacts were fragments from miniature Inca bowls. Such vessels were common components of Inca offerings.

One of the units near the center of the plaza revealed the straight edge of a pit cut into bedrock. Excavations in this area were expanded with an adjacent 2 × 2 m unit, which exposed a 60 × 50 cm rectangular pit carefully cut 60 cm into bedrock, as well as several other shallow depressions. Although this area of the plaza has been badly disturbed by looters, it seems certain that the rectangular pit once held offering materials. Bandelier documents that some of the offerings in the Sacred Rock area were placed in stone chests, and he purchased one from the hacienda owner (Bandelier 1910, plate LXI). A nearly identical chest from the Island of the Sun had been bought four years earlier, in 1891, by George Dorsey for the 1892–1893 World Columbian Exposition in Chicago. This chest measures 39 × 24 × 25 cm and can be found within the holdings of the Field Museum of Natural History (Photo 7.28).[42] Although we will never know for certain, one can speculate that the deeply cut rectangular pit in the plaza once held such a chest.

PHOTO 7.28. Bandelier reports that some of the offerings in the Sanctuary area were buried in stone chests. One stone chest from the Island of the Sun was sent by Bandelier to the American Museum of Natural History. A second stone chest from the island (seen in this photograph) was purchased by George Dorsey in 1891 for the World Columbian Exposition in Chicago and is now part of the Field Museum's holdings (artifact number A4248).

The plaza-testing program also exposed the remains of a small stone canal, first identified in units near the Inca wall. Additional excavations were conducted to follow the course of this canal and to better understand its function. Although the exact origin point of the canal could not be identified due to extensive looting, it appears to have begun somewhere near the concave section of the Sacred Rock. The canal sloped slightly downhill from the Sacred Rock, crossed the plaza in a straight, although not rigid, line, and passed under the Inca wall some two meters south of the doorway. Buried at the time of use, the canal survives in varying states of presentation. In several areas we found it complete with cap stones and a channel measuring 20 cm wide and 30 cm deep (Photo 7.29). In other areas, the canal is damaged (Photo 7.30).

Given the general origin point of the canal near the concave area of the rock, and the fact that there is no natural source of water in the plaza area, it is clear that this canal was built by the Inca to drain liquid offerings from the plaza. Descriptions of such offerings can be found in the conquest and early colonial accounts of the Sanctuary. For example, the first Europeans to arrive

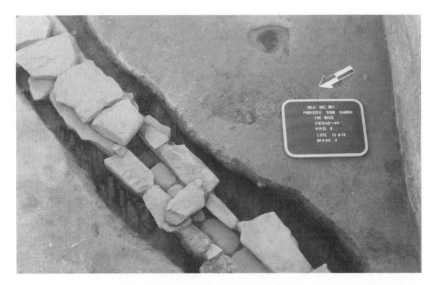

PHOTO 7.29. Excavations in the Sacred Rock plaza found the remains of a stone canal. In some areas the canal was still complete with cap stones.

PHOTO 7.30. The plaza area has been badly looted. In many places looting has damaged the Inca canal that once drained liquid offerings from near the Sacred Rock. In this photograph, the cap stones of the canal have been lost.

in the Lake Titicaca region state that there were a large number of "women who make *chicha* [corn beer] in order to throw it upon that stone"[43] (Sancho de la Hoz 1917:163 [1534: Ch. 18]). Furthermore, both Ramos Gavilán (1988: 116 [1621: Bk. 1, Ch. 17]) and Cobo (1990:96–97 [1653: Bk. 13, Ch. 18]) note that large amounts of corn beer were poured into a stone basin that was directly in front of the sacred rock.

Although the upper portions of the plaza have been destroyed by plowing and looting, at a depth of 60 cm below the modern ground surface, the testing program identified well-preserved stratified levels near the Inca wall. These strata began 20 cm above bedrock. They passed below the wall foundation and were cut by the construction of the canal. There were at least two thin lenses of dark brown silty clay mixed with small flecks of carbon, separated by levels of finely laminated sandy silt. The clay lenses appeared to be prepared floors that once covered the plaza area. The most remarkable find, however, was a floor of crushed greenstone[44] and silty clay found below these thin lenses and above the natural subsoil.[45]

The greenstone floor was more than 3 cm thick in the west, but grew gradually thinner in the east. The greenstone varied in size from minute to some pieces as large as 4 mm. The floor is cut by the canal, indicating that it was built before the canal was made. No artifacts were found in association with the floor, but flecks of carbon collected from it yielded an AMS date of 450 ± 50 BP (AD 1500 ± 50).[46] This date places the construction of the floor during the Inca occupation of the island. As this floor was placed directly above bedrock, it seems that the Inca leveled the area before they began construction.

Three test units were also dug on the west side of the Inca wall. No evidence of the greenstone floor was found there, and no artifacts were recovered. However, excavations did reveal a continuation of the canal. Furthermore, it seems that the drainage of the canal was remolded at some time, since we also found a section of an abandoned canal.

Finally, we conducted a 6 × 5 m excavation directly in front of the concave area of the Sacred Rock. Unfortunately, this area had been extensively looted and all evidence of prehispanic activities was destroyed. We did, however, encounter various small slab cists, which held modern offerings to the rock. Some of the offerings were made within this decade, though others appeared to be much older.[47]

Astronomical Research on the Island of the Sun
and the Copacabana Peninsula

The best-documented examples of Inca astronomy are from Cuzco, where the Inca used the movements of the Sun across the horizon to organize their ritual calendar. We know, for example, that various solar markers (or pillars) were used during the enormous public rituals that were held in Cuzco (Bauer and Dearborn 1995:50–53; Bauer 1998). These solar markers were rectangular structures, which were built in pairs on the horizon to frame the sunrise or sunset on specific dates. For example, Cobo (1990:25 [1653: Bk. 13, Ch. 13]) indicates that a pair of pillars on a hill called Quiangalla marked the June solstice.[48] Another set of twin pillars marked the location of the December solstice sunset. It has also been documented that the Inca used light and shadow casting to keep track of time (Dearborn and White 1983). In these procedures, the path of light (cast from a window or natural hole) or the path of a shadow (cast from a gnomon) was traced across a calibrated surface (Bauer and Dearborn 1995).

As part of our research program on the Islands of the Sun and the Moon, we surveyed their prehispanic remains for evidence of astronomical activities. As ritual centers related to the emergence of the Sun, the sacred islands of Lake Titicaca were prime candidates for finding evidence of Inca solar astronomy. The results of our investigation are outlined below as well as those of Rivera Sundt on the Copacabana Peninsula.

The June Solstice Sunrise and the Horca del Inca

Just south of the city of Copacabana on the summit of a steep, rocky hill is an unusual archaeological site called the Horca del Inca (Gallows of the Inca). Nestled within a number of mammoth outcrops are two closely spaced crags. The area between these twin crags has been carved to hold a stone lintel (Photo 7.31). The bedrock at the base of the crag has also been carved to provide the footing for a stone wall, which is now destroyed. Although Cobo (1990:91 [1653: Bk. 13, Ch. 18]) noted the presence of this site in 1618 and Wiener (1880: 437) provides the first illustration of it, the function of the Horca del Inca remained unknown.[49] In 1978, however, Oswaldo Rivera Sundt (1984b) documented that a hole in another crag some twenty meters away casts a well-defined spot of light onto the center of the lintel on the morning of the June solstice (Photo 7.32, Figure 7.11). Since Rivera Sundt's discovery, interest in this marker has grown and officials of Copacabana now hold a celebration at the site each year on the June solstice.

The June Solstice Sunset and the Sacred Rock

Ramos Gavilán (1988:176 [1621: Bk. 1, Ch. 29]) notes that the Inca held large celebrations at the site of Kasapata on the Island of the Sun during the solstices. The results of our work on the island indicate that the Inca also made astronomical observations from the Sacred Rock. Research on the Island of the Sun by David Dearborn found that the June Sun sets over a ridge, called Tikani, less than a kilometer northwest of the plaza of the Sacred Rock. On this ridge, there are two structures that flank the position at which the Sun sets on the June solstice as seen from the plaza (Photos 7.33–7.35). In other words, ev-

PHOTO 7.31. The Horca del Inca consists of two stone crags that are crossed by a lintel. These remains may have helped the Inca mark the June solstice sunrise.

PHOTO 7.32. On the morning of the June solstice, light passes through this small hole and shines on the lintel of the Horca del Inca.

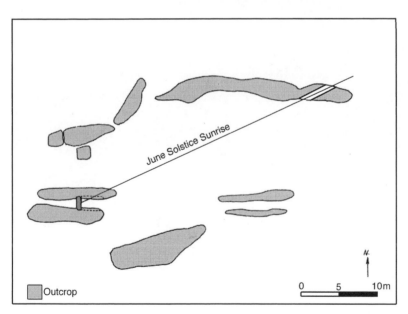

June Solstice Sunrise

Outcrop

0   5   10m

N.

FIGURE 7.11. At the Horca del Inca, outside of Copacabana, light is cast through a small hole onto a lintel on the morning of the June solstice (after Rivera Sundt 1984b).

PHOTO 7.33. The ridge of Tikani. Even today, the remains of two structures built on this ridge are clearly visible from the plaza area.

PHOTO 7.34. The June solstice sunset as seen from the plaza of the Sacred Rock.

eryone located in the plaza could see the sunset between the structures on that date. As the use of horizon markers is well documented in the Inca capital, and the structures on the Tikani ridge exactly frame the setting Sun on the June solstice, it seems certain that these structures were used by the Inca as part of their June solstice celebrations on the Island of the Sun (Dearborn et al. 1998).

PHOTO 7.35. The sun sets directly between two structures (marked by flags) on a ridge northwest of the Sacred Rock on the June solstice.

A Pilgrim's Perspective of the June Solstice Sunset

The chroniclers state that only a few of the pilgrims who crossed the island were allowed to approach and worship at the Sacred Rock itself. Most visitors had to be content to view the Sacred Rock from a distance. These accounts may help to explain the remains of a small Inca platform, Site 19, that we found adjacent to the Sanctuary wall.

The Sacred Rock and ridge of Tikani are visible from this platform (Photo 7.36). The frontage width of the platform is just over 30 meters, matching the separation between the pillar foundations on the ridge, as well as the width of the Sacred Rock plaza. The location and size of this platform are such that most of the people on it would have seen the Sun setting over the rock and the plaza, as well as between the pillars, for dates near the June solstice. We propose that by standing at this structure, pilgrims who were not allowed direct access into the Sanctuary could have still participated with priests and other elites in the plaza area in observing the Sun return to earth between the horizon pillars (Dearborn et al. 1998).

PHOTO 7.36. The Sanctuary area as seen from the platform (Site 19). From this platform, the only structure built along the Sanctuary wall, the June solstice sun sets over the Sacred Rock and the plaza, and between the two ridge structures.

This adds a dimension to the practice of the solar cult that was not explicitly recorded in the accounts of state rituals. Though both elite and non-elite groups participated in solar worship, the non-elites simultaneously offered respect to the Sun and to the Inca elites. This physical organization emphasized that the Inca alone held direct and undisputed access to the powers of the Sun. With this authority, they controlled time and regulated social activities through the seasons. The physical separation of both groups also served to reinforce class distinctions in Inca society. The nobility stood near the spot where the Sun was born and witnessed the solstice from that location. The plaza was large enough that the lesser nobility, including the priests and attendants from the elite Cuzco kin groups, could also participate in the ceremony. Simultaneously, the commoners could partake, but at a distance. Like a serf standing at the back entrance of a medieval church, they had the right, perhaps even the obligation, to witness the ceremony. In medieval society, the closer one was to the altar, the higher one's relative social position. Similarly, in the Inca state, the ruling Inca and the highest nobility stood in the center of the plaza and in front of the Sacred Rock. The lesser nobility were farther from the center, and the non-elite were on the edge of the Sanctuary: a physical arrangement of people that mirrored their status within the state itself.

8 | THE PILGRIM'S PROGRESS

An Archaeological and Historical Perspective

THE SPANIARDS of the Early Colonial Period were no strangers to pilgrimages. Spain, like all of Europe, contained a host of local and regional shrines that were visited by the pious. Christian pilgrimages to the Holy Land, first established in the early fourth century AD, continued throughout the Middle Ages, despite the area's incorporation into the Arab world. Furthermore, within the first few years of Spanish occupation in the Andes, Christian saints were credited with various miracles, and specific places became associated with these divine events. Wondrous appearances, supernatural powers associated with specific places and objects, and religious journeys were all part of the European worldview when the Spaniards disembarked on the shores of the New World.

Within this cultural context, the Spaniards were not surprised to find that the indigenous people of Peru also traveled to shrines in acts of devotion. For example, while describing Coricancha, Pachacamac, and the Islands of the Sun and the Moon, Cobo notes:

> These were rich, magnificent temples, and like sanctuaries that were widely venerated; people went to them on pilgrimage from every part of the Peru, much in the same way that Christians customarily visit the Holy Sepulcher of our Savior, the temple of the Apostles Saint Peter and Saint Paul, and the famous sanctuary of Santiago in Galicia. (Cobo 1990:48 [1653: Bk. 13, Ch. 12])[1]

In the first part of this chapter, we reconstruct the pilgrimage route that individuals took from the Copacabana mainland to the Island of the Sun in late prehispanic times. In doing so, we rely heavily on the archaeological findings presented in the previous chapter and on information provided by Ramos Gavilán and Cobo. In the second half, we address a series of related questions, including when the visits were made, what was offered to the shrines, and who maintained the temples. In addition, we discuss the religious activities that took place on the islands and describe similar rites that occurred elsewhere in the empire, particularly in Cuzco. For these comparative discussions, we use information offered by a number of early writers, including Blas Valera, Pedro de Cieza de León, Garcilaso de la Vega, and Pedro Pizarro.

Arriving at Copacabana

During the period that the Inca controlled the Lake Titicaca Basin, individuals from across the empire traveled to the Islands of the Sun and the Moon to see and pay homage to the shrines built on them. According to Cobo, the pilgrims first arrived at the town of Yunguyu, about an hour from Copacabana (Map 8.1). He notes that a wall was constructed near Yunguyu and that guards were stationed at the gates to inspect travelers wishing to enter the Copacabana area:

MAP 8.1. The pilgrims' route from Yunguyu to the Island of the Sun.

Since the area starting from the straits or isthmus which I mentioned above between Yunguyo and Copacabana was considered to be a sacred place, the Inca
had this entrance closed off with a wall which he had made from one beach to
the other. He had gates put along the wall with watchmen and guards to look
over the people who came to the sanctuary on pilgrimages. (Cobo 1990:94
[1653: Bk. 13, Ch. 18])[2]

Later in his account, Cobo (1990:96 [1653: Bk. 13, Ch. 18]) states that to gain
access to Copacabana, the pilgrims spoke with a confessor and did penance.
They also abstained from salt, meat, and chili peppers. Interestingly, nearly
four and a half centuries later, the Copacabana Peninsula is still separated
from the rest of the mainland by the national border between Peru and Bolivia.
A modern wall and arch stand on a ridge at the border just outside of Yunguyu,
and visitors must still pass through immigration guards and seek permission
to continue their journey.

Ramos Gavilán characterizes the pilgrims' route in even more detail. He begins by describing a specific kind of public building that the Inca built for the
pilgrims' lodging:

There were so many people from the entire kingdom subject to the Inca that
visited this shrine, that he ordered public hostelries made where the pilgrims
gathered. Here in Peru, they usually call these hostelries (which were large
structures) *tambos,* and they named those that were made for the people that
visited the shrines *corpaguasi,*[3] which means the same as "pilgrims' house," in
our vernacular, where they [were] provided for during the time of their pilgrimage. (Ramos Gavilán 1988:127 [1621: Bk. 1, Ch. 20]; authors' translation)[4]

Ramos Gavilán also relates that as the pilgrims passed from Yunguyu to Copacabana they were provided with food and supplies from royal storehouses at a
place called Loca. Apparently, the social and political status of the pilgrims determined the nature of these gifts. Ramos Gavilán writes:

Coming from Yunguyo, they arrived first at Copacabana, where each one was
given, according to their status, the necessary food and drink, and if they were
poor, they were given some clothes. For this the Inca had in a place of Loca, a
half league from Copacabana, some storehouses, or granaries, that the Indians
call *colcas,* where all the food was collected, as much for the sustenance of the
soldiers as for the ministers of the temples and for the pilgrims that attended

them. These deposits are seen about Copacabana, on the lower slopes of the hills. (Ramos Gavilán 1988:127 [1621: Bk. 1, Ch. 20]; authors' translation)[5]

The community and storehouses of Loca are probably those mentioned in a 1548 Copacabana *encomienda* document that describes "another small town in which there are certain storehouses, that is between the town of Copacabana and Yunguyu, with seventeen Indians of service and nine widows and elders (Espinoza Soriano 1972a:10)."[6] Cobo also saw these imperial storehouses, for he writes: "In order to keep them [inns for the pilgrims] supplied, the Inca had large storehouses built near Copacabana for provisions of food, clothing, and other supplies. The ruins of these storehouses remain to this day, and I have seen them myself" (Cobo 1990:93 [1653: Bk. 13, Ch. 18]).[7] The village of Loca still exists between Yunguyu and Copacabana, near the Peru-Bolivia border.

The Journey from Copacabana to the Sanctuary of the Sun

During Inca times the town of Copacabana served as the regional administrative center for the peninsula and was responsible for guarding and controlling access to the sacred islands. The ruling elite, many of whom may have been from important kin groups of Cuzco, lived in the town and traveled out to the islands on specific ritual occasions. The pilgrims, after arriving at Copacabana, rested for several days and prayed at the local temples and shrines before proceeding to the Island of the Sun (Ramos Gavilán 1988:171–172 [1621: Bk. 1, Ch. 28]; Cobo 1990:96 [1653: Bk. 13, Ch. 18]).

A number of Inca sites in the Yunguyu-Copacabana area appear to have ritual functions. Escalante Moscoso (1994:370–375) has described several of these. The site of Khopakati, for instance, is near the border. This site has numerous Inca-style cut stone blocks and may have been an important stop on the pilgrimage route. About two hundred meters from these cut stones is the site of Pasankallani that Escalante Moscoso (1994:373) interprets to be a possible habitation area associated with Khopakati.

Near Copacabana there is the famous outcrop known as the Horca del Inca, which was used by the Inca to record the June solstice sunrise (Rivera Sundt 1984b). In addition, a set of cut outcrops known as Intinkala, just outside modern Copacabana, is typical of cut stones in the Cuzco area, and other such cut stones are found throughout the Copacabana area. Hyslop (1990:121), in fact, notes that the Copacabana area contains one of the highest densities of Inca-style carved rocks of anywhere in the empire.

From Copacabana, the pilgrims walked toward the port of Yampupata, some three hours away, on a well-paved road.[8] According to Ramos Gavilán (1988:127 [1621: Bk. 1, Ch. 20]), while en route to Yampupata the pilgrims passed through two additional checkpoints, with warehouses holding corn, other crops, and dried meat (*charque*). There may also have been a place at Yampupata for the pilgrims to spend the night before crossing over to the Island of the Sun (Squier 1877:327).[9] There is a small Inca site near the modern port that may be associated with this lodging.

The crossing of the strait from Yampupata to the Island of the Sun was an integral part of the pilgrimage process (Photos 8.1 and 8.2). Here, the Inca authorities were able to control absolutely the movement of pilgrims along the prescribed pilgrimage route.[10] The Inca landing place on the Island of the Sun is simply called Puncu (Entrance). It is at the extreme southeastern tip of the island, the point of land closest to the mainland. Squier offers a detailed description of the port as well as a small plan of the structures it comprised (Figure 8.1).[11] Thirty years after Squier's report, these structures were barely visible (Bandelier 1910:187, 191), and today only a few walls and a light scatter of Inca pottery remain to mark this important debarkation point.

From the landing place, the pilgrims began their trip to the opposite end of the island. The remains of the prehispanic road that began at Puncu can still be seen on the hillside (Photo 8.3). Traveling on this road, the pilgrims soon passed the impressive site of Pilco Kayma (Photo 8.4). Terraces surround this two-story, multichambered structure, and there is a small group of outlying buildings to its north.

We do not know if the pilgrims continued directly to the summit of the island from Pilco Kayma or if they first passed by the Fountain of the Inca to the east. The area of the Fountain of the Inca is shaped like a natural amphitheater and is covered with well-made agricultural terraces. High on the slope is a three-spout fountain that emerges out of the hill. Today, the Fountain of the Inca is the primary landing spot for tourists and the principal port for local boat owners. On the beach, there is a set of niches in an Inca wall, and in Inca times the site may have held a large structure as well (Bandelier 1910:197). Our archaeological survey indicates that there were no habitation sites adjacent to the fountain, although several sites can be found on the nearby slopes. The role of the fountain area is not mentioned in the chronicles, but we believe that its terraces were reserved for special agricultural products, perhaps the sacred maize for which the island was famous.

PHOTO 8.1. View from Yampupata to the Island of the Sun.

PHOTO 8.2. A small channel separates the Island of the Sun (foreground) from the Copacabana mainland (background). During Inca times, pilgrims crossed this channel in reed boats.

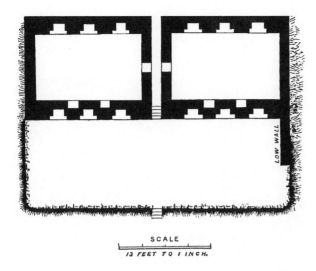

SCALE

/3 FEET TO 1 INCH.

FIGURE 8.1. The Inca site of Puncu marks the beginning of the
pilgrimage road on the Island of the Sun (Squier 1877:333).

Regardless of whether the pilgrims visited the fountain area or not, they
would have continued their trip to the Sacred Rock by climbing the slope near
Yumani. At the summit of the island, they would have walked along the ridge
for approximately seven kilometers. On this route they would have passed one
of the largest Inca villages on the island, a site now called Apachinacapata
(Photo 8.5).[12]

From Apachinacapata, travelers could have continued along the ridge to the
Sanctuary area at the far northern end of the island, or they could have taken
another road that led past several Inca villages along the northeast lakeshore.
Our survey work on the ridge between the site of Apachinacapata and the
Sacred Rock identified a series of low, rectangular platforms with light scatters
of Inca pottery along the road (Photo 8.6). These platforms may have served as
offering spots along the pilgrimage route.

For the Inca, the two most important lakeside settlements on the island
were Challapampa and Kasapata. Challapampa is located on a narrow spit of
land between two large bays, and surface collections indicate that the site was
built by the Inca (Photo 8.7).[13] It may have been the town that Cobo (1990:94
[1653: Bk. 13, Ch. 18]) credits to Topa Inca Yupanqui, writing: "He made a moderate-sized town one league from the temple, and the majority of the inhab-

PHOTO 8.3. A prehistoric road runs from Puncu, at the far southeast tip of the Island of the Sun, toward the modern village of Yumani. Note the remains of Pilco Kayma near the lake below the road, and the Copacabana mainland in the distance.

PHOTO 8.4. The north side of Pilco Kayma in 1877. (Photograph by Wiener. Courtesy of the Peabody Museum, Harvard University [catalog number H9831].)

PHOTO 8.5. The site of Apachinacapata.

PHOTO 8.6. A series of Inca platforms is located along the pilgrimage route.

itants were mitimaes of Inca blood and lineage. And he had a dwelling built there for them to live in."[14]

The site of Kasapata is situated on a wide and extensively terraced isthmus, a short walk from the Sanctuary area (Photo 8.8). During Inca times, Kasapata was larger and more important than Challapampa.[15] Ramos Gavilán (1988:86 [1621: Bk. 1, Ch. 12]) refers to this site when he writes that Topa Inca Yupanqui "founded a moderate-sized town, half league, or almost, before the rock and shrine, and built his royal palace in it."[16] It is also referred to by Cobo (1990: 93 [1653: Bk. 13, Ch. 18]), who states that "one quarter of a league before one reaches the temple, there was an impressive tambo or inn for the pilgrims to stay in."[17]

Surface collections and excavations at Kasapata both by Bandelier (1910: 203–213) and by our project have yielded elegant Inca ceramics as well as evidence of large trash middens. Work at the site has also documented the remains of various Inca buildings, including one that measures approximately forty meters long. The building has five doorways and is specifically mentioned by Ramos Gavilán when he discusses the Inca solstice celebrations held on the island.

> When the Indians celebrated the solemn festivals of the Sun, particularly that of Capac Rayme [Royal Festival; i.e., December solstice], and that of Intip Rayme [Sun Festival; i.e., June solstice], those of the lineage of the Incas put all the idols in their litters (that they call rampa[18]) and adorned them with many flowers, gold and silver plates, and many feathers. Performing their dances and festivals, they all went to the island, and put them in a place called Aucaypata, where there was a great square, and where they held the festivals. *There was a large temple with five doors.* No Colla Indian was permitted to attend or be found at these festivals nor enter until they were finished. (Ramos Gavilán 1988:176 [1621: Bk. 1, Ch. 29]; authors' translation, emphasis added)[19]

We can infer from this quote that Kasapata contained a large plaza. The plaza was called Aucaypata (Terrace of Tranquillity), which was also the name of the central plaza of Cuzco where the major celebrations of the imperial capital were held. The plaza of Kasapata and its adjacent temple were important ritual focal points for the Inca elites who arrived on the island carried in their litters. We also learn from Ramos Gavilán that a certain group of natives, the Colla (most likely a gloss for mainland natives in general), were not allowed to participate in the rituals or even enter the plaza until the festivals were completed.

PHOTO 8.7. Challapampa can be seen in the lower right of this photograph. It is located on a narrow spit of land between two large bays.

PHOTO 8.8. The site of Kasapata. The building of five doorways is located near the center of this photograph.

The Entrance to the Sanctuary Area

A paved road heading north from Kasapata leads directly to the Sanctuary area. Again, both Ramos Gavilán and Cobo furnish similar, although not identical, reports on this area of the island. Cobo states that there was a single entrance to the Sanctuary, a gateway called Intipuncu (Door of the Sun), that was located some two hundred paces from the Sacred Rock (see Maps 7.5 and 7.6). According to Cobo, it was at this portal that visitors to the shrine removed their sandals. Cobo implies that most pilgrims were not allowed to approach the rock directly, traveling only as far as the Intipuncu, where they handed their offerings to the attendants who resided in the Sanctuary. He also includes a detailed description of a set of "footprints" and Inca structures that were near this gate. The "footprints," in fact, are natural inclusions in the bedrock and can be seen today:

> The entrance to all of these constructions was through that gate called Intipuncu, located two hundred paces from the crag [the Sacred Rock]. A living stone [exposed bedrock] was located between this gate and the constructions mentioned, and the road that leads to the sanctuary passes through this stone. On it was what appear to be the traces of certain enormous footprints left by Indian sandals. The old Indians thought that these were miraculous footprints that remained there from the extremely obscure times of their heathendom. However, they are really watermarks on the stone itself. To one side of the entrance mentioned above, certain old buildings can be seen which, according to what the Indians say, were lodgings for the attendants and servants of the temple. (Cobo 1990:97 [1653: Bk. 13, Ch. 18])[20]

Ramos Gavilán's description of the Sanctuary entrance is more extensive than Cobo's, although somewhat confusing. Ramos Gavilán suggests that the pilgrims had to pass through not one, but three, closely spaced gateways to enter the Sanctuary, and that at each gateway they held an audience with a priest. He indicates that the first gateway was called Pumapuncu [Door of the Puma]. The second gateway, Kentipuncu [Door of the Hummingbird], was covered with hummingbird feathers. We know that this is the same gateway that Cobo calls Intipuncu, since both authors indicate that there were Inca structures near it and footprints in the bedrock after it.[21] The third and final gateway, Pillcopuncu [Door of the Pillco], was adorned with pillco feathers.[22] Ramos Gavilán (1988:94 [1621: Bk. 1, Ch. 15])[23] first describes the second gateway, Kentipuncu, correctly, noting that it was on the northeast side of the island facing the Umasuyu road,[24] and then he returns to characterize each of the three gateways in order:

> One enters all this by the aforementioned door Kentipuncu, which is two hundred paces before the rock where the Inca removed his shoes and placed his feet for the first time . . . at its right can be seen some old houses, that at that time were residences of the sanctuary priests and the virgins dedicated to the Sun. A bit further (past the door), there is a rock outcrop over which the trail passes to the false sanctuary. This rock shows the tracks of human footsteps that we mentioned before.
>
> Before reaching this shrine, one had to pass through three doors a bit more than twenty paces apart from each other. The first was called Pumapuncu, which means the same as Door of the Lion because there was a stone lion there that was said to guard the entrance. At this door, before entering, one atoned for one's sins, confessing them to the priest who resided there.
>
> The second door was called Kentipuncu, as it was completely covered with the feathers of hummingbirds they called Kenti. Here they again confessed their sins to another priest who guarded that door. He counseled the pilgrims to go about their worship devoutly if they wished to be favored by the Sun.
>
> The third door's name was Pillcopuncu, which means Door of Hope. It was adorned with the green feathers of a prized and brilliant bird brought from Los Chunchos, called Pillco. At this last door, its custodian priest effectively persuaded the pilgrim to examine his conscience thoroughly because there was no passing [this last door] with a burdened one. (Ramos Gavilán 1988:94 [1621: Bk. 1, Ch. 15]; authors' translation)[25]

Through a careful inspection of the Sanctuary area, one can still find vestiges of the three entrances mentioned by Ramos Gavilán.[26] The Sanctuary is separated from the rest of the island by the Sanctuary wall, described in the last chapter, through which the road from Kasapata passes (Photo 8.9). It is at this point that one gains the first view of the Sacred Rock (Photo 8.10). This entrance may be that which Ramos Gavilán (1988:94 [1621: Bk. 1, Ch. 15]) describes as Pumapuncu, the first of three gateways that led into the Sanctuary area. It is also most likely the gateway through which the non-elite could not pass.

A series of large stone steps leads from the gateway of the Sanctuary down the hill slope (Photo 8.11). At the bottom of the hill, a seasonal spring crosses

PHOTO 8.9. The Sanctuary is separated from the rest of the island by a low wall.

PHOTO 8.10. The pilgrims first viewed the Sacred Rock from the entrance to the Sanctuary. One side of the rock descends toward the lake. Ramos Gavilán and Cobo suggest that this side was covered in fine cloth.

the road in a channel and flows some 250 meters to the lake. Also at the bottom of this hill is the site of Mama Ojlia. As mentioned above, our excavations indicate that this site was occupied exclusively during the Inca Period.

As the road rises on the opposite slope toward the Sacred Rock, it passes over an expanse of bedrock on which there are two large, natural marks that have long been described as the supernatural footprints (Photo 8.12). Just before the footprints are the faint remains of a wall running roughly perpendicular to the road. A clear gap in the wall, where the road passed through it, and three stone steps mark the location of a former doorway (Photo 8.13). The proximity of this doorway to the footprints indicates that this is the entrance that Cobo calls Intipuncu and that Ramos Gavilán names Kentipuncu. Indeed, this area of the road retained the name of Kentipuncu well into the nineteenth century (Bandelier 1910:216–217).

PHOTO 8.11. A series of large stone steps leads from the gateway of the Sanctuary down the hill slope. The stone footprints are on the exposed bedrock at the lower right. The site of Mama Ojlia can be seen in the center.

PHOTO 8.12. An area of exposed bedrock contains large, natural marks that have long been described as supernatural footprints.

PHOTO 8.13. A gap in the wall, where the road passed through it, and three stone steps mark the location of a former gateway called Kentipuncu by Ramos Gavilán and Intipuncu by Cobo. The footprints lie on the bedrock just beyond the steps.

Approximately fifty meters beyond the footprints the road levels off and enters the plaza of the Sacred Rock. Although there are no foundations at this point to mark a formal gateway, the leveling of the road and its entrance into the sacred plaza clearly mark a transitional zone. This area could be interpreted as representing a third gateway and is perhaps the place that Ramos Gavilán calls Pillcopuncu (Photo 8.14).

It is also important to mention that although Ramos Gavilán's and Cobo's accounts of the entrance to the Sanctuary on the Island of the Sun differ in details, they are not unlike those offered by Garcilaso de la Vega for priests entering the Coricancha in the heart of Cuzco. Garcilaso de la Vega (1966:186, 187, 359 [1609: Pt. 1, Bk. 3, Ch. 23; Bk. 6, Ch. 21]) notes several times that individuals visiting the temple had to remove their sandals when they were within two hundred steps of the Coricancha. Furthermore, Garcilaso de la Vega specifically states that only the highest Inca royalty, accompanied by the priests of the Sun, could enter the temple area. Visitors of lower status could only approach the entry gate of the temple, where they passed their offerings to the priests. Cobo describes similar ritual exclusion taking place on the Island of the Sun:

PHOTO 8.14. The entrance to the plaza before the Sacred Rock may have marked the place that Ramos Gavilán called Pillcopuncu.

But no one was permitted to come empty-handed up close enough to see the sacred crag, much less anyone who had not been fully approved of by the confessors who were stationed at the above-mentioned places for this purpose. Moreover, they did not get close to the crag; they were only allowed to view it from the gateway called Intipuncu, and there they handed over their offerings to the attendants who resided there. (Cobo 1990:96 [1653: Bk. 13, Ch. 18])[27]

The lowest-status pilgrims to the Sanctuary, like the Colla who were excluded from participating in the solstice rituals at Kasapata, were not able to pass through the first gate. Our astronomical research indicates, however, that these visitors could have followed the Sanctuary wall uphill to a platform on the crest of the island. From this platform the commoner could have watched the elite perform their rituals within the Sacred Rock plaza and simultaneously have witnessed the June solstice Sun set between two markers beyond the nobles on the distant border of the Sanctuary area (Dearborn et al. 1998).

The Sanctuary Area

The Sacred Rock from which the Sun first rose is a large exposed outcrop of reddish sandstone near the center of the Sanctuary area (Photos 8.10 and 8.15). Ramos Gavilán states that the broad descending side of the outcrop was covered with fine Inca cloth (*cumbi*), "the most subtle, and delicate that was ever seen in the Indies."[28] He also indicates that the other side of the rock, the shape of which is noticeably concave, was faced with plates of silver and gold and that an altar was located in a prominent concavity near its center (Ramos Gavilán 1988:115–116, 149, 150 [1621: Bk. 1, Chs. 17, 24]).

Ramos Gavilán (1988:93 [1621: Bk. 1, Ch. 13]) indicates that many gold idols, ceramic vessels, and other items had already been found by treasure hunters in the Sanctuary plaza. He also states that there was a large stone basin directly in front of the Sacred Rock into which corn beer offerings were poured. Ramos Gavilán adds that there were still fragments of corn beer vessels on the surface of the plaza, and that the round offering stone had been used as a base for a cross that was erected in the plaza (1988:93, 116 [1621: Bk. 1, Chs. 13 and 17]).

Cobo is even more specific in his description of the Sacred Rock:

The front of it faces north, and the back faces south; there is not much to the concave part of it, which is what they worshipped. The altar of the Sun was inside. The convex part is the living stone, whose slopes reach out as far as the

PHOTO 8.15. The Sacred Rock. Ramos Gavilán and Cobo suggest that this face of the rock, which is slightly concave, was covered with gold and silver.

water, where there is a cove made by the lake. The adornment was a covering over the convex part, a curtain of *cumbi,* which was the finest and most delicate piece [of cloth] that has ever been seen. And the entire concave part of it was covered with sheets of gold, and they threw the offerings into some holes that can still be seen now. Ahead of this crag and altar a round stone can be seen which is like a basin, admirably wrought, about as large as a medium-sized millstone, with its orifice; the stone is used as the foot of a cross now. The *chicha* for the Sun to drink was tossed into this orifice. (Cobo 1990:96–97 [1653: Bk. 13, Ch. 18])[29]

Although the stone basin mentioned by both Ramos Gavilán and Cobo has long since been removed from the plaza area, our excavations found the remains of a stone canal, which drained the offerings away from the Sacred Rock.

The Island of the Moon and the Return Home

Ramos Gavilán (1988:170–171 [1621: Bk. 1, Ch. 28]) states that after visiting the Island of the Sun, many pilgrims traveled to the Island of the Moon. Cobo concurs and adds the following information: "Upon finishing their prayers and offerings at this sanctuary of Titicaca, they continued on to Coata Island, which was considered to be the second station. And since a visit to these sanctuaries was sold to them at such a high price, the result was that such visits were held in higher esteem" (Cobo 1990:96 [1653: Bk. 13, Ch. 18]).[30] Unfortunately, little is known about the status of the pilgrims after their return. We can only speculate that it must have been great, since Garcilaso de la Vega (1966:191 [1609: Pt. 1, Bk. 3, Ch. 25]) notes that "any Indian who could get a grain of that maize or any seed [from the Island of the Sun] to cast in his barn thought he would never want for bread for his whole life."[31] Surely a person who had journeyed to the origin place of the Sun itself would have held considerable standing in the community.

When Did the Visits Occur and What Was Offered?

The island sanctuaries were maintained year-round by *mitimaes* of the Copacabana region. Garcilaso de la Vega (1966:190 [1609: Pt. 1, Bk. 3, Ch. 25]) suggests that once a year all the provinces subdued by the Inca sent offerings to the Island of the Sun, but he does not provide information about when the pilgrimages occurred. Nevertheless, there are several reasons to speculate that journeys to the Lake Titicaca shrines were concentrated in the dry season (May–August). First, travel across the high Andes is easiest during the dry season. Second, travel during this time would have correlated with the period of least agricultural work in the homeland regions. Third, dry-season visits could have been timed to correlate with the June solstice festival (Inti Raymi), one of the largest and most important celebrations of the Inca Empire (Bauer and Dearborn 1995).

The arrival of pilgrims at the Sacred Rock, and the offering of their gifts, is not well described by the chronicles. One could suggest, however, that the presentation of offerings took the same form on the Island of the Sun as it did in Cuzco. With this in mind, we can turn to Garcilaso de la Vega's description of visits to the Coricancha:

> The Inca offered the vessels of gold used for the ceremony with his own hands. The remaining Incas gave their vessels to the Inca priests appointed and dedicated to the service of the Sun: those who were not priests, even though they were of the Sun's blood, were seculars and not permitted to perform the functions of priests. After offering up the vessels of the Incas, the priests went outside [the Coricancha] to collect the *curacas'* [local lords'] vessels. The *curacas*

approached in order of seniority according to the period when their people had been incorporated in the empire and they handed over their vessel and other objects of gold and silver which they had brought from their own province to present to the Sun. (Garcilaso de la Vega 1966:359 [1609: Pt. 1, Bk. 6, Ch. 21])[32]

As mentioned above, visitors to the Coricancha and the Sacred Rock removed their sandals about two hundred paces before these shrines. Furthermore, in each of these cases, only the most worthy could enter the inner sanctum and approach the altars.

Ramos Gavilán (1988:148–157 [1621: Bk. 1, Ch. 25]) is the lone writer to describe some of the events that took place on the Island of the Sun during the course of the year. For example, he includes the following list of items offered to the Sun during the month of April:

> The month of April had the name Atiguayquin, they offered one hundred sheep [llamas] (that they call *moromoros* [of various colors][33]), and with their blood they made libations to the shrine of the Sun, offering much wealth, like gold, silver, shell, and many feathers of various and very showy birds. They offered much coca and during all of the sacrifices made to the Sun, it was customary to put very rich and showy fabrics of *cumbi* [fine cloth] on the shrine of the Sun. Those who presented themselves at the ceremony went with tokens and signs of devotion, and they kept their silence. The animals to be offered were adorned with roses of various colors. (Ramos Gavilán 1988:151 [1621: Bk. 1, Ch. 25]; authors' translation)[34]

Dances and songs were also an integral part of the rituals performed at the Sacred Rock. The most complete description of these is contained in Ramos Gavilán's account of the Inti Raymi activities in the Sanctuary that occurred near the time of the June solstice:

> They were adorned with very rich vestments, and did a dance called *cayo*, covering the roads where they passed (with) many flowers. The Indians got dressed in the most curious clothes, and almost all of the women were elaborately made up, and the principal people put some gold medallions in their beards. All went in this way to the shrine of the Sun, to offer their sacrifices. They all kept to a rhythm in the great dances and festivities; the animals that were to be sacrificed wore tassels, with their faces dyed red. The crag of the temple was decorated with admirable and careful workmanship. . . . The shepherds danced in one way, the warriors another, and the Incas another, and each na-

tion was differentiated from the others in their dances. There was great drunkenness because there was general license to drink. (Ramos Gavilán 1988:153 [1621: Bk. 1, Ch. 25]; authors' translation)[35]

We also know from descriptions of the Sanctuary that large amounts of corn beer were offered to the Sacred Rock. This corn beer was poured into what Cobo and Ramos Gavilán describe as a carved stone basin with a hole in its center. Such maize beer offerings were not limited to ritual activities on the Island of the Sun. Pedro Pizarro, cousin of Francisco Pizarro and an eyewitness to the conquest, gives an account of corn beer offerings made to the mummified ancestors of the Inca in the central plaza of Cuzco: "When these *verquis* [large pitchers] were filled, they emptied them into a round stone in the middle of the plaza, and which they held to be an idol, and it was made around a small opening[36] by which it [the corn beer] drained itself off through some pipes which they had made under the ground" (Pizarro 1921:251–252 [1571]).[37] Garcilaso de la Vega also describes the offering of corn beer to the Sun in the central plaza of Cuzco as he recalls the June solstice celebrations: "After the invitation to drink, the Inca poured the contents of the vessel in his right hand, which was dedicated to the Sun, into a gold basin, and from the basin it flowed along a beautifully made stone-worked channel which ran from the square to the house of the Sun" (Garcilaso de la Vega 1966:358–359 [1609: Pt. 1, Bk. 6, Ch. 21]).[38] Although the stone basin that once stood near the Sacred Rock has been lost, excavations in the plaza revealed the remains of a stone channel that led from the Sacred Rock to a low walled area to the northwest and was used to drain the liquid offerings from the Sacred Rock.

Other objects were buried in the plaza. Many of the most elaborate items contained in the Garcés collection, including the two well-known silver camelids (Photos 8.16 and 8.17), may well be such offerings. Child sacrifices were most likely also conducted at the rock (Ramos Gavilán 1988:51, 149, 154 [1621: Bk. 1, Chs. 6 and 24]). In this respect, Ramos Gavilán (1988:108–109 [1621: Bk. 1, Ch. 16]) tells a story of a young girl who was spared from being sacrificed after a priest found a small mole on her breast. The mole, a sign of an imperfect offering, rendered her unfit as a sacrifice.[39] Since nearly all of the major early colonial writers described child sacrifice as occurring on a limited scale in the Inca Empire, it would not be surprising if such offerings also took place on the sacred islands of Lake Titicaca.

PHOTO 8.16. This large silver llama was found on the Island of the Sun. It may have come from near the Sacred Rock.
(Neg. No. 327112. [Photo by Rota.] Courtesy American Museum of Natural History Library.)

PHOTO 8.17. A large silver alpaca from the Island of the Sun. It may have come from near the Sacred Rock.
(Neg. No.322739. [Photo by Lee Boltin.] Courtesy American Museum of Natural History Library.)

Who Maintained the Shrines on the Islands of the Sun and the Moon?

From the fragmentary historical information we have, it is difficult to state when or how often pilgrims visited the islands. Nevertheless, we do know that these island sanctuaries were occupied and maintained year-round. The most frequently mentioned shrine attendants are an elite group of women called Mamacona and the colonists referred to as *mitimaes*.

The Mamacona

The Mamacona were women selected by the state at a young age and trained to hold a number of important roles, including serving the state temples. Pedro Pizarro (1921:255–256 [1571]) indicates that there were some two hundred Mamacona, all daughters of important natives, who slept in the Temple of the Sun in Cuzco. The production of food and corn beer for the Sun and its servants occupied much of their time: "And those who were dedicated to the Sun went to live in his houses, which were very large and very well enclosed [with walls], the women busying themselves with making chicha, which was a kind of beverage which they made from maize and drank as we do wine, and with preparing the food as well for the Sun and for those who served him" (Pizarro 1921:257 [1571]).[40]

As the Inca expanded across the Andes, they constructed a series of provincial centers. They built temples in most of these centers, each of which was assigned a large number of women for their maintenance. For example, Cieza de León writes: "Here in Huancabamba there was a temple of the Sun with many women. From all these regions they came to worship in this temple and bring their offerings; the virgins and attendants who resided in it were held in high esteem and reverence" (Cieza de León 1976:92 [1553: Pt. 1, Ch. 58]).[41]

Ramos Gavilán suggests that the female workers on the Island of the Sun were grouped into three classifications, and that there was a single, high-ranking woman in charge of them all:

> [There were] three kinds of virgins, some very beautiful that were called Guay-ruro,[42] others not so beautiful that had the name Yuracaclla, others that were less beautiful named Paco[c]aclla.[43] Each one of these had as an abbess, an old Indian women who was also a virgin. She guarded all those of her monastery, and distributed to them the thread and cloth that they were required to make.
> (Ramos Gavilán 1988:118 [1621: Bk. 1, Ch. 18]; authors' translation)[44]

Not all the Mamacona were selected from provincial villages of the empire. Many came from Cuzco itself and even from the noble Inca lineages. In this regard it is worth mentioning that Ramos Gavilán (1988:185 [1621: Bk. 1, Ch. 31) states that Huayna Capac, the last Inca to rule a united empire, sent two of his daughters to serve the Island of the Sun.[45]

According to the first report on the Island of the Sun, there were some "six hundred Indians serving in this place, and more than a thousand women who make corn beer in order to throw it upon that stone Tichicasa" (Sancho de la Hoz 1917:163 [1554: Ch. 18]).[46] Although the number of female attendants for the shrine seems high, this account emphasizes the importance that the Mamacona played in maintaining the Sacred Rock. Some of these women most likely lived in the Chincana, while others may have lived in Kasapata or Challapampa.

Mitimaes

Although the Inca policy of *mitimaes* (the replacement of one population with another) was a widely used administrative technique, the Island of the Sun was especially affected by resettlement policies. Both Ramos Gavilán (1988:41, 85 [1621: Bk. 1, Chs. 4 and 20]) and Cobo (1990:94 [1653: Bk. 13, Ch. 18) indicate that after the Inca Conquest of the area, the Inca removed the local population from the islands, as well as the surrounding mainland, and resettled them in Yunguyu. These writers and other early colonial sources indicate that the Inca then repopulated the Copacabana region with colonists from all parts of the empire.[47]

The archaeological survey of the Island of the Sun reveals evidence of a massive reorganization of island populations at the time of the Inca Conquest (see Maps 6.6 and 7.1). The largest Altiplano Period site, Kurupata, was abandoned. If the chronicles are correct in stating that the Inca removed the indigenous population from the island, these people were resettled on the mainland. There was also a large-scale creation of new villages on the island. The three largest Inca Period occupations on the Island of the Sun, Apachinacapata, Challapampa, and Kasapata, show no surface evidence of Altiplano Period remains. These communities appear to have been built by the Inca. According to Cobo (1990:94 [1653: Bk. 13, Ch. 18]), at least one was inhabited by "mitimaes of Inca blood and lineage."[48]

The mainland was also greatly affected by forced colonization by the Inca. When García de León received Copacabana as an *encomienda* in 1548, it had a population of 739 taxpayers as well as 334 elders and widows. The *encomienda* document specifically states that "all of the above-mentioned Indians are mitimaes, put there by the Lords of the Cuzco for the service of the House of the Sun that they had in the lake" (Espinoza Soriano 1972a:10).[49] If each household held three children, Espinoza Soriano (1972a:4) estimates that the total number of inhabitants in 1548 was around 3,300. By 1572 the population had grown as high as 5,970 (Espinoza Soriano 1972a:6). Within this population there were still 953 *mitimaes* and 88 resident Urus (Espinoza Soriano 1972b: 131–132).

Ramos Gavilán (1988:172–173 [1621: Bk. 1, Ch. 28]) puts the population of *mitimaes* in the region at the time of the Inca at around 2,000. A similar population estimate is provided by Salas (1901:19 [1628]), who suggests that the islands and the Copacabana Peninsula held 2,000 inhabitants, as well as by the first Europeans at Lake Titicaca, who suggest that there were some 1,600 individuals in the region. The primary task of the imported population was to serve and maintain the religious facilities on the Islands of the Sun and the Moon. This work was considered so important that the Copacabana population was exempted from all other taxes and tributes normally demanded by the Inca state (Ramos Gavilán 1988:172–173 [1621: Bk. 1, Ch. 28]).

The ethnic affiliations of the peoples that the Inca brought into the Copacabana area is open to question. Martín de Murúa (1946:202 [1590: Pt. 1, Ch. 15]) indicates that Copacabana was populated with many groups, including Inca, Cañares, and Chachapoyas. Ramos Gavilán (1988:84–85 [1621: Bk. 1, Ch. 20]) is more specific, noting that there were representatives from forty-two different "nations" in Copacabana. Ramos Gavilán also provides the following list of groups from across the empire (Map 8.2):

> The Inca transported here (taking them from their homelands) the Anacuscos, Hurincuscos, Ingas, Chinchaisuyos, Quitos, Pastos, Chachapoyas, Cañares, Cayambis, Latas, Caxamarcas, Guamachucos, Guaylas, Yauyos, Ancaras, Qui-

Facing page

MAP 8.2. Ramos Gavilán (1988:84–85 [1621: Ch. 20]) includes a list of different groups that served as *mitimaes* in the Copacabana area. From this list it is clear that colonists were brought in from across the Andean highlands.

chuas, Mayos, Guancas, Andesuyos, Condesuyos, Chancas, Aymaras, Ianaguaras, Chumbivilcas, Padre[,] Chilques, Collaguas, Hubinas, Canches, Canas,
Quivarguaros, Lupacas, Capancos, Pucopucos, Pacajes, Iungas, Carangas, Quillacas, Chichas, Soras, Copayapos, Colliyungas, Guánucos, and Huruquillas.
(Ramos Gavilán 1988:84–85 [1621: Bk. 1, Ch. 20]; authors' translation)[50]

A less reliable source on the inhabitants of the Copacabana Peninsula is Salas. He states that the total population of the Island of the Sun was around 400
individuals (2,000 for the region as a whole) and that these were drawn from
a pool of seventy-two groups.[51] Salas indicates that 20 individuals came from
twenty different groups every two years. He also suggests that five groups of Ya-
nacona [government servants] sent 7 individuals for seven-year rotations:

> The privileged and priestly families that live on and serve the Island of Titicaca
> come every two years from the seventy-two ayllus [kin groups] in which twenty
> from twenty families alternate, in addition to five of Yanaconas that alternate
> seven every seven years. In total they compose about 400 souls, and the island
> does not admit more. (Salas 1901:3 [1628]; authors' translation)[52]

Although more than five hundred years have passed since the Inca took control
of the Copacabana area, the results of their resettlement program can still be
seen. Most specifically, there continues to be a village on the lakeshore called
Chachapoyas and another village called Collasuyu.

9 | PILGRIMAGE AND RITUAL
IN THE ANCIENT ANDES

THE ISLANDS of the Sun and the Moon in Lake Titicaca were two of the most sacred locations in the Inca Empire. There was a pan-Andean belief that the islands marked the origin place for the Sun and the Moon, and early Spanish explorers of the region stated that the islands were visited by pilgrims from across the Inca realm. In this book, we have examined the degree to which the use of the islands as a pilgrimage center during Inca times was founded on and developed from earlier religious traditions of the Lake Titicaca region. We have incorporated the historic information on the islands handed down to us from early colonial sources as well as recent archaeological data recovered from surveys and excavations on the islands.

The survey and excavation data provide a fascinating corroboration of key late-sixteenth- and early-seventeenth-century documents describing the Islands of the Sun and the Moon as an important pilgrimage center in the Inca Empire. They also provide insights into the pre-Inca use of the islands and raise the compelling possibility that the religious significance of the islands is of great antiquity and that the shrine areas were associated with earlier complex polities. This chapter provides a summary of our research findings.

Lake Titicaca, 3,810 meters above sea level, represents a unique center of ancient Andean civilizations. First occupied as early as 5000 BC, the region has witnessed the growth, development, and expansion of numerous villages, chiefdoms, and complex societies. Throughout time, people have also been drawn to the many islands in the lake. As early as 2000 BC, people were living and exploiting the rich resources of the Island of the Sun. At that time, it was occupied by small groups of hunter-gatherers who traveled to the island by boat and settled in its richest ecological areas. There was most likely marginal population growth on the island throughout the Early Formative Period (2000–1300 BC), although the settlement pattern remained relatively unchanged, even with the advent of agriculture and the appearance of ceramic technologies.

It was during the Middle Formative Period (which on the islands is called the Early Titinhuayani Period [1300–500 BC]) that ranked societies first developed in the Lake Titicaca region, characterized by elaborate exchange relationships (Browman 1978, 1981), a ritual complex known as Yaya-Mama (Chávez and Chávez 1975), the development of a standardized corporate architectural style (Stanish 1993), and the development of site-size hierarchies (Albarracin-Jordan and Mathews 1990; Stanish et al. 1997). The settlement pattern for this period on the Island of the Sun is marked by site-size hierarchies and a population concentration in the maize-producing and lakeside fishing areas. Some occupations were established on the northern end of the island, but we currently see no evidence suggesting that these sites were anything more than small homesteads. Likewise, there is no clear evidence suggesting that the island held an important shrine during this period.

The nature of the Sacred Rock area changed, however, during the Upper Formative Period (locally called the Late Titinhuayani Period [500 BC–AD 400]). We suggest that during this period political centers developed in both the Challa and Yumani areas, and a ritual center developed at the site of Chucaripupata near the Sacred Rock. The recovery of elite and ceremonial materials from Chucaripupata may reflect the emergence of the Sacred Rock area as a local shrine for the island peoples. We also see the development of a ritual focus on the Island of the Moon during the Upper Formative, suggesting that both of the islands were gaining importance during this period.

By AD 600 or so, the islanders came into contact with the emergent Tiwanaku state. Within two or three generations, the Tiwanaku peoples had incorporated the Island of the Sun into their state and converted its northern end into a great regional shrine. Although the majority of the Tiwanaku occupations on the island were established in economically rich areas, a major cluster of Tiwanaku settlements developed near the Sacred Rock, including the site of Chucaripupata, the second-largest Tiwanaku occupation on the island. Recent excavations at Chucaripupata recovered elaborate ceremonial ceramics, and both gold and silver Tiwanaku offerings were recovered in the area by Bandelier. The use of offering materials imported from the mainland, if not the capital city of Tiwanaku itself, and the construction of a large site in view of the Sacred Rock indicates that this area held special importance for the Tiwanaku state. Similarly, elaborate Tiwanaku offerings have been recovered from the Island of the Moon, suggesting that this island was developing ritual significance as well.

The Islands of the Sun and the Moon may have represented local shrines before the era of Tiwanaku control, but there is no evidence indicating that they were of regional importance. In contrast, with the development of the Tiwanaku state and the incorporation of the islands into this expansionist polity, the importance of the shrines dramatically increased. Simultaneous with Tiwanaku control of the Islands of the Sun and the Moon, the first formalized pilgrimage route to the Sacred Rock area was established. The Tiwanaku state also invested large amounts of time, energy, and materials in maintaining shrines on both islands. We believe that the incorporation of local shrines on the Islands of the Sun and the Moon, and their promotion through the creation of a state pilgrimage route to them and the presentation of elaborate, imported offerings at the shrines, was an integral part of the process of Tiwanaku imperialism as it expanded throughout the Lake Titicaca region and beyond.

The Altiplano Period (AD 1100–1400) settlement pattern on the Island of the Sun is radically different from either the preceding Tiwanaku or the later Inca settlement patterns. The abrupt settlement changes on the island indicate substantial disruptions in both the local and regional political organizations. The development of numerous fortified hilltop sites on the mainland suggests internecine conflict throughout the Lake Titicaca region during this period.[1] The same is true for the Island of the Sun, which witnesses the construction of at least one large fortified site. The regional importance of the Sacred Rock also appears to have been affected during this turbulent period. Altiplano Period settlements on the northern end of the Island of the Sun dramatically decline, and there is scant evidence of the Sanctuary area being used at this time.

During the period of Inca rule (AD 1400–1532) the political and ideological importance of the islands grew to unprecedented levels. This is clearly reflected in the Inca settlement pattern on the Island of the Sun. Archaeological data indicate that there was a substantial increase in the settlement density of the island in the Inca Period. As described in the early Spanish documents, the Inca relocated existing communities on the Island of the Sun to the mainland and then imported *mitimaes* from throughout the empire to maintain their interests on the island. As during the earlier Tiwanaku Period, many of the most impressive Inca sites were located in the Sanctuary area. However, the Inca greatly expanded the Sanctuary area, building a number of state installations within this remote and agriculturally poor area of the island. Likewise, the Inca built a large ritual complex on the Island of the Moon. In short, the archaeological evidence unambiguously supports the historical documents: the

Inca controlled the sacred islands of Lake Titicaca and built there a massive pilgrimage complex.

Shrine Worship and Regional Control for the Inca Empire

Throughout this work we have taken a modified "Durkheimian" perspective, rather than a "Turnerian" approach, to understanding the religious complex in the southern Lake Titicaca Basin. As with any conceptual dichotomy designed to model a continuum of cultural behavior, the Durkheim/Turner dichotomy, we recognize, is incapable of explaining all instances of pilgrimage and certainly unable to express the meaning associated with, and imparted by, a shrine for all of its participants. But we also view this dichotomy as providing the best means of understanding the origins of such pilgrimage centers with the methodology adopted here.

We address the issues of the origin and maintenance of the shrines in the Lake Titicaca Basin within the confines of the development of complex polities. At the time of the Spanish invasion, the Lake Titicaca shrine complex was fundamentally an Inca state institution, but with local roots. The shrine complex was also designed to project certain meanings associated with Inca culture and political ideology, and the experience of the pilgrims as they traveled through the shrine area was carefully orchestrated by the Inca state.

Ideology and Polity

One useful definition of ideology is that, as a system of symbols, signs, beliefs, and understandings, it is a theory of the social and physical world that surrounds us. In this light, Alan Fiske has argued that "people must use some kind of models of and for social relations to guide their own social initiatives and to understand and respond appropriately to the social action of others" (1991:3). He outlines four basic models by which social relationships are structured and demonstrates how these "implicit models are the psychological foundations of social relations and society." In each of these models, there exists an ideology of shared, or at least mutually intelligible, sets of beliefs about what constitutes a proper social order.

Within expanding states such as the Inca, there is considerable competition between internal elites, conflict with incorporated territories, and other social tensions between classes, kin groups, and the like. These tensions are generally reflected in the various ideologies that exist in such a multiethnic, heterogeneous state. We argue that ideology can be a powerful means of imperial expansion as the state moves into foreign territories. Ideology does not conquer armies, but an ideology of legitimacy and power is a necessary condition for successful consolidation of new territories. Conquered territories must be incorporated not only militarily and politically, but also ideologically.

Settlement and excavation data indicate that the use of the islands of the Sun and the Moon as shrines by the Inca was founded on ancient Lake Titicaca Basin traditions as well as those of the Cuzco state. Moreover, it is apparent that the use of the islands as religious sanctuaries throughout prehistory directly corresponds to the peaks of complexity of contemporary cultures on the mainland. There was little activity on the northern end of the island during the earliest periods. We have evidence that the first ritual activities began to occur in the Sanctuary area on the Island of the Sun as well as at Iñak Uyu on the Island of the Moon as the population increased and as ranked societies began to emerge both on the mainland and on the islands. These ceremonial manifestations become unmistakable in the Late Formative with the development of complex societies throughout the Lake Titicaca region and reached a zenith during the period of Tiwanaku rule. Then, with the fall of Tiwanaku, the regional importance of the sacred islands also waned. With the incorporation of the lake region into the Inca Empire, the islands once again became the focus of major ritual activities, and state facilities on a heretofore unseen scale were constructed on them. These patterns suggest that control of the sacred islands played an important role in regional statecraft. We believe that the elite of the earliest state-level Lake Titicaca society, Tiwanaku, not only sponsored pilgrimages to, and financed religious facilities at, the Sacred Rock, but that they may also have attempted to use the religious importance of the island as the origin place of the Sun, as the Inca did later, to help legitimate their privileged position within their own social hierarchies.

The shrines of the Islands of the Sun and the Moon were consciously maintained by the Inca state to impart a sense of legitimacy to their rule in Collasuyu in particular, and throughout the empire in general. The overriding purpose of the complex was to impart a sense of political legitimacy to their control of the region. By controlling the Islands of the Sun and the Moon, the Inca successfully competed with local elites, specifically the Lupaqa nobility, for ideological hegemony in the region. At the same time, they converted the islands into a great pilgrimage center, which had profound effects on their attempts to create and exert control over the ideology of the conquered provinces in all of their empire.

There is a tendency in contemporary scholarship to downplay the role of hierarchies or, at the very least, inflate the role of non-elites in various forms of resistance to state authority. There is no question that commoner populations successfully resist elite hegemony, particularly ideological hegemony in state and imperial contexts. That resistance oftentimes takes its most successful form as "unofficial" or "illegal" religions. We also recognize that such resistance took place in the Inca state, alongside that of overt political resistance to state control. However, we would locate ideological resistance to state control in the local shrines maintained by non-elite populations under Inca authority rather than in the panregional pilgrimage centers under the direct control of the state.

Resistance to the Catholic Church's domination of religious practices in the Andes offers a useful analogy. Overt resistance to Spanish ideology was widespread in the countryside, where people continued to worship "pagan" shrines. The extirpation of idolatry by Spanish religious authorities, backed by the power of the state, focused on rural and semirural communities where such practices persisted. In other words, some of the most significant resistance to ideological hegemony was in the areas where it was strongest: the rural countryside where "unofficial" religious ideological practices continued to be observed.

We reject a Turnerian perspective that classifies a pilgrimage center such as the Islands of the Sun and the Moon as a counterhegemonic phenomenon. Rather, the Island of the Sun and its sister/wife shrine, the Island of the Moon, was a state construction designed and perpetuated to maintain state ideological and political control. The Inca appropriated a ritual center of earlier cultures, and they expanded and elaborated it on a scale unseen in Lake Titicaca Basin history. In other words, a religious center was not only taken over but was turned into a center of unprecedented scale and importance.

Under Inca tutelage, the Islands of the Sun and the Moon reached a pan-Andean level of importance that was impossible under the Tiwanaku state. At the time of the European invasion, the Islands of the Sun and the Moon were ritually and politically significant not only for the Aymara speakers of the Lake Titicaca Basin, but for all the peoples of the Inca Empire, even for those who may never have visited the area. The Inca state converted what was essentially a regional shrine into an imperial pilgrimage destination. A shrine of significance to an earlier and smaller state (Tiwanaku) and later to a conflict-ridden local polity (the Lupaqa) was converted into the birthplace of the cosmos and the origin of the founding lineage of Tawantinsuyu. In this masterstroke, Inca elites not only co-opted a shrine of regional importance in what was arguably their richest highland province, Collasuyu, but converted it into a center that sanctified the very founding and existence of their state in Cuzco.

The shrine complex on the Islands of the Sun and the Moon was a fundamental element of the expansion process of the Inca Empire as it incorporated the heartland of the great administrative quarter called Collasuyu. As such, the journey to the islands served both overt and covert political ends. Simultaneously, the pilgrimage complex was also of profound religious significance to the thousands of people who visited it. During Inca times, and most likely well before in the Tiwanaku Period, these islands were the final destination point of pilgrims on a religious journey. This journey took them through a uniquely Andean landscape. At the same time, many aspects of the trip mirrored elements of pilgrimages worldwide. This ritualized movement, from the ordinary to the divine, is especially clear in the pilgrim's progress to the Islands of the Sun and the Moon. It was a highly structured passage through a series of gates, ports, and landings of increasing sanctity. The pilgrims entered the Copacabana Peninsula through the guarded Yunguyu gates and spent several days journeying across *mitima*-controlled lands to the port of Yampupata. After traveling by boat to the southeast tip of the Island of the Sun, they traveled on foot to the Sanctuary area on its northwest end. The fact that the pilgrimage destinations were islands served physically, and perhaps spiritually, to separate them from the mainland. In this sense, the use of an island as a pilgrimage destination provided a clear separation between the most sacred and the less sacred, with the act of taking a boat ride mediating this divide.

The pilgrims approached the area of the Sacred Rock by passing through one or more doorways, where they finally handed their offerings to the resident priests. It is not by chance that the final destination of the pilgrims was on the point of land farthest from the mainland, on the northwest side of the Island of the Sun. The Sanctuary was, like many pilgrimage centers of the world, situated in a remote location that served to emphasize its otherworldliness. A trip to the island Sanctuary was to leave the recognizable shores of the mainland, and therefore the ordinary, behind and to journey to the point of cosmic origins.

Travel through the sacred landscape of Copacabana and the islands was not casual or incidental; rather, it reflected a highly regulated set of movements that stressed the special nature of the journey. Pilgrims gave confessions and abstained from certain foods as they passed through the various entrances, thereby physically and spiritually cleansing themselves. As the pilgrims trekked across the region, they were supervised and monitored by the priests and attendants of the shrines. Through the tightly controlled access to the Copacabana area and the preparatory rites that the visitors underwent, the pilgrims' journey was transformed beyond simple travel and became a ritual itself (Coleman and Elsner 1995:25). Furthermore, by completely controlling access to the region and the sanctuaries, and by dictating the manner in which the pilgrims must pass through each of the various entrances, the state was able to impose its own ideological character on the shrines. By imposing conformity on the ritual actions of the pilgrims, the state constrained, if not largely determined, the visitors' experiences at the shrines (Eade and Sallnow 1991:11).

Coleman and Elsner's discussion of the sixth-century Christian pilgrimage of St. Catherine in Mount Sinai provides what we believe to be an excellent analogy to the pilgrimage center in the southern Lake Titicaca Basin. Their discussion demonstrates how the state or church elite can impose an ideology on the pilgrims without overt political or religious propagandizing. Rather, the very act of the pilgrimage involves several levels of meaning and significance to the participants:

> The sixth-century fixtures, images and buildings of Sinai acted both to channel pilgrims from a wide variety of provenances through its sacred places and to locate the process of Sinai pilgrimage in a Christian interpretative frame. The pilgrim's journey consisted not only of the voyage to the monastery, but also of a number of other controlled journeys, of less distance but ever increasing theological significance: the journey through the monastery to the burning bush, the path up the mountain to Elijah's cave, and finally to the summit, where Moses received the tablets of the law. (Coleman and Elsner 1994:84)

The analogy to the southern Lake Titicaca Basin Sanctuary is very appropriate. Progressively more sacred destinations line the pilgrimage route: the entrance to the Copacabana Peninsula, the boat trip to the Island of the Sun, the journey to the northern end of the island, and finally the arrival at the Sacred Rock. These "controlled journeys" encouraged the visitor to "interpret the various sites . . . not so much as part of an intellectual process but through physical action and practice" (Coleman and Elsner 1994:84).

The Inca state was heavily invested in the maintenance of the Lake Titicaca island sanctuaries. The Inca elite performed a number of annual rites, including the December and June solstices, on the Islands of the Sun and the Moon. They presented a wide range of offerings, from *chicha* to children, to the Sacred Rock. The Inca removed the existing population of the islands and the surrounding mainland, replacing them with colonists from across the empire. They also established a group of women on the islands whose singular role was to serve the sanctuaries. Furthermore, they built many state facilities on the mainland and on the islands, including temples, storehouses, specialized housing for the attendants, and lodging of the pilgrims.

The Sanctuary area was extensively modified by the Inca state. The convex side of the rock held an elaborate metal altar and a stone offering place, and the opposite side was covered with fine textiles produced by the servants of the state. A plaza area was built in front of the rock, and various state structures were constructed in the Sanctuary. With each of these additions, the state altered the contents of the Sanctuary area. Likewise, the trip to the rock was also controlled and shaped by the state. Pilgrims were granted permission to enter the Copacabana area by official guards, and once inside, they were fed and clothed from state warehouses and housed in state hostels. The Inca imparted a sense of their own political legitimacy not by a raw and obvious display of power, but through more subtle means that reached the individual. The ideology of the Inca Empire was made material in the pilgrimage, which provided a means for the individual pilgrim to incorporate that ideology within his or her own view of the new cultural order. In other words, the pilgrims traveled through a sacred landscape, but the panorama, both physical and ideological, was filled with symbols of the state. The powers of the state and those of the sacred locations, points of intense religious devotion, became intermixed and inseparable.

Radiocarbon Dates from the Islands
of the Sun and the Moon

Site	Lab No.	Radiocarbon Age	Calendar	(Calibrated)[1]
Chincana	I-18,556	340 ± 80 BP	AD 1610 ± 80	68.2% Confidence
				AD 1480 (68.2%) AD 1640
				95.4% Confidence
				AD 1400 (92.6%) AD 1700
				AD 1750 (2.8%) AD 1850
Chincana	I-18,555	220 ± 80 BP	AD 1730 ± 80	68.2% Confidence
				AD 1720 (27.8%) AD 1820
				95.4% Confidence
				AD 1490 (95.4%) AD 1960
Ch'uxuqullu	I-18,314	3780 ± 170 BP	1830 ± 170 BC	68.2% Confidence
				2470 BC (66.0%) 2010 BC
				2000 BC (2.2%) 1970 BC
				95.4% Confidence
				2700 BC (95.4%) 1600 BC
Ch'uxuqullu	I-18,402	2770 ± 100 BP	820 ± 100 BC	68.2% Confidence
				1020 BC (68.2%) 810 BC
				95.4% Confidence
				1220 BC (94.3%) 780 BC
				1260 BC (1.1%) 1230 BC

[1]Calibration estimates have been conducted using OxCal Program v3.4.

Site	Lab No.	Radiocarbon Age	Calendar	(Calibrated)[1]
Ch'uxuqullu	I-18,401	2110 ± 100 BP	160 ± 100 BC	68.2% Confidence 240 BC (57.6%) AD 10 360 BC (10.6%) 290 BC 95.4% Confidence 390 BC (95.4%) AD 70
Chucaripupata[2]	OS 12671	1420 ± 40 BP	AD 530 ± 40	68.2% Confidence AD 600 (68.2%) AD 660 95.4% Confidence AD 540 (95.4%) AD 680
Chucaripupata	OS 12678	1370 ± 35 BP	AD 580 ± 35	68.2% Confidence AD 643 (68.2%) AD 684 95.4% Confidence AD 600 (92.0%) AD 720 AD 740 (3.4%) AD 770
Chucaripupata	OS 12676	1310 ± 40 BP	AD 640 ± 40	68.2% Confidence AD 660 (48.4%) AD 720 AD 740 (19.8%) AD 770 95.4% Confidence AD 640 (95.4%) AD 780
Chucaripupata	OS 12675	1140 ± 35 BP	AD 810 ± 35	68.2% Confidence AD 880 (68.2%) AD 980 95.4% Confidence AD 780 (95.4%) AD 990

[2]Radiocarbon dates from Chucaripupata are provided by Seddon (1998:510).

Site	Lab No.	Radiocarbon Age	Calendar	(Calibrated)[1]
Chucaripupata	OS 12672	475 ± 35 BP	AD 1475 ± 35	68.2% Confidence
				AD 1416 (68.2%) AD 1445
				95.4% Confidence
				AD 1400 (95.4%) AD 1480
Chucaripupata	OS 12677	540 ± 35 BP	AD 1410 ± 35	68.2% Confidence
				AD 1330 (16.8%) AD 1345
				AD 1395 (51.4%) AD 1430
				95.4% Confidence
				AD 1380 (64.6%) AD 1440
				AD 1300 (30.8%) AD 1360
Iñak Uyu	I. 18,554	1310 ± 80 BP	AD 640 ± 80	68.2% Confidence
				AD 640 (68.2%) AD 810
				95.4% Confidence
				AD 590 (94.3%) AD 900
				AD 920 (1.1%) AD 950
Iñak Uyu	I. 18,629	410 ± 80 BP	AD 1540 ± 80	68.2% Confidence
				AD 1430 (45.5%) AD 1530
				AD 1570 (22.7%) AD 1630
				95.4% Confidence
				AD 1400 (95.4%) AD 1660
Iñak Uyu	AA34942	445 ± 45 BP	AD 1505 ± 45	68.2% Confidence
				AD 1420 (68.2%)
				95.4% Confidence
				AD 1400 (87.6%) AD 1530
				AD 1580 (7.8%) AD 1630
Iñak Uyu	AA34943	470 ± 50 BP	AD 1480 ± 50	68.2% Confidence
				AD 1405 (68.2%) AD 1470
				95.4% Confidence
				AD 1320 (3.7%) AD 1350

Site	Lab No.	Radiocarbon Age	Calendar	(Calibrated)[1]
				AD 1390 (88.2%) AD 1520
				AD 1590 (3.5%) AD 1630
Kasapata	I-18,557	270 ± 80 BP	AD 1680 ± 80	68.2% Confidence
				AD 1480 (59.1%) AD 1680
				AD 1770 (7.3%) AD 1810
				AD 1930 (1.9%) AD 1950
				95.4% Confidence
				AD 1400 (95.4%) AD 2000
Mama Ojlia	LLNL 23788	370 ± 60 BP	AD 1580 ± 60	68.2% Confidence
				AD 1450 (37.7%) AD 1530
				AD 1560 (30.5%) AD 1630
				95.4% Confidence
				AD 1430 (95.4%) AD 1650
Mama Ojlia	LLNL 2378	9420 ± 60 BP	AD 1530 ± 60	68.2% Confidence
				AD 1420 (56.9%) AD 1520
				AD 1590 (11/3%) AD 1630
				95.4% Confidence
				AD 1410 (95.4%) AD 1640
Pilco Kayma	AA34944	420 ± 60 BP	AD 1530 ± 60	68.2% Confidence
				AD 1420 (56.9%) AD 1520
				AD 1590 (11/3%) AD 1630
				95.4% Confidence
				AD 1410 (95.4%) AD 1640
Pilco Kayma	AA34945	470 ± 50 BP	AD 1480 ± 50	68.2% Confidence
				AD 1415 (68.2%) AD 1485
				95.4% Confidence
				AD 1390 (85.0%) AD 1530
				AD 1570 (10.4%) AD 1630

Site	Lab No.	Radiocarbon Age	Calendar	(Calibrated)[1]
Sacred Rock	Beta 10253	1450 ± 50 BP	AD 1500 ± 50	68.2% Confidence
				AD 1415 (68.2%) AD 1485
				95.4% Confidence
				AD 1390 (85%) AD 1530
				AD 1570 (10.4%) AD 1630
Sacred Rock	LLNL 23790	modern	modern	modern
Tikani ridge	LLNL 23786	1840 ± 60 BP	AD 110 ± 60	68.2% Confidence
				AD 80 (7.4%) AD 110
				AD 120 (60.8%) AD 250
				95.4% Confidence
				AD 20 (1.0%) AD 40
				AD 50 (94.4%) AD 350
Tikani ridge	LLNL 23787	modern	modern	modern

1. Inca Shrine Worship in the Andes

1. "La [veneración] fué tan grande, que de todas partes acudían en peregrinación a él, donde era muy extraordinario el concurso que siempre había de gentes extranjeras; con que vino a ser tan célebre y famoso, que vivirá su memoria entre los indios todo lo que ellos duraren" (Cobo 1964 :192 [1653: Bk. 13, Ch. 18]). Also see Ramos Gavilán (1988:25 [1621: Bk. 1, Ch. 1]).

2. "Antes que fueran sujetadas por los reyes Incas" (Cobo 1964:190 [1653: Bk. 13, Ch. 18]).

3. The term "Inca" refers to the emperor, the people, and the empire of Tawantinsuyu.

4. "El templo más rico, suntuoso y principal que había en este reino era el de la ciudad del Cuzco, el cual era tenido por cabeza y metrópoli de su falsa religión y por el santuario de más veneración que tenían estos indios, y como tal era frecuentado de todas las gentes del imperio de los Incas, que por devoción venían a él en romería. Llamábase *Coricancha,* que quiere decir 'casa de oro' por la incomparable riqueza de este metal, el que había enterrado por sus capillas y en las paredes, techo y altares" (Cobo 1964:168 [1653: Bk. 13, Ch. 12]).

5. Among the many descriptions of Pachacamac are those by Cieza de León (1976: 334–337 [1553: Pt. 1, Ch. 72]), Hernando Pizarro (1959:82–83 [1553]), Santillán (1950:58–59 [1564]), Pedro Pizarro (1921:244 [1571]), Albornoz (1984:214 [ca. 1582]), Cabello Valboa (1951:338 [1586]), Huarochirí Manuscript (1991:111–113 [ca. 1608: Ch. 22]), and Calancha (1981 [1638]).

6. "Después del soberbio templo del sol tenía el segundo lugar de grandeza, devoción, autoridad y riqueza el de Pachacama; al cual, como a santuario universal, venían en peregrinación las gentes de todo el imperio de los Incas y ofrecían en él sus votos" (Cobo 1964:186 [1653: Bk. 13, Ch. 17]).

7. "El capitán disimuló con ellos y dijo que quería ir a ver aquel ídolo que tenían, . . . El estaba en una buena casa bien pintada, en una sala muy escurra, hedionda muy cerrada; tienen un ídolo hecho de palo muy sucio y aquél dicen que es su dios el que los cría y sostiene y cría los mantenimientos. A los pies del [ídolo] tenían ofrecidas algunas joyas de oro. Tiénenle en tanta veneración, que solos sus pajes y criados que dicen que él señala, esos le sirven; y otro no osa entrar, ni tienen a otro por digno de tocar con la mano en las paredes de su casa . . . Vienen a este diablo en peregrinación de trescientas leguas con oro y plata y ropa, y los que llegan van al portero y piden su don, y él entra, y habla con el ídolo, y él dice que se lo otorga" (Xérez 1985:136–137 [1534]).

8. In early records, Lake Titicaca is called both Lake of Chucuito, after the capital of the adjacent Lupaqa kingdom, and Lake Titicaca, after its largest and most important island.

9. "Tenía este santuario el tercero lugar en reputación y autoridad cerca destos indios peruanos, el cual (dado que tratamos del como si fuera solo uno) comprendía dos magníficos templos, puestos en dos islas distintas de la laguna de Chucuito; y por estar ambas cerca del pueblo de Copacabana, le damos el nombre sobredicho. La una destas islas se decía Titicaca, y la otra, Coatá; aquélla era dedicada al sol y ésta a la luna" (Cobo 1964:189 [1653: Bk. 13, Ch. 18]).

10. See Meiklejohn (1988) for a discussion of the relationship between the Church and the Lupaqa peoples in the Early Colonial Period.

11. "La luna, que era hermana y mujer del sol, y que le había dado *Illa Tecce* parte de su divinidad, y héchola señora de la mar y de los vientos, de las reinas y princesas, y del parto de las mujeres y reina del cielo. A la luna llamaban *Coya,* ques reyna" (Valera 1950:136 [ca. 1585]).

12. ". . . todos los hombres adorasen al sol por criador dellos porque era tradición de sus antepasados que el sol crio a los hombres en su oriente en titicaca y los crio con calsones que llaman carabillac y a las mugeres mandaba adorar la luna como a madre y criadora de las mugeres y guarda las comidas y les da bestidos . . ." (in Duviols 1986:151).

13. "Sacaban también una figura de mujer, que era la *huaca* de la Luna, la cual llamaban Pacsamama (madre Luna) teníanla a cargo mujeres, y así cuando salían de la casa del Sol, donde tenía su aposento para sí, a donde ahora es el mirador de Santo Domingo, la sacaban ellas en hombros. La razón porque la tenían a cargo mujeres; porque decían era mujer, como en su figura parece" (Molina 1943:49–50 [ca. 1575]).

Cobo (1990:29 [1653: Bk. 13, Ch. 6]), who took much of his information on the Inca from Molina, includes a similar statement concerning the priestesses of the Moon.

14. "La una cuadra de aquellas estaba dedicada para aposento de la luna, mujer del sol, y era la que estaba más cerca de la capilla mayor del templo; toda ella y sus puertas estaban aforradas con tablones de plata, porque por el color blanco viesen que era aposento de la luna; teníanla puesta su imagen y retrato como al sol, hecho y pintado un rostro de mujer en un talbón de plata. Entraban en aquel aposento a visitar la luna, y a encomendarse a ella, porque la tenían por hermana y mujer del sol, y madre de los Incas, y de toda su generación; y así la llamaban Mamaquilla, que es madre luna; no le ofrecían sacrificios como al sol. A una mano y a otra de la figura de la luna estaban los cuerpos de las reinas difuntas puestas por su orden y antigüedad" (Garcilaso de la Vega 1963:113–114 [1609: Vol. 1, Bk. 3, Ch. 21]).

15. "La razon por donde no hacen mucha cuenta los indios de las mujeres en el numerar sus anales es tradicion antigua porque ni el Inga hizo mucha cuenta de la adoracion de la Luna por ser a cargo de las mujeres . . ." (in Duviols 1986:466).

2. The Lake Titicaca Basin and Its Prehistory

1. "Esta parte que llaman Collas es la mayor comarca a mi ver de todo el Perú, y la más poblada. Desde Ayauire comiençan los Collas, y llegan hasta Caracollo. Al oriente tienen las montañas de los Andes: al poniente las cabeçadas de las sierras neuadas, y las ver-

tientes dellas que van a para a la mar del sur. Sin la tierra que ocupan con sus pueblos y labores ay grandes despoblados y que están bien llenos de ganado syluestre. Es la tierra del Collao toda llana, y por muchas partes corren ríos de buen agua. Y en estos llanos ay hermosas vegas muy espaciosas: y que siempre tienen yerua en cantidad, y a tiempos muy verdes aunque en el estío se agosta como en españa. El inuierno comiença (como ya he escripto) de Octubre, y dura hasta Abril. Los días y las noches son casi yguales: y en esta comarca haze más frío que en ninguna otra de las del Perú, fuera los altos y sierras neuadas: y cáusalo ser la tierra alta: tanto que ayna emparejara con las sierra. Y cierto si esta tierra del collao fuera vn valle hondo, como el de Xauxa, o Choquiabo, que pudiera dar mayz, se tuuiera por lo mejor y más rico de gran parte destas Indias . . . pero como sea tan fría no da fructo el mayz, ni ay ningún género de árboles. Antes es tan estéril, que no da fructas de las muchas que otros valles produzen y crían" (Cieza de León 1984: 271–272 [1553: Pt. 1, Ch. 99, f. 125–125v]).

2. ORSTOM—Institut Français de Recherche Scientifique pour le Développement en Cooperation; UMSA—Universidad Mayor de San Andrés, La Paz, Bolivia.

3. The discrepancies in the dates given in the two cited publications are probably the result of additional cores being analyzed and included in the 1991 publication. We therefore follow the later publication.

4. The first modern census of the circum-Titicaca region is found in an early ethnography by David Forbes (1870). He gives a figure of around 700,000 Aymara speakers for Peru and Bolivia (Forbes 1870:200–202). Later, Marroquín (1944:1) noted that the Peruvian Department of Puno had 600,000 people in the 1940s. Likewise, Tschopik (1946:506) suggested figures of approximately 500,000 to 750,000 Aymara speakers between the mid nineteenth century and 1935.

These population figures generally coincide with the results of censuses conducted in the Early Colonial Period by Diez de San Miguel (1964 [1567]) in the Lupaqa province and by Viceroy Francisco de Toledo (1975 [1573]) across the Andes. Their reports suggest a population of around 100,000 for Lupaqa and a total of some 260,000 individuals in the immediate lake region. The late-prehispanic figures were most certainly higher, as a combination of Old World diseases, wars, economic changes, and forced migrations to mining areas greatly reduced indigenous population levels at the time of European contact.

5. According to moderately reliable census figures from Peru and Bolivia, there are currently approximately 1,000,000 Aymara speakers living in both nations.

6. See La Barre (1941:496) for a more detailed historical summary.

7. Bouysse-Cassagne has also argued that the term "Urukilla" was used in pre-1600 documents to refer to Uru people or the language in the southwest basin.

8. Today, people who are called Uru are famous for living on artificial islands, subsisting on lake resources and tourist income. Nowadays, they speak Aymara and Spanish; they do not have a separate language. The theme that the Uru are poor and live on or near the lake runs consistently through the early documents of the region. For example, a 1567 inspection of Lupaqa Province, on the western shores of the lake, has numerous references to the Uru as marginalized populations, including the following:

"These uros that do not go to Potosí serve in the *tambos* [way stations] like the aymaraes and that these uros gather lake grass for the *tambos* and they also help in the fields of the *caciques* [lords] and they give fish for the tribute to the priests and when they build churches they [the urus] perform the labor and they go to the *yungas* [lowlands] for wood and they do not pay anything else because they are poor." (authors' translation)

("Estos uros que no van a Potosí sirven en los tambos como los aymaraes y que estos uros cogen la yerba de la laguna para el servicio de los tambos y que también ayudan a hacer las chácaras de los caciques y dan pescado para la ración de los frailes y que cuando se hacen iglesias trabajan en la obra y van por madera a los yungas y que no pagan otra cosa porque son pobres." [Diez de San Miguel 1964:196 (1567)])

At first analysis, it appears that the Uru were merely an impoverished ethnic group, speaking their own language and existing on the margins of the dominant Aymara, Pukina, and Quechua societies. This is the prevailing view among many scholars of the region today. This may not, however, be the case. One hypothesis suggested by recent research, such as that of Julien (1983), Wachtel (1986), Torero (1987:332–338), and Mannheim (1991:50), is that the designation of "Uru" reflected a social status and tax category as opposed to an ethnic one. In this perspective, the Uru were simply Aymara speakers who were placed in a different social classification and, by extension, tax category. The term "Uru" was used as a social designation rather than an ethnic one, and it indicated poor, landless persons who did not pay taxes in animals or wool, but rather provided labor to meet their tribute obligations. Bouysse-Cassagne (1987:128–136) argues for an early migration of "Urukilla"-speaking Uru peoples. Later, Aymara peoples migrated into the Titicaca Basin and referred to other ethnic groups as Uru. In her model, the term "Uru" came to mean "non-Aymara."

9. It is also important to remember that lake levels may have been much lower at this time. If this is true, then many of the Late Archaic and Early Formative sites are now under water.

10. This empirical pattern is virtually identical to that of the Inca Period.

11. The largest cultural division in the Lake Titicaca Basin is that of Umasuyu and Urcosuyu. In the most general terms, Umasuyu corresponds to the eastern and northeastern side of the lake, and Urcosuyu refers to the western and northwestern side. The division follows more or less the middle of the lake, the Desaguadero River, and Lake Poopó. Some of the ethnic groups themselves were divided in half by the region's bifurcation. For example, the Canas were divided into Canas Umasuyu and Canas Urcosuyu. Likewise, the Pacajes were divided into Pacajes Umasuyu and Pacajes Urcosuyu. Curiously, the Lupaqa polity was not bipartite (Bouysse-Cassagne 1986:202–203).

12. We use the spelling of *pucara* with a "c" to refer to the fortified sites of the Altiplano Period. We use the spelling of Pukara with a "k" to refer to the site and culture of the Formative Periods.

3. Inca and Early Colonial Activities in the Lake Titicaca Basin

1. Antonio de la Calancha (1981 [1638]) describes the early history of the Augustinians; however, his sections on the Lake Titicaca region were copied directly from Ramos

Gavilán. Calancha offers little in the way of new or original information on the sacred islands.

2. See Espinoza Soriano (1972b) for a detailed account of the life and times of Ramos Gavilán.

3. "A la cual isla se fué Viracocha y mandó que luego saliese el sol, luna y estrellas y se fuesen al cielo para dar luz al mundo; y así fué hecho. Y dicen que crió á la luna con más claridad quel sol, y que por esto el sol invidioso al tiempo que iban á subir al cielo le dió con un puñado de ceniza en la cara, y que de allí quedó obscurecida de la color que agora parece" (Sarmiento de Gamboa 1906:26 [1572: Ch. 7]).

4. Ramos Gavilán (1988:163 [1621: Bk. 1, Ch. 26]) indicates that on the Island of Titicaca, "there was a great rock and in it a clear and small hole, which by tradition was seen as the opening from where the Sun left" (estava una gran peña y en ella un claro y pequeño hueco, que tenía por tradición aver sido puerta por donde avía salido el Sol).

5. "El adoratorio del sol que estaba en la isla de Titicaca, era una grande y firme peña, cuya veneración y motivo porque la consagraron al sol, tiene por principio y fundamento una novela bien ridícula, y es que los antiguos afirman que habiendo carecido de luz celestial muchos días en esta provincia, y estando todos los moradores della admirados, confusos y amedrentados de tan oscuras y largas tinieblas, los que habitaban la isla sobredicha de Titicaca vieron una mañana salir al sol de aquella peña con extraordinario resplandor, por lo cual creyeron ser aquel peñasco la casa y morada verdadera del sol o la más acepta cosa a su gusto de cuantas en el mundo había; y así se lo dedicaron y edificaron allí un templo suntuoso para en aquellos tiempos, aunque no lo fué tanto como después que los Incas lo engrandecieron e ilustraton" (Cobo 1964:190 [1653: Bk. 18. Ch. 18]).

6. "Otro desvarío es que cuando el Criador del mundo . . . mandó al sol, luna y estrellas irse a la isla de Titicaca, que está en la laguna deste nombre, y que desde allí se subiesen al cielo; y que al tiempo que se quería partir el sol en figura de un hombre muy resplandeciente, llamó a los Incas, y a Manco Cápac, como a hermano mayor, habló desta manera: "Tú y tus descendientes habéis de sujetar muchas tierras y gentes y ser grandes señores; siempre me tened por padre, preciándoos de ser hijos míos, sin jamás olvidaros de reverenciarme como a tal"; y que acabando de decir esto, le dió las insignias de rey, que desde entonces usó él y sus sucesores, y se subió luego al cielo con la luna y estrellas a ponerse cada cual en el lugar que tienen; y que luego incontinenti, por mandado del Hacedor, se sumieron debajo de tierra los hermanos Incas, y fueron a salir a la dicha cueva de Pacarictampu" (Cobo 1964: 62–63 [1653: Bk. 12, Ch. 3]).

7. Garcilaso de la Vega (1966:111–114 [1609: Vol. 1, Bk. 2, Ch. 20]) places the conquest of the Collao region considerably earlier, during the reign of Lloque Yupanqui, the third Inca king. It should be noted, however, that Garcilaso de la Vega (1966:190 [1609: Vol. 1, Bk. 3, Ch. 25]) did not visit the area himself, but relied on the now-lost writing of Blas Valera. Sarmiento de Gamboa (1906:75–77 [1572: Ch. 37]) and Cobo (1979:138–141 [1653: Bk. 12, Ch. 13]) support Cieza de León's suggestion that Pachacuti Inca Yupanqui conquered the lake region. According to Polo de Ondegardo (1916: 50–51 [1571]), Pachacuti conquered up to the Villcanota pass, on the far northern frontier of Collao. Only in the time of his son, Topa Inca, was the empire extended into the Lake Titicaca area. Betanzos

(1996:145–146 [1557: Pt. 1, Ch. 34]) and Ramos Gavilán (1988:32, 36 [1621: Bk. 1, Ch. 3]) also state that Topa Inca was the first Inca to defeat the Titicaca Basin. Murúa (1946:199 [1590: Pt. 3, Ch. 15]) places the conquest of the area later in time, during the rule of Huayna Capac.

8. It is worth noting that the necessity of a reconquest of the Colla indicates that the initial "conquest" was less than complete.

9. Hatuncolla during the Inca Empire was approximately 0.8 km² in size. Huánuco Pampa, another major Inca administrative center, was around 2 km² (Morris and Thompson 1985:86).

10. "Entró en la gran laguna de Titicaca y miró las yslas que en ella se hazen, mandando hazer en la mayor dellas templo del Sol y palaçios para él y sus deçendientes" (Cieza de León 1985:151 [1554: Pt. 2, Ch. 52, f. 61]).

11. Cieza de León (1976:249 [1554: Pt. 2, Ch. 63]) also indicates that several years later, when the next king of Cuzco, Huayna Capac, was entering the region, "He went to the island of Titicaca, and ordered great sacrifices performed" (En la ysla de Titicaca entró y mandó hazer grandes sacrefiçios [Cieza de León 1985:182 (1554: Pt. 2, Ch. 63, f. 76]).

12. "Algunos señores del Collao se ofreçieron de yr por sus personas con el mismo Ynga, y con los que señaló entró en el palude de Titica[ca] y loó a los que entendían en las obras de los edefiçios que su padre mandó hazer quán bien lo avían hecho" (Cieza de León 1985:176–177 [1554: Pt. 2, Ch. 61, 73v]).

13. Cabello Valboa (1951:362–363 [1586: Pt. 3, Ch. 21]) notes that Huayna Capac visited the Island of the Sun, but this information was copied from either Sarmiento de Gamboa or Molina. Acosta (1940:72 [1590: Bk. 2, Ch. 6]) suggests that the islands were abandoned immediately after Spanish contact, but he offers no proof of this statement. For additional references to Lake Titicaca and the Island of the Sun, see Las Casas (1958, 2:163 [ca. 1550: Ch. 182]), Cieza de León 1976:27 (1554: Pt. 2, Ch. 5), Betanzos (1996:7 [1557: Pt. 1, Ch. 1]), Pizarro (1921:193 [1571: Pt. 1]), Sarmiento de Gamboa (1906:28, 105 [1572: Chs. 7, 59]), Molina 1943:79 [ca. 1575]), Murúa (1946:201, 407 [1590: Pt. 3, Ch. 25; Pt. 4, Ch. 13]), Gutiérrez de Santa Clara (1963:209 [ca. 1600: Bk. 3, Ch. 49]), Oliva (1895: 33–37, 51–52 [1613: Chs. 2, 9]), and Santa Cruz Pachacuti Yamqui Salcamayhua (1950:213 [1613]).

14. Ramos Gavilán (1988:185, 189 [1621: Bk. 1, Ch. 31]) indicates that Paullu Inca, who ruled the Inca Empire under Spanish control, traveled to Copacabana to find a daughter of Huayna Capac who had been sent to serve on the Island of the Sun.

15. "[El inca] pasó adelante y quiso de camino visitar el templo de Titicaca. Tuviéronle los de la provincia prevenidas muchas balsas para el pasaje a aquella isla, en la cual se detuvo algunos días, mandando edificar un suntuoso palacio y otros edificios reales; y habiendo sacrificado al sol, prosiguió su viaje" (Cobo 1964:84 [1653: Bk. 12, Ch. 13]).

16. While in Cajamarca, Sancho de la Hoz was responsible for recording the distribution of Atahualpa's ransom among the Spaniards. His principal account, however, begins around June 14, 1533, with the departure of Hernando Pizarro to Spain with the king's portion of the ransom, and finishes just over a year later in the city of Jauja on July 15, 1534.

17. Pedro Pizarro (1921:279 [1571: Pt. 1]) provides the names of these first European visitors to Lake Titicaca: Diego de Agüero and Pedro Martínez de Moguer.

18. "Dicen los indios que hay en ella una laguna grande de agua dulce, y en medio tiene dos islas. Para saber el estado de esta tierra y su gobierno, mandó el Gobernador dos cristianos que le trajesen de ello larga información, los que partieron á principios de Diciembre. . . . Los dos cristianos que fueron enviados á ver la provincia del Collao tardaron cuarenta días en su viaje, y vueltos luego á la ciudad del Cuzco donde estaba el gobernador, le dieron nueva y relación de todo lo que habían visto y entendido que es ésta que aquí abajo se declara . . . en medio de la provincia hay una gran laguna de grandor casi cien leguas: y la tierra más poblada es alrededor de la laguna, en el medio de ella hay dos isletas pequeñas, y en una hay una mezquita y casa del sol que es tenida en gran veneración, y á ella van á hacer sus ofrendas y sacrificios en una gran piedra que está en la isla que llaman Tichicasa, en donde, ó porque el diablo se esconde allí y les habla, ó por costumbre antigua como es, ó por otra causa que no se ha aclarado nunca, la tienen todos los de aquella provincia en grande estima, y le ofrecen oro, plata y otras cosas. Hay más de seiscientos Indios sirviendo en este lugar, y más de mil mujeres que hacen chicha para echarla sobre aquella piedra Tichicasa" (Sancho de la Hoz 1898:405, 413, 415 [1534: Chs. 16 and 18]).

19. The validity of Viscarra's research is difficult to assess, since his primary source is a confused chronicle by an obscure Augustinian, Baltasar de Salas, which Viscarra has rendered even more difficult to use through disjointed editing. See Espinoza Soriano (1972b:172–176) for additional information on Baltasar de Salas.

20. The exception to this statement would be if this group had been part of Diego de Almagro's exploration of the regions south of Cuzco from July 1535 to April 1537.

21. However, it should also be noted that the 1536 date correlates with the year in which Salas (1901:33 [1618]) indicates that the Franciscans first arrived on the peninsula with the Captains Illescas and Anzurez, and with information presented by Ramos Gavilán (1988:164 [1621: Bk. 1, Ch. 26]), who states that the first Spaniards in the area were led by Illescas.

22. ". . . á una isla que se dice Titicaca, que es en el Collao, donde decían que había mucho oro é plata, é á buscarlo por toda la tierra" (Espinal 1959:363 [1539]).

23. During one of these two trips to Copacabana, Paullu Inca fathered Francisco Tito Yupanqui as well as a number of other children.

24. *Encomiendas* included the exclusive rights to the labor or produce from specific communities. They were granted by the Spanish Crown to many of the early Spaniards.

25. The inhabitants of the Copacabana region, like all indigenous people of the Andes, hated the imposed Potosí labor tax, which resulted in the death of many members of their communities. Ramos Gavilán (1988:172–173 [1621: Bk. 1, Ch. 28]) suggests that the Copacabana residents argued against this tax, stating that if during the time of the Inca they were granted exemption from all state taxes to serve a false god, they should be granted the same status to serve the "mother of the real God." Their request was denied.

26. "La gran laguna del Collao tiene por nombre Titicaca, por el templo que estuuo

edificado en la misma laguna. De donde los naturales tuuieron por opinión vna vanidad muy grande, y es: que quentan estos Indios que sus antiguos lo afirmaron por cierto, como hizieron otras burlerías que dizen, que carescieron de lumbre muchos días: y que estando todos puestos en tinieblas y obscuridad, salió desta ysla de Titicaca el Sol muy resplandeciente: por lo qual la tuuieron por cosa sagrada: y los Ingas hizieron en ella el templo que digo: que fue entre ellos muy estimado y venerado a honrra de su Sol: poniendo en él mugeres vírgines y sacerdotes con grandes thesoros. De lo qual puesto que los Españoles en diuersos tiempos han auido mucho, se tiene que falta lo más" (Cieza de León 1984:281 [1553: Pt. 1, Ch. 103, f. 128v]).

27. Although Toledo passed through the Lake Titicaca region in 1572, there is no evidence that he visited the Islands of the Sun and the Moon.

28. Also see Morales Figueroa (1866:41 [1591]).

29. Francisco Tito Yupanqui's daughter, a great-granddaughter of Huayna Capac, was called María Pillcosisa. She died in Copacabana in 1617 (Ramos Gavilán 1988:185, 189 [1621: Bk. 1, Ch. 31]).

30. MacCormack (1984) provides a detailed analysis of the relationship between the Inca worship of the Island of the Sun and the Spaniards' establishment of the Virgin of Copacabana.

31. Numerous gold and silver objects were buried on the Islands of the Sun and the Moon. Santos Escobar (1986) documents one figurine that was found in 1740. Even today, metal figurines continue to be found in plowed fields and in erosion cuts. Many locals have donated the objects they have found to the community museum of Challapampa.

32. "Comoquiera que haya sido el principio y origen deste santuario, él tenía muy grande antigüedad y siempre fué muy venerado de las gentes del Collao, antes que fueran sujetadas por los reyes Incas" (Cobo 1964:190 [1653: Bk. 13, Ch. 18]).

33. See Gutiérrez Flores et al. (1970) for a secret report on Dominican activities in the Lake Titicaca region that was prepared for Viceroy Toledo in 1572.

34. The most notable Early Colonial offerings to survive from the Island of the Sun are six ponchos purchased by Bandelier (1910:221, 232) from Miguel Garcés, owner of the Challapampa hacienda. Two lesser-known ponchos were recovered from the Island of the Moon (Posnansky 1957:137–138). There is no doubt that most, if not all, of these ponchos were produced after the conquest, since several have European design elements.

4. The Islands of the Sun and the Moon Today

1. Pentland (1827: f. 84v) estimates the island population to be about 120 in 1827.

2. In Bandelier's (1910:50) time, Coati was considered part of Sampaya, and both were owned by Dr. W. del Carpio.

3. A flood in 1985 destroyed the remains of the former hacienda house and the barracks for the political prisoners.

4. "Los reyes Incas, demás del templo y su gran ornato, ennoblecieron mucho aquella isla por ser la primera tierra que sus primeros progenitores, viniendo del cielo, habían pisado como ellos decían. Allanáronla todo lo que ser pudo quitándole peñas y peñascos;

hicieron andenes, los cuales cubrieron con tierra buena y fértil, traída de lejos para que pudiese llevar maíz, porque en toda aquella región, por ser tierra muy fría, no se coge de ninguna manera; en aquellos andenes lo sembraban con otras semillas, y con los muchos beneficios que le hacían cogían algunas mazorcas en poca cantidad, las cuales llevaban al rey por cosa sagrada, y él las llevaba al templo del sol, y de ellas enviaba a las vírgenes escogidas que estaban en el Cozco, y mandaba que se llevasen a otros conventos y templos que por el reino había; un año a unos y otro año a otros, para que todos gozasen de aquel grano, que era como traído del cielo. Sembraban de ellos en los jardines de los templos del sol, y de las casas de las escogidas en las provincias donde las había, y lo que se cogía se repartía por los pueblos de las tales provincias. Echaban algunos granos en los graneros del sol y en los del rey, y en los pósitos de los concejos, para que como cosa divina guardase, aumentase y librase de corrupción el pan, que para el sustento común allí estaba recogido. Y el indio que podía haber un grano de aquel máiz o de cualquiera otra semilla para echarlo en sus orones, creía que no le había de faltar pan en toda su vida; tan supersticiosos como esto fueron en cualquiera cosa que tocaba a sus Incas" (Garcilaso de la Vega 1963:120 [1609: Pt. 1, Bk. 3, Ch. 25]).

5. There is some disagreement as to what the term *yatiri* means. For some, a *yatiri* is a specific term denoting a ritual specialist in any community, usually referring to just one of a handful of elderly women and men who have earned the right to conduct rituals. For others, the term *yatiri* is more like the word *doctor* in Western society and denotes a person of some recognized scholarly or professional status, such as a dentist, a professor, a physician, or a member of some other respected profession.

6. In Mesa and Gisbert (1972) the figures are erroneously attributed to Wiener (1880); however, in Mesa and Gisbert (1973: Pl. 5) d'Orbigny is correctly credited.

7. The figures of Pilco Kayma and Iñak Uyu are reversed in the 1854 edition.

8. For additional information on Squier's photographs, see McElroy (1986). Some of Squier's photographs are currently housed in the Latin American Library of Tulane University.

9. These photographs are cataloged as anonymous. However, a comparison of Wiener's engravings and individual photographs in the collection reveals that the engravings were made from the photographs.

10. The Islands of the Sun and the Moon were also visited by E. Pickering of the Harvard University Observatory in 1892. He took a series of photographs, including the earliest picture of the Sacred Rock, which are currently held by the Peabody Museum at Harvard University.

11. Only one of these photographs has been published (Bingham 1922).

12. Photographs from Bingham's expeditions are stored in the Peabody Museum at Yale University as well as in the National Geographic Society in Washington, D.C.

13. A similar pendant has been found on a child sacrifice found in 1985 on the mountain of El Plomo (Schobinger 1991:63).

14. See D'Altroy and Bishop (1990) and Julien (1993) for additional information on the ceramics in the Bandelier collection at the American Museum of Natural History.

15. It should be noted, however, that some of the metal objects in the collection came

from other sites on the island and some of the Inca ceramics came from Yunguyu (Bandelier 1910:27, 227).

16. Bandelier's book (1910:221, 225, 232) and his correspondence provide apparently contradictory information about the original locations of the other five tunics. In his book, Bandelier suggests that many, or all, of the tunics were recovered on the Island of the Sun, whereas in a letter dated July 22, 1895, he states that five of the tunics came from Copacabana.

17. See Ponce Sanginés et al. (1992) for an extensive bibliography and summary of recent research on the islands.

18. Many museums across the world hold objects reported to be from the Islands of the Sun and the Moon. Posnansky (1957:61–62) illustrated a Tiwanaku *kero* (drinking vessel) and a bowl, given to the British Museum in 1828, perhaps by Pentland, which were found in a tomb on the Island of the Sun. Posnansky (1957:65–71) also drew seven Early Colonial wooden *keros* from the sacred islands (four from the Island of the Sun and three from the Island of the Moon) that are held by the National Museum and the Tiwanaku Institute of Anthropology in La Paz. The Museum für Völkerkunde has an impressive set of objects from the sacred islands (Eisleb and Strelow 1980), many of which were collected by Uhle. Furthermore, the Staatliches Museum für Völkerkunde (Munich), holds about twenty objects collected in 1914 from the islands. Posnansky (1957:61) drew a Tiwanaku bowl from this collection. The Peabody Museum of Archaeology and Ethnology at Harvard University also holds a small set of artifacts collected in 1875 and 1892–1893 from the islands. Most importantly, the American Museum of Natural History houses the bulk of Bandelier's artifacts from the islands as well as the Garcés collection, including its rare Lake Titicaca region tunics. An additional Early Colonial tunic, said to have been found on the Island of the Moon, is held by the Museum of the American Indian, and another tunic, also said to be from the Island of the Moon, is illustrated in Posnansky (1957:137–138).

19. We did not survey within the boundaries of modern cemeteries. We likewise did not go inside modern house compounds without permission.

20. The first pottery on the Island of the Sun therefore overlaps with the Pasiri Period and the Early Sillumocco Period, as defined in the Juli region.

21. This is curious because whole vessels from the Bandelier collection, supposedly obtained from the Island of the Sun, were used by Wallace (1957) to define this pottery style.

22. We were able to locate all of the sites discussed by Bandelier, in virtually all cases corroborating his observations and in most cases augmenting them.

5. The Island of the Moon

1. ". . . halló buena comodidad en una isla, que dista de Titicaca una legua y más, hazia en Oriente, mediana, de buen temple, y poblada de alguna arboleda aunque sin agua vezina. Esta isla dedicó a la luna, y allí le hizo altar donde puso un vulto de oro a la traça de una Coya, que representava la muger del Sol, llamóla Coata, o Coyata que es tano como Reyna. Esta era la segunda romería después de aver llegado a la isla, y era muy celebrada" (Ramos Gavilán 1988:170 [1621: Bk. 1, Ch. 28]).

2. "En la isla Coata se hallan grandes edificios, porque el Inga Guaynacapac, quiso aventajarse a su padre, y assí intentó cosas nuevas por señalarse, edificó una casa, para vivienda de las Vírgines dedicadas al Sol, para que cuydasen del adorno de su templo, y de su esposa la Luna, que en aquesta isla, . . . Tocante a esta isla . . . se hallaron labradas en piedra muchas figuras de animales diversos, casi semejantes, a las que los Españoles hallaron en México quando ganaron aquella tierra . . . Al monasterio, o casa donde estavan estas Vírgines llamavan Acllaquasi (que suena lo mismo, que casa de escogidas). Cada casa destas tenía su Vicario, o Governador, el qual vivía no muy distante della, llamávanle Apopanaca" (Ramos Gavilán 1988:120 [1621: Bk. 1, Ch. 18]).

3. "Avía muchas, y muy frequentes missiones de una isla, a otra, y grandes retornos, fingían los ministros del un templo, y del otro, que la Coya muger del Sol, teniendo las vezes de la luna le embiava sus recados, y que el Sol se los retornava con caricias de recíproca afición, yvan y venían brevajes, y hazían tiempo para bever a una. Demás desto para representar las figuras al vivo se componían en cada uno de los adoratorios, un ministro mayor, y una Mamacona que hazían los personages del Sol, y de la luna, cubiertos con láminas de oro el que representava el Sol, y el de la luna con sus planchas de plata, brindávanse, regalando la Coya al Sol, pidiéndole tiempo fértil, y apacible, y que sustentasse en regalada vida al Inga, y a los demás que con tanta fe, y devoción empleavan sus voluntades en su servicio" (Ramos Gavilán 1988:171 [1621: Bk. 1, Ch. 28]).

4. "Los sacerdotes y ministros deste adoratorio y del de Coatá tenían muy grande comunicación, y había muchas y muy frecuentes misiones de una isla a la otra con grandes retornos, fingiendo los ministros del un santuario y del otro que la mujer del sol, así como lo pudiera a su parecer hacer la luna, le enviaba sus recaudos; los cuales el sol le retornaba con caricias de tierna afición y recíproco amor; y en esto gastaban mucho tiempo, ocupando en su ministerio gran cantidad de balsas, que iban y tornaban de una isla a otra; y para representar esto al vivo, se componía en el un adoratorio el ministro mayor, que representaba la persona del sol, y en el otro una india, que hacía el personaje de la luna. Brindábanse el uno al otro y la que representaba a la luna acariciaba al que figuraba al sol, pidiéndole con caricias se les mostrase cada día claro y apacible y que nunca ocultase sus rayos, para que fertilizasen los sembrados hasta el tiempo en que fuesen necesarias las lluvias. Demás desto, le pedía que conservase en vida, salud y reposo al Inca y a los demás que con tanta fe y devoción se ocupaban en su servicio y culto; y el que en nombre del sol se fingía, respondía con regaladas palabras, suficientes a satisfacer" (Cobo 1964:193–194 [1653: Bk. 13, Ch. 18]).

5. "Pero, no contento con lo hecho para ornamento y lustre deste santuario, juzgando todavía que no satifacía enteramente a su obligación y que no acudía con prudencia al servicio del sol si no le señalaba mujer, y aun mujeres, para su uso y servicio, acordó de hacerlo; y estando en esta determinación, halló una buena comodida para efectuarla, que fué la isla de Coatá, or Coyatá, denominado de *Coya,* que es tanto como reina, y labró en ella un suntuoso templo, donde puso una estatua de mujer, de la cintura para arriba de oro, y de la cintura para abajo, de plata, la cual era de la grandeza de una mujer y representaba ser imagen de la luna. De manera que demás de las mujeres vivas que en Titicaca estaban dedicadas al sol para su servicio, lo era este ídolo con nombre de esposa

suya, en representación de la luna. Aunque otros quieren que esta figura y estatua se llamaba Titicaca, y dicen que representaba Titicaca, y dicen que representaba a la madre de los Incas. Sea lo uno o lo otro, la estatua fué llevada a la ciudad del Cuzco por el marqués don Francisco Pizarro, que envió a tres españoles por ella" (Cobo 1964:192 [1653: Bk. 13, Ch. 18]).

6. This information was most likely taken from Pedro Pizarro's account.

7. "En esta laguna ay una ysla que se dize Titicaca, donde tenían por ydolo una muger, de la çinta arriua de oro y de la çinta auaxo de plata, de la estatura de una muger mediana" (Pizarro 1986:46 [1571:28]).

8. ". . . cuando llegaron á la Península los Capitanes Alzures y los Illescas, con los Padres franciscanos, aunque intentaron en 1536, no pudieron llegar á esta, por falta de tiempo, y porque la creyeron como á la del Sol estar yerma y desierta" (Salas 1901:33 [1618]).

9. In Cobo (1964:194 [1653: Bk. 13, Ch. 18]), the year is listed as 1617: "La fama que yo oí estando en esta provincia el año de mil y seiscientos y diez y siete, es que hay gran riqueza en la isla de Coatá; a cual fueron entonces ciertos españoles en un barco y no pudieron hallar cosas."

10. Salas (1901:31 [1618]) reports that the construction of the boats began on July 26, 1617, a full ten months before the trip started.

11. Many of the reed boats would have been small, capable of holding only one or two people.

12. Although it is difficult to say how much validity one should ascribe to Salas, it is worth noting that he states that there were still two ñustas (women of royal blood) living on the island at the time of his visit, some eighty-six years after the Spanish invasion. While this seems most unlikely, it is remotely possible that very young girls who had arrived on the island near the time of the conquest could still have been alive in 1618. The elder of the two women, Coyllor Lulu, with a reported age of 132, is said to be the sister of Huayna Capac and the great-aunt of Francisco Tito Yupanqui. Salas (1901:35, 280 [1618]) presents her as well versed in the history of the Inca and in the art of quipu reading. Because Huayna Capac, the final Inca to reign over a unified Inca Empire, died in middle age around 1528, it seems impossible that a sister of his could have survived until 1618.

According to Salas, the younger ñusta was Ana Cusiur Lulu, who is said to have been 92 years old. She is reported to have been the sister of Francisco Tito Yupanqui, the well-known maker of the Image of Copacabana, who was himself the son of Paullu Inca. She would have thus been the granddaughter of Huayna Capac. As there are no other documents attesting to these individuals, their existence is open to question.

13. Researchers have recovered various stone chests on the Island of the Sun as well as in the lake near this island.

14. Earlier researchers refer to this site by a number of names, including Temple of the Moon and Palace of the Virgins of the Sun. In this work, we accept the name reported by Bandelier, Iñak Uyu, which continues to be used today.

15. As with his description of the Sacred Rock on the Island of the Sun, Bandelier was

disoriented in his description of Iñak Uyu. Throughout his discussions he refers to the south component of the site as the western part.

16. Bandelier (1910:265, plate LXXIII) suggests that the complex at one time may have been more elaborate, citing evidence of a small structure behind the principal building.

17. E. Pickering, of the Harvard University Observatory, visited the Island of the Moon in 1892. His photographic collection in the Peabody Museum at Harvard University contains a dark, offshore picture of the Iñak Uyu terraces (catalogue number H9605).

18. Bandelier (1910, plate LXXIXa) also recovered an Inca-style pedestal cooking pot at Iñak Uyu, although he does not say precisely where it was located.

19. Two similar gold pumas were recovered in stone boxes in Lake Titicaca near the Island of the Sun (Ponce Sanginés et al. 1992:739), and four additional metal pumas from the Island of the Moon are in the Museum für Völkerkunde in Berlin (Eisleb and Strelow 1980:94–95).

20. "La principal de ellas es una escultura en forma de clava, que representa una figura zoomorfa en forma de cara, con las orejas gachas, y que termina en forma de una punta por el otro extremo (41 cm de altura y 26 de extensión de la cabeza)."

21. Also see the drawing in Rivero and Tschudi (1851).

22. Polo de Ondegardo (1916:109–110 [1571]) states that the central plaza of Cuzco contained a level of sand.

23. Similar puma-head incense burners have been recovered in Lake Titicaca near the Island of the Sun (Ponce Sanginés et al. 1992; Reinhard 1992a, 1992b).

24. Teledyne I-18,554. All radiocarbon samples reported in this study were treated for the removal of carbonates and humic acids. The Libby half-life of 5,568 years was used to calculate the ages. Calibration dates are provided using OxCal.v3.4.

25. Teledyne I-18,629; wood charcoal. See Appendix for calibrated dates.

26. Arizona AA 34942; *ichu* grass. See Appendix for calibrated dates.

27. Arizona AA 34943; *ichu* grass. See Appendix for calibrated dates.

28. Bandelier (1910:273–274, 280–281) calls this site Chichería.

29. Bandelier (1910, plate LXXII) also notes the presence of three small structures on a terrace near the northwest end of the island. These buildings are no longer recognizable.

30. David Dearborn studied the remains of Iñak Uyu in 1996 and found no significant relationship between the orientation of its buildings and the movements of the Moon.

31. These pumas are virtually identical to ones found on the Island of the Sun (Eisleb and Strelow 1980:95), in the lake near the Island of the Sun (Ponce Sanginés et al. 1992; Reinhard (1992a, 1992b), and at the site of Tiwanaku itself (Posnansky 1957, plate XCII).

32. In some areas, the sand fill was more than one meter deep.

6. The Pre-Inca Occupations on the Island of the Sun

1. The three radiocarbon samples dated are: 3780 ± 170 BP (Teledyne I-18,314; wood carbon); 2770 ± 100 BP (Teledyne I-18,402; wood carbon); and 2110 ± 100 BP (Teledyne I-18,401; wood carbon). See Appendix for calibrated dates.

2. His wording in this matter is unclear: ". . . there are remains designated as Chullpa (andenes and burials) about the heights of Santa Bárbara (12) and at Titin-Uayani, near Kea (29). At the latter place we excavated a number of graves, obtaining skulls, pottery of the coarser kind . . ." (Bandelier 1910:172). It is not quite clear if Bandelier meant that he excavated at sites near Kea (Kea Kollu Chico or the sides of Kea itself) or Titinhuayani. Bandelier rarely mentions the site after that. Furthermore, the number that he places after Kea, 29, is incorrectly placed on his map. However, the collections at the American Museum of Natural History have materials that appear to be from Titinhuayani, including Tiwanaku vessels. It is most likely that Bandelier excavated at this site. It is also possible that he combined the work from Kea Kollu Chico, where he also excavated, with that of the slopes of Titinhuayani, since these sites are close to each other.

3. This work was for his thesis at the Universidad Mayor San Andrés, La Paz, Bolivia.

4. It is possible that the Middle Formative occupation also contained complex architecture, but it was not recognizable in our limited test excavations.

5. Bandelier's description of Chucaripupata is somewhat confusing, probably due to the fact that there are two sites close to each other, one called Chucaripu, which contains ruins, and the other called Chucaripupata, which contains a large set of terraces. Bandelier distinguishes between them on his map but not in his text.

The suffix *pata* means, among other things, "place of terraces," as Bandelier (1910:5) well understood. Nevertheless, Bandelier calls both ruins as well as the terraces Chucaripupata. In spite of this mistake in nomenclature, we, like Seddon (1998), follow Bandelier's name for the ruins to avoid even more confusion.

6. Our data are sparse at the present time. However, it is likely that Late Archaic–style projectile points coexisted with the earliest pottery in the region during the first centuries of the second millennium BC.

7. Camelid bones were discovered in the Ch'uxuqullu middens.

8. The earliest pottery located to date in the Titicaca Basin has been identified by Steadman (in press) at the site of Quelcatani. This site, excavated by Aldenderfer, provides a C-14 date of 3660 ± 60 BP, a date that calibrates to around 2000 BC.

9. This interpretation is supported by the absence of sites in the southern Challa area. This area is a productive agricultural area, with no obvious impediments to human occupation. Indeed, later sites were founded in this region. Yet Middle Formative populations chose not to live in this area, a fact that left a geographical separation between the Challa cluster of sites and the southernmost group on the island. This is a classic indicator of a social or political boundary.

10. These areas, in fact, could not be exploited effectively for any period of time without the use of terraces.

11. The Early and Late Titinhuayani Periods correspond to Early and Late Sillumocco from the Juli area. Late Titinhuayani ceramic diagnostics include some Qeya fragments and other styles defined by Steadman (1994) for Tumatumani during this period. Diagnostic Qeya shards included the feline incense burners with a buff paste, occasionally tempered with light fiber. A few Qeya bottle fragments were also discovered on Qeya Kollu.

12. In other areas of the Titicaca Basin that have been intensively surveyed, there is a general pattern in which population totals and site sizes increase, but total site numbers decrease during the Upper Formative Period (Albarracin-Jordan and Mathews 1990; Stanish et al. 1997; Stanish n.d.).

13. The horizontal exaggeration of the oblique view of the island on Map 6.5 distorts the distance of Wakuyu and Apachinacapata from the Challa Bay.

14. In the Late Titinhuayani Period, Titinhuayani is 4.0 hectares and the other three are 3.0 hectares in size.

15. It is important to point out that excavation evidence from Iñak Uyu on the Island of the Moon and from Chucaripupata on the Island of the Sun suggests that both of the islands were simultaneously gaining in ritual importance in the Upper Formative. Excavations at the Inca temple of Iñak Uyu recorded a large Upper Formative occupation and recovered numerous high-prestige and ceremonial objects.

16. Perrín Pando (1957) excavated at Wakuyu and discovered several burials containing classic Tiwanaku vessels. He also noted that the hill was artificial and that there was at least one major wall at the site.

17. Curiously, there is no line of Tiwanaku sites along the low northeastern side of the island where a second Inca road was constructed.

18. Bermann (1990:323) places the end of the Tiwanaku Period (his Tiwanaku V phase) as late as AD 1200.

19. "Y el vno de ellos entró en la laguna de Titicaca: y que halló en la ysla mayor que tiene aquel palude gentes blancas, y que tenían baruas: con los quales peleó de tal manera que los pudo matar a todos. Y más dizen, que passado esto, tuuieron grandes batallas con los Canas y con los Cánchez" (Cieza de León 1984:274 [1553: Pt. 1, Ch. 100, f. 125v]).

In the same section of his book, however, Cieza de León relates that there was subsequent fighting with the Canas and Canchis, followed by the famous meeting of Viracocha Inca with the Lupaqa king in Chucuito. If we take the sequence of events as generally correct chronologically, then the Island of the Sun could have been conquered by either polity. However, if we assume that the death of the Colla leader at the hands of the Lupaqa at Paucarcolla meant that the Colla lost regional influence, then it would be likely that the Island of the Sun fell under Lupaqa control just before Inca forces entered the Lake Titicaca region.

7. The Island of the Sun under Inca Rule

1. We recorded eighty-two Inca Period sites on the Islands of the Sun, the Moon, Chuyú, Kenata, and Pallalla.

2. Early colonial accounts suggest that during Inca times the Copacabana area, including the islands, was administratively distinct from the territories that surrounded it. For example, a comprehensive 1567 report on Lupaqa Province ends at Yunguyu (Diez de San Miguel 1964 [1567]). Copacabana is also specifically listed as an area apart from Chucuito in other early documents (Gutiérrez Flores et al. 1970:5 [1572]). Furthermore, the separation of Copacabana from the rest of the mainland was clearly demarcated by a wall near Yunguyu.

3. This is a similar pattern to the Juli-Pomata settlement data (Stanish et al. 1997).

4. The Juli-Pomata survey and the survey on the Island of the Sun used identical methodologies for defining sites.

5. Some possible factors that would artificially inflate the Inca Period population include the ubiquity and distinctiveness of Inca pottery diagnostics and the better preservation of these more recent sites. Even with the biases, it is clear that there was a major increase in population on the island during Inca times.

6. The foreground and background elements are decorative.

7. Squier (1877:367) notes that Antonio Raimondi, who was traveling with him, also made a map of the site.

8. Ramos Gavilán (1988:163-164 [1621: Bk. 1, Ch. 26]) also states that there were painted figures on some of the temple walls on the Island of the Sun.

9. Arizona AA 34945; *ichu* grass. See Appendix for calibrated dates.

10. Arizona AA AA34944; *ichu* grass. See Appendix for calibrated dates.

11. Trimborn (1967:34–41) describes Kasapata and illustrates several fragments of Inca pottery from it. He also erroneously describes the large cut stone near the center of the site as a stela with two human faces. Squier (1877:369) and Bandelier (1910:205) correctly describe this monolith, which can still be seen today, as a simple carved stone.

12. The site has further deteriorated since Bandelier's time. Among the features illustrated by Bandelier (1910:204 and plate LII) that have since been lost are a large trapezoidal niche and an impressive gateway.

13. Teledyne I-18,557; wood charcoal. See Appendix for calibrated dates.

14. "Formó un moderado pueblo, media legua, o casi, antes de la peña, y adoratorio, y en él labró su Real Palacio" (Ramos Gavilán 1988:86 [1621: Bk. 1, Ch. 12]).

15. "Un grandioso *tambo* o mesón para hospedaje de peregrinos" (Cobo 1964:191 [1653: Bk. 13, Ch. 18]).

16. Also see Bandelier (1910:215).

17. "Casas de habitación de los ministros del santuario, y de las vírgenes dedicadas al Sol" (Ramos Gavilán 1988:94 [1621: Bk. 1, Ch. 15]).

18. ". . . eran aposentos de los ministros y sirvientes del templo" (Cobo 1964:193 [1653: Bk. 13, Ch. 18]).

19. Bandelier (1910:294) states that local traditions on the Island of the Sun assigned the name Mama Ojlia to the mother of Manco Capac (and of the Sun). This name is not found in other documents pertaining to the island.

20. The name Mama Ojlia is no longer used; the largest building is now simply known as *kayma* (temple). The name Mama Ojlia most likely refers to the sister/wife of the mythical Manco Capac, the first Inca, who is generally called Mama Ocllo.

21. We found no portion of this structure to be particularly suited for Sun observations.

22. This area represented approximately 14 percent of the building's interior.

23. The earliest possible date for the floor is Inca, since the pottery below it dated to that period. It is possible that the floor is a post-Inca feature, but the available data are inconclusive.

24. LLNL 23788; wood charcoal. See Appendix for calibrated dates.

25. LLNL 23789; wood charcoal. See Appendix for calibrated dates.

26. Hyslop (1990:76) suggests that these buildings served as the Temple of the Sun. Squier (1877:338) and Bandelier (1910:216–217), following the chroniclers, propose that they served as the residences of the priests, attendants, and Mamaconas of the shrine.

27. "Más adelante dellas, en la barranca que cae en frente del camino (entre Juli, y Pomata) está la despensa del Sol, que si el tiempo no la uviera desvaratado, tenía la vista en qué entrenerse en sus edificos, y traça, que era como un laberinto, por los innumerables retretes que tenía, que los Indios llaman Chingana, que quiere dezir, lugar donde se pierden. Tiene en medio un vergel con su alameda de alisos, cuya continua frescura sustenta un dulce manantial de agua, que allí rebienta. A lo sombrío destos árboles labró el Inga unos curiosos baños de piedra para el Sol, y su culto" (Ramos Gavilán 1988:93 [1621: Bk. 1, Ch. 13]).

28. "Y cerca del templo se ven ruinas de la despensa del sol, cuyos retretes imitan al laberinto de Creta. En los paredones y rastros que hoy quedan en pie se echa de ver el primor que tuvo todo el edificio deste supersticioso adoratorio; y asimismo se ve la traza de un vergel que hubo con su alameda de alisos, a la sombra de los cuales estaban unos baños de piedra bien labrada, que el Inca mandó hacer, diciendo eran para que el sol se bañase" (Cobo 1964:193 [1653: Bk. 13, Ch. 18]).

29. "Hay señales de un gran edificio, que era el recogimiento de las *Mamaconas*, mujeres consagradas al sol, las cuales servían de hacer brebajes y telas de curiosidad que en aquel ministerio del adoratorio se gastaban. Estaba esta casa de las *Mamaconas* en el mejor lugar de la isla" (Cobo 1964:193 [1653: Bk. 13, Ch. 18]).

30. The general orientation of the rooms in the Chincana is to an azimuth of 235°. The complex offers an impressive southwesterly view, but the orientation is too far south of west to have been directed toward any sunset. Many of the walls still stand to full height, but as expected in a cool climate, there are few windows. The windows that do exist are mainly between rooms in the complex, and according to our measurements, are not oriented in interesting directions. Based on an absence of well-oriented windows, anomalous rooms, or alignments carved in stone, we cannot propose that any area of the Chincana is particularly suited for monitoring the solar motion.

31. The Peabody Museum at Harvard University has a series of photographs of the Chincana taken by Wiener (catalog numbers H9828, H9829, H9834, H9835, H9836).

32. Other notable photographs of the Chincana can be found in Posnansky (1912, 1957).

33. Teledyne I-18,556; wood charcoal. See Appendix for calibrated dates.

34. Teledyne I-18,555; wood charcoal. See Appendix for calibrated dates.

35. ". . . en la barranca que cae en frente del camino (entre Juli, y Pomata) está la despensa del Sol, . . . que era como un laberinto, por los innumerables retretes que tenía, que los Indios llaman Chingana" (Ramos Gavilán 1988:93 [1621: Bk. 1, Ch. 13]).

36. "Y cerca del templo se ven ruinas de la despensa del sol, cuyos retretes imitan al laberinto de Creta" (Cobo 1964:193 [1653: Bk. 13, Ch. 18]).

37. ". . . las ventanas, alhacenas o nichos que por las paredes había" (Cobo 1964:193 [1653: Bk. 13, Ch. 18]).

38. ". . . hacer brebajes y telas de curiosidad que en aquel ministerio del adoratorio se gastaban" (Cobo 1964:193 1653: Bk. 13, Ch. 18]).

39. OS 12672; wood charcoal (Seddon 1998:510). See Appendix for calibrated dates.

40. OS 12677; wood charcoal (Seddon 1998:510). See Appendix for calibrated dates.

41. The cluster of andesite blocks is not present in Pickering's 1892 photographs of the plaza (Photo 7.24), but they can be seen in pictures taken about ten years later by Gregory (1913a). Perhaps the stones were assembled in one place after Bandelier's 1895 excavations.

42. Max Portugal Ortiz (1992:652–566, figures 4.8–4.12) and Reinhard (1992a:473, figure 3.12) describe other stone containers recovered underwater between the islands of Khoa and Pallalla.

43. ". . . mujeres que hacen chicha para echarla sobre aquella piedra Tichicasa" (Sancho de la Hoz 1898:415 [1534: Ch. 18]).

44. Munsell Color Chart 1994: light greenish gray 7/1.

45. Green shale is found in abundance on the island, although not within the immediate area of the rock sanctuary.

46. Beta 102531; wood charcoal. See Appendix for calibrated dates.

47. Two of the small slab cists contained pairs of miniature vessels. The style of the vessels was unknown to our eldest workers, suggesting that the offerings were certainly more than fifty years old.

48. ". . . donde estaban dos mojones o pilares que tenían por señales que, llegando allí el sol, era el principio de verano" (Cobo 1964:172 [1653: Bk. 13, Ch. 13]).

49. Also see Trimborn (1959:6–8) and Hyslop (1990:228–229).

8. The Pilgrim's Progress

1. ". . . eran templos muy suntuosos, ricos, y como santuarios de general devoción, adonde de todas las partes del Perú iban en romería, al modo que los cristianos suelen visitar el Santo Sepulcro de nuestro Redentor, el templo de los apóstoles San Pedro y San Pablo, y el célebre santuario de Santiago de Galicia" (Cobo 1964:167 [1653: Bk. 13, Ch. 12]).

2. "Por comenzar a ser tenido por lugar sagrado desde que se pasaba el estrecho de tierro o istmo, que arriba dije estar entre Yunguyo y Copacabana, hizo el Inca cerrar esta entrada con una cerca que sacó de la una playa a la otra, y poner en ella sus puertas, porteros y guardas que examinasen a los que en romería venían a este santuario" (Cobo 1964:191 [1653: Bk. 13, Ch. 18]).

3. The early Quechua dictionaries provide similar, although not identical, names for pilgrims' houses. For example, González Holguín (1989:625 [1608]) writes, "Peregrinos aluergar, o hospedar = Corpacani huaciyman hamuyñini," and in the Aymara dictionary of Ludovico Bertonio (1984:361 [1612]) we find the word "Corpachatha" for lodging given to pilgrims.

4. "Era tanta la gente, que de todo el Reyno sugeto al Inga acudía a este adoratorio, que mandó se hiziessen, hospederías públicas, donde se recogiessen los peregrinos. A estas hospederías (que eran unos galpones grandes) llaman acá en el Pirú comúnmente tambos, y a los que se hazían, para los que acudían a los adoratorios, nombravan corpaguasi, que suena lo mismo, que en nuestro vulgar, casa de peregrinos, donde eran regalados, mientras durava el tiempo de su romería" (Ramos Gavilán 1988:127 [1621: Bk. 1, Ch. 20]).

5. "Viniendo de Yunguyo, llegavan primero a Copacabana, donde cada uno era regalado, según la calidad de su persona, dándoles lo necessario de comida, y bevida, y si eran pobres se les dava algún vestido. Para esto tenía el Inga, en un lugar de Loca, media legua de Copacabana, unas albóndigas, o graneros, que los Indios llaman colcas, donde se recogía toda la comida, assí para el sustento de la gente de guerra, como para los ministros de los templos, y para los peregrinos, que a ellos acudían, destos depósitos se ven alrededor de Copacabana, por las faldas de los cerros" (Ramos Gavilán 1988:127 [1621: Bk. 1, Ch. 20]).

6. "Y otro pueblezuelo en que están ciertos depósitos, que está entre el pueblo de Copacaguana y Yunguyo, con cuarenta indios de servicio y diez y siete viejos y viudas" (Espinoza Soriano 1972a:10).

7. ". . . para el aviamiento de los cuales hizo en el contorno de Copacabana grandes depósitos así de mantenimientos como de ropas y otras cosas de provisión, cuyas ruinas duran hasta hoy, y yo las he visto" (Cobo 1964:191 [1653: Bk. 13, Ch. 18]).

8. Sections of the Inca road can still be seen between Copacabana and Yampupata.

9. Along the way, they most likely passed a number of other small shrines, although these have not been precisely located. For example, they passed the site of Kusijata, which contains cut stones that may be Inca in date (Escalante Moscoso 1994:371). In addition, a major Christian shrine is found today in a valley near the Inca road. This shrine was most likely patterned after Inca ones in the area.

10. Squier made the one-to-two-kilometer trip across the strait in 1864 and supplies an important description by someone who experienced the trip in a reed boat:

"Leaving behind the little playa or beach [of Yampupata], our Indian boatmen pushed along under a steep, rocky cliff, until they reached the point where the strait between the mainland and the island is narrowest. The water at the foot of the cliff is very deep, but wonderfully transparent. We were more than two hours in propelling the balsa across the strait, a distance which an ordinary oarsman in a Whitehall boat would get over in fifteen minutes, and landed on the island under the lee of a projecting ledge of rocks, full in view of the Palace of the Inca [Pilco Kayma] and the terraces surrounding it, half a mile to our right." (Squier 1877:329)

Squier traveled in a particularly small boat, but he notes that there were larger vessels on the lake, some of which could be rigged with a sail and were capable of carrying as many as sixty people. Although Squier appears to have viewed the slow crossing of the lake as a fault of the boatmen, the reality is that the lake is extremely difficult to navigate. Modern motor-driven boats take almost an hour to go from Yampupata to the Island of the Sun. The lake is usually wind-swept and currents are strong. In Inca times, the trip would have been very difficult, and we suspect that an oarsman from Whitehall would have found this trip far more difficult than the experienced raftsmen of Copacabana.

11. Squier writes: "They told us that they had mules ready for us beyond the rocks, up and through which we clambered by a steep and narrow path, worn in the stone by the feet of myriads of pilgrims. This leads to a platform 73 feet [22 m] long and 45 feet [14 m] broad, faced with rough stone carefully laid and reached by a flight of steps. Above this is another platform, ascended in like manner, on the farther side of which are the remains of two rectangular buildings, each 35 feet [11 m] long by 27 feet [8 m] broad, with a narrow passage between them.

"The front of each building is much ruined, but is relieved by reentering niches of true Inca type, and characteristic of Inca architecture. Midway from the passage between the buildings, which is only thirty inches wide, doors open into each edifice, which is composed of but a single room. The farther sides of these have niches corresponding with those of the exterior. Opposite them, and designed apparently more for use than ornament, are two lesser and plain niches, like closets stuck in the wall. If there were any windows, they were in the upper portions of the walls, now fallen. Both buildings are of blue limestone, roughly cut, and laid in a tough clay. They were probably stuccoed." (Squier 1877:333-334)

12. Surface collections at Apachinacapata indicate that it was continuously occupied from the Middle Formative to Inca times.

13. Challapampa continued to play a prominent role in the Early Colonial Period as the center of one of the two haciendas established on the island. Today, the village of Challapampa is the third-largest community on the island. Ramos Gavilán provides the following information on Challapampa:

"Antes que los Religiosos de nuestro Padre San Agustín, cuydassen de aquesta dotrina de Copacabana, eran muchos los Indios que gustavan vivir en esta isla, y por quitar inconvenientes los an trasladado al mismo pueblo, solamente an permitido en Challapampa hasta treynta casas, donde se recogen los Indios en tiempo de sus sementeras. Es este lugarejo de gran recreación, donde tienen una capilla dedicada al glorioso Santiago." (Ramos Gavilán 1988:199 [1621: Bk. 1, Ch. 33])

("Before the Augustinians were in charge of the Copacabana shrine, there were many Indians that enjoyed living on the island [of the Sun], and in order to take care of some problems they were moved to the same town [Copacabana], and only thirty households were permitted to live in Challapampa where they worked their fields during the agricultural season. It is in this important place where there is a shrine dedicated to the Blessed Santiago." [authors' translation])

14. "De los mitimaes, que la mayor parte eran de la sangre y linaje de los Incas, formó un moderado pueblo media legua antes del templo, y en él mandó labrar casa de su habitación" (Cobo 1964:191 [1653: Bk. 13, Ch. 18]).

15. Kasapata now contains only a few families and is a political annex of Challapampa.

16. ". . . formó un moderado pueblo, media legua, o casi, antes de la peña, y adoratorio, y en él labró su Real Palacio" (Ramos Gavilán 1988:86 [1621: Bk. 1, Ch. 12]).

17. ". . . un cuarto de legua antes de llegar al templo, un grandioso tambo o mesón para hospedaje de peregrinos" (Cobo (1964:191 [1653: Bk. 13, Ch. 18]).

18. González Holguín (1989:331 [1608]) writes, "Rampa. Las andas en que lleuauan al Inca a hombros." Similarly, Bertonio (1984:188 [1612]) defines *lampa* as "Litera. La de los Caciques antiguos era como una grande hanega, de mimbres, o ramos delgados, con fus palos para lleuarla." Both of these definitions refer to a litter made of thin logs or reeds and used to carry nobility.

19. "Quando los Indios celebravan las fiestas solenes del Sol, particularmente la del Capacrayme, y la del Intip rayme, los de la parcialidad de los Ingas, ponían todos los Idolos en sus andas (que ellos llaman rampa) y adornándolas con muchas flores, y planchas de oro, y plata, y mucha plumería, hazían sus bayles, y fiestas yvan todos hazia la isla, y las ponían en un lugar llamado Aucaypata, donde estava una gran plaça, y allí se hazían las fiestas. Avía un templo grande con cinco puertas, y no se permitía a ningún Indio Colla, assistir ni hallarse a estas fiestas, ni entrar hasta que fuesen acabadas" (Ramos Gavilán 1988:176 [1621: Bk. 1, Ch. 29]).

20. "A todos los cuales se entraba por aquella puerta dicha Intipuncu, doscientos pasos distante de la peña. Entre esta puerta y los edificios dichos estaba una peña viva, por la cual pasa el camino que va al santuario, y en ella están ciertas señales que parecen del calzado de los indios, grandísimas, las cuales creían los indios viejos ser pisadas milagrosas que allí quedaron de aquellos más que tenebrosos tiempos de su gentilidad, siendo como son aguajes de la misma peña. A un lado de la puerta sobredicha se ven ciertos edificios viejos, que, según los indios cuentan, eran aposentos de los ministros y sirvientes del templo" (Cobo 1964:193 1653: Bk. 13, Ch. 18]).

21. Ramos Gavilán (1988:63 [1621: Bk. 1, Ch. 8]) suggests that these were the footprints of Tunupa, the Aymara creator god, rather than those of the first Inca, as suggested by Cobo (1990:97 (1653: Bk. 13, Ch. 18).

22. González Holguín (1989:285 [1608]) writes, "Apillco ppichu. Un pájaro de los Andes colorado preciado por las plumas" (Apillco ppichu. A colored Andean bird, esteemed for its feathers).

23. Also see Ramos Gavilán (1988:87 [1621: Bk. 1, Ch. 12]).

24. Two great Inca roads bordered Lake Titicaca. The Umasuyu road ran along the east side of the lake, and the Urcosuyu road ran along the west side.

25. "A todo esto se entra por aquella puerta ya dicha Kentipuncu, que está dozientos passos antes de la peña, donde el Inga se descalçó la primera vez, que allí puso los pies . . . al lado derecho de la qual se ven ciertos caserones, que eran aquel tiempo casas de habitación de los ministros del santuario, y de las vírgenes dedicadas al Sol. Poco adelante (passada la puerta) parece una peña viva, sobre que passa la senda hazia el falso santuario en esta peña están los rastros de pies humanos, de que ya emos tratado. Antes de llegar a este adoratorio, se avía de passar por tres puertas, que distavan las unas de las otras poco más de veynte passos; la primera, se llamava Pumapuncu, que suena lo mismo, que puerta del León porque avía allí un León de piedra, que dezían guardava la entrada, y en ésta antes de passar, se hazía una expiación de pecados, confessándolos al Sacerdote que allí residía.

"La segunda puerta, tenía por nombre Kentipuncu, por estar matizada toda de plumas de tominejos, a quien ellos llaman Kenti, aquí bolbían de nuevo a confessarse con otro Sacerdote, que guardava aquella puerta, éste aconsijava a los peregrinos fuessen con devoción si querían ser favorecidos del Sol a quien yvan a adorar.

"De la tercera puerta era el nombre Pillco-puncu, que suena puerta de esperança, estava adornada con plumas verdes de un pájaro muy estimado, que se trae de los Chunchos llamado Pillco, que haze muchos visos, en esta puerta que era la úlitma, el Sacerdote custodio della persuadía con gran eficacia, al peregrino, hiziesse muy riguroso examinen de conciencia, porque no avía de passar teniéndola agravada." (Ramos Gavilán 1988:94 [1621: Bk. 1, Ch. 15])

26. It is worth noting that Cobo selected to paraphrase the first part of Ramos Gavilán's description and to change the name of Kentipuncu to Intipuncu. Cobo then chose to ignore the information provided by Ramos Gavilán on the other two gateways.

27. "Pero a ninguno era permitido llegar a vista de la peña sagrada con las manos vacías, ni menos que muy aprobados por los confesores que para esto había en los lugares referidos. Ni tampoco llegaban cerca de la peña, sino a sólo darle una vista desde la puerta llamada Intipuncu, y en ella entregaban las ofrendas a los ministros que allí residían" (Cobo 1964:192 [1653: Bk. 13, Ch. 18]).

28. ". . . el más súbtil, y delicado, que jamás se vio en Indias" (Ramos Gavilán 1988:116 [1621: Bk. 1, Ch. 17]).

29. "Tiene su frente que mira al norte, y las espladas al sur; lo cóncavo della, que es lo que se veneró, no es mucho, estaba dentro del altar del sol. El convexo es de peña viva, cuyas vertientes llegan a comunicarse con el agua en una ensenada que la laguna hace. El adorno que tenía era que la parte convexa estaba cubierta con una cortina de *cumbi,* el más sutil y delicado que jamás se vió; y todo lo cóncavo della cubierto de láminas de oro. Delante de la dicha peña y altar se ve una piedra redonda al modo de bacía, admirablemente labrada, del tamaño de una piedra de molino mediana, con su orifico, que ahora sirve al pie de una cruz, en que echaban la *chicha* para que el sol bebiese" (Cobo 1964:193 [1653: Bk. 13, Ch. 18]).

30. "Acabada su oración y sacrificios en este santuario de Titicaca, pasaban a la isla de Coatá, que tenían por segunda estación; y como se les vendía tan cara la visita destos santuarios, era causa de que fuesen en mayor estima" (Cobo 1964:192 [1653: Bk. 13, Ch. 18]).

31. "Y el indio que podía haber un grano de aquel máiz o de cualquiera otra semilla para echarlo en sus orones, creía que no le había de faltar pan en toda su vida; tan supersticiosos como esto fueron en cualquiera cosa que tocaba a sus Incas" (Garcilaso de la Vega 1963:120 [1609: Pt. 1, Bk. 3, Ch. 25]).

32. "El Inca ofrecía de su propia mano los vasos de oro en que había hecho la ceremonia; los demás Incas daban sus vasos a los sacerdotes Incas que para servicio del sol estaban nombrados y dedicados, porque a los no sacerdotes, aunque de la misma sangre del sol (como a seglares), no les era permitido hacer oficio de sacerdotes. Los sacerdotes, habiendo ofrecido los vasos de los Incas, salían a la puerta a recibir los vasos de los *curacas,* los cuales llegaban por su antigüedad como habían sido reducidos al imperio y daban sus

vasos y otras cosas de oro y plata que para presentar al sol habían traído de sus tierras" (Garcilaso de la Vega 1963: 220–221 [1609: Pt. 1, Bk. 6, Ch. 21]).

33. González Holguín (1989:252 [1608]), "Muru muru. Cosa de varias colores o manchada de colores."

34. "El mes de Abril tenía el nombre Atiguayquin, ofrecían cien carneros listados (que llaman moromoros), y con la sangre de ellos, regavan el adoratorio del Sol, ofreciendo muchas riquezas, assí de oro, como de plata, conchas, y mucha plumería de pájaros diversos, y muy vistosos. Ofrecían mucha coca y en todos los sacrificios que hazían al Sol, era costumbre poner muy ricas, y vistosas telas de cumbi, sobre el adoratorio del Sol, los que al sacrificio acudían, yvan con muestras, y señales de devoción, por el silencio que guardavan. Los animales que avían de ser ofrecidos, estavan adornados con rosas de varios colores" (Ramos Gavilán 1988:151 [1621: Bk. 1, Ch. 25]).

35. "Adornávanlas con muy ricas vestiduras, y hazían un bayle llamado cayo, estendiendo por los caminos por donde passavan, muchas flores. Vestíanse los Indios las más curiosas ropas, y por el consiguiente las mugeres, y casi todos se afeytavan, y la gente principal se ponía, unas patenas de oro en la barba, y todos yvan desta manera al adoratorio del Sol, a ofrecer sus sacrificios. Llevavan a compás de grandes bayles, y regozijos, los animales que se avían de ofrecer, que yvan con muchas borlas, y los rostros embijados, teñidos de rojo. La peña del adoratorio, se adornava con admirable artificio, y curiosidad. . . . Los pastores baylavan de una manera, los guerreros de otra, y los Ingas de otra, y cada nación en sus bayles se diferenciava de las otras. Era grande la embriaguez porque avía licencia general para bever" (Ramos Gavilán 1988:153 [1621: Bk. 1, Ch. 25]).

36. This basin is mentioned again by Pedro Pizarro (1921:253–254 [1571]) as he describes burnt offerings to the Sun in the plaza of Cuzco: "All the ashes which were left over from these fires they threw into the round stone trough shaped like a teat which, as I say, was in the middle of the plaza and into which they threw the [chicha]" [Todas estas çeniças que quedauan de estos fuegos que hazían, las echauan en este pilón que digo estaua en mitad de la plaça y piedra rredonda a manera de teta donde echauan la [chicha] (Pizarro 1986:91 [1571:54]).

37. "Pues llenos estos *birques,* los derramauan en una piedra rredonda que tenían por ydolo, en mitad de la plaça y hecha alrrededor una alberca pequeña, donde se consumía por unos caños que ellos tenían hechos por deuaxo de tierra" (Pizarro 1986:90 [1571: 53v]).

38. "Hecho el convite del beber, derramaba el vaso de la mano derecha, que era dedicado al sol, en un tinajón de oro, y del tinajón salía a un caño de muy hermosa cantería que desde la plaza mayor iba hasta la casa del sol" (Garcilaso de la Vega 1963:220 [1609: Pt. 1, Bk. 6, Ch. 21]).

39. This story is retold by Cobo (1990:99 [1653: Bk. 13, Ch. 18]).

40. "Y los que heran para el sol estauan en sus casas, que heran muy grandes y muy çercadas, ocupándose las mugeres en hazer chicha, que es una manera de breuaxe que hazían del maíz, que beuían este breuaxe como nosotros vino, y en guisar de comer para el sol y para los que le seruian" (Pizarro 1986:93 [1571:55v]).

41. "Auía en esta Guancabamba templo del sol con número de mugeres. De la co-

marca destas regiones venían a adorar a este templo y a ofrecer sus dones. Las mugeres vírgines y ministros que en él estauan eran reuerenciados y muy estimados" (Cieza de León 1984:184 [1553: Pt. 1, Ch. 58, f. 84v]).

42. Bertonio (1984:157 [1612: Bk. 2]) defines "Huayruru" as "A very beautiful thing."

43. Bertonio (1984:242 [1612: Bk. 2]) defines "Pacohakhlla" as "Moza hermosa en positivo grado. Hanko hakhlla: Hermosa en mayor grado. Huayruru: Moza hermosa en sumo grado, y las mas de estos tres generos estaban guardadas por mandato del Inga. Hahuatahuaco: Eran las de mas mozas que no se contaban por hermosas y que tenian alguna falta que las aseaba" [Pacohakhlla: Beautiful girl in certain degree. Hanko hakhlla: Beautiful in a greater degree. Huayruru: Beautiful girl of highest degree, and the best of these three kinds were cared for by the orders of the Inca. Hahuatahuaco: These were the rest of the girls that were not considered beautiful because they had some fault that distinguished them].

44. "[Había] tres géneros de Vírgines, unas muy hermosas que llamavan Guayruro, otras no tan hermosas, que tenían por nombre Yuracaclla, otras que eran menos hermosas, que nombravan Pacoaclla. Cada una destas tenía, una como Abadessa, que era una India anciana, que también avía de ser Virgen, la qual cuydava de todas las de su monasterio, y les repartía el hilado, y ropa que avían de hazer" (Ramos Gavilán 1988:118 [1621: Bk. 1, Ch. 18]).

45. According to Ramos Gavilán (1988:189 [1621: Bk. 1, Ch. 31]), Paullu Inca visited the Copacabana area after the arrival of the Spaniards and married one of these women and fathered a number of offspring, including Francisco Tito Yupanqui, who later produced a daughter called Doña María Pillcosisa. She would have been the great-granddaughter of Huayna Capac Inca. Ramos Gavilán states that Pillcosisa died in 1617. This was the very year that preparations were begun for Salas's trip to the Island of the Moon (see Chapter 6).

46. "Hay más de seiscientos Indios sirviendo en este lugar, y más de mil mujeres que hacen chicha para echarla sobre aquella piedra Tichicasa" (Sancho de la Hoz 1898:415 [1554: Ch. 18]).

47. Lizárraga (1908 [1605]), while recognizing the fact that the Inca sent *mitimaes* to the Copacabana region, incorrectly suggests that they were all sent to the Island of the Sun (Espinoza Soriano 1972a:2). Garcilaso de la Vega (1966:190 [1609: Pt. 1, Bk. 3, Ch. 25]), citing the earlier, now-lost chronicle of Blas Valera, indicates that there were *mitimaes* in Copacabana. Diez de San Miguel (1964:81 [1567]) notes that there were more than one thousand *mitimaes* in Copacabana, some of whom were from the Lupaqa area to the immediate west of the lake.

48. ". . . eran de la sangre y linaje de los Incas" (Cobo 1964:191 [1653: Bk. 13, Ch. 18]).

49. "Todos los cuales dichos indios som mitimaes, puestos allí por los señores del Cuzco para el servicio de la casa del Sol que ellos tenían dentro de la laguna de Titicaca" (Espinoza Soriano 1972a:10).

50. "Trasplantó aquí el Inga (sacándolos de su natural) a los Anacuscos, Hurincuscos, Ingas, Chinchaisuyos, Quitos, Pastos, Chachapoyas, Cañares, Cayambis, Latas,

Caxamarcas, Guamachucos, Guaylas, Yauyos, Ancaras, Quichuas, Mayos, Guancas, Andesuyos, Condesuyos, Chancas, Aymaras, Ianaguaras, Chumbivilcas, Padre [,] Chilques, Collaguas, Hubinas, Canches, Canas, Quivarguaros, Lupacas, Capancos, Pucopucos, Pacajes, Iungas, Carangas, Quillacas, Chichas, Soras, Copayapos, Colliyungas, Guánucos, y Huruquillas" (Ramos Gavilán 1988:84–85 [1621: Bk. 1, Ch. 20]).

51. Elsewhere Salas (1901:488 [1628]) seems to suggest that there were seventy-five *ayllus* involved in maintaining the Island of the Sun.

52. "Las familias privilegiadas y sacerdotales que en esta Isla del Titikaka existen y sirven, son venidas cada dos años de los setenta y dos Ayllos, que de á veinte en veinte familias se turnan, sobre cinco de Yanaconas que vienen de siete en siete años, con que todas componen como cuatrocientas almas, y que la Isla no admite más" (Salas 1901:3 [1628]).

9. Pilgrimage and Ritual in the Ancient Andes

1. This vision of the Altiplano Period in the Lake Titicaca region as a time of intensive conflict, if not outright warfare, is supported by several other archaeological investigations conducted in the region (Lumbreras 1974a; Hyslop 1976; Stanish et al. 1997).

Abbott, Mark B., M. Binford, M. Brenner, and Kerry Kelts
1997   A 3500 ^{14}C high-resolution record of water-level changes in Lake Titicaca, Bolivia/Peru. *Quaternary Research* 47: 169–180.

Acosta, José de
1940   *Historia natural y moral de las Indias* [1590]. Edited by Edmundo O'Gorman. Mexico City: Fondo de Cultura Económica.

Albarracin-Jordan, Juan
1996   *Tiwanaku: Arqueología regional y dinámica segmentaria*. La Paz: Editores Plural.

Albarracin-Jordan, Juan, and James Edward Mathews
1990   *Asentimientos prehispánicos del Valle de Tiwanaku*. Vol. 1. La Paz, Bolivia: Producciones CIMA.

Albornoz, Cristóbal de
1984   Instrucción para descubrir todas las guacas del Pirú y sus camayos y haziendas [ca. 1582]. In "Albornoz y el espacio ritual andino prehispánico," edited by Pierre Duviols. *Revista Andina* 2 (1): 169–222.

Alconini Mujica, Sonia
1993   La cerámica de la pirámide akapana y su contexto social en el estado de Tiwanaku. Tesis de Licenciatura, Universidad Mayor de San Andrés, La Paz.

Aldenderfer, Mark S.
1988   Middle Archaic Period domestic architecture from southern Peru. *Science* 241: 1828–1830.

1989   Archaic Period settlement patterns in the sierra of the Osmore Basin. In *Ecology, settlement, and history in the Osmore drainage, Peru,* edited by Don S. Rice, Charles Stanish, and Philip Scarr, pp. 129–166. BAR International Series 545. Oxford: British Archaeological Reports.

1991   Informe preliminar sobre las excavaciones de Quelcatani, Sub-Región de Puno, Región José Mariátegui. Report submitted to the Instituto Nacional de Cultura, Lima.

1998   *Montane foragers: Asana and the south-central Andean Archaic.* Iowa City: University of Iowa Press.

Almagro, Diego de
1873   Acusación contra Don Francisco Pizarro á S. M., por Don Diego de Almagro. In *Colección de documentos inéditos relativos al descubrimiento, conquista y organización de las antiguas posesiones españolas de América y Oceanía sacados de los archivos del reino,* vol. 20, edited by D. Joaquín F. Pacheco, Francisco de Cárdenas, and Luis

Torres de Mendoza, pp. 217–380. Colección de Documentos Inéditos de Indias. Madrid: Imprenta del Hospicio.

Anderson, Karen, and Ricardo Céspedes Paz

1998   Late Formative to Middle Horizon transition in Cochabamba, Bolivia. Paper delivered at the Society of American Archaeology annual meeting, Seattle, Washington.

Anonymous

1942   Memoria exacta i completa de los repartimientos desta ciudad del Cuzco así vacos como los que tienen dueños [1548]. In *Documentos para la historia del Perú: Alardes y derramas,* edited by Rafael Loredo, pp. 126–134. Lima: Gil S. A. Impresores.

Anonymous Chronicler

1906   Discurso de la sucesión y gobierno de los yngas [ca. 1570]. In *Juicio de límites entre el Perú y Bolivia; prueba peruana presentada al gobierno de la República Argentina,* vol. 8, edited by Víctor M. Maúrtua, pp. 149–165. Madrid: Tipografía de los Hijos de M. G. Hernández.

Bandelier, Adolph F. A.

1910   *The islands of Titicaca and Koati.* New York: The Hispanic Society of America.

Bauer, Brian S.

1988   Pacariqtambo and the mythical origins of the Inca. Paper presented at the 46th International Congress of Americanists, Amsterdam, The Netherlands.

1991   Pacariqtambo and the mythical origins of the Inca. *Latin American Antiquity* 2 (1): 7–26.

1992a   *The development of the Inca state.* Austin: University of Texas Press.

1992b   *Avances en arqueología andina.* Cuzco, Peru: Centro de Estudios Regionales Andinos "Bartolomé de Las Casas."

1996   The legitimization of the Inca state in myth and ritual. *American Anthropologist* 98 (2): 327–337.

1998   *The sacred landscape of the Inca: The Cusco ceque system.* Austin: University of Texas Press.

Bauer, Brian S., and David S. P. Dearborn

1995   *Astronomy and empire in the ancient Andes.* Austin: University of Texas Press.

Bennett, Wendell C.

1933   Archaeological hikes in the Andes. *Natural History* 33 (2): 163–174.

1934   Excavations at Tiahuanaco. *Anthropological Papers of the American Museum of Natural History* 34 (3): 359–494.

1936   Excavations in Bolivia. *Anthropological Papers of the American Museum of Natural History* 35 (4): 329–507.

1950   Cultural unity and disunity in the Titicaca Basin. *American Antiquity* 16 (2): 89–98.

Bermann, Marc

1990   Prehispanic household and empire at Lukurmata, Bolivia. Ph.D. diss., Department of Anthropology, University of Michigan.

1994   *Lukurmata: Household archaeology in prehistoric Bolivia.* Princeton, N.J.: Princeton University Press.

Bertonio, Ludovico

1984   *Vocabulario de la lengua Aymará.* Cochabamba, Bolivia: Centro de Estudios de la Realidad Económica y Social.

Betanzos, Juan de

1987   *Suma y narración de los Incas* [1557]. Prólogo, transcripción y notas por María del Carmen Martín Rubio; estudios preliminares de Horacio Villanueva Urteaga, Demetrio Ramos y María del Carmen Martín Rubio. Madrid: Atlas.

1996   *Narrative of the Incas* [1557]. Translated and edited by Roland Hamilton and Dana Buchanan from the Palma de Mallorca manuscript. Austin: University of Texas Press.

Binford, Michael, and Mark Brenner

1989   Resultados de estudios de limnología en los ecosistemas de Tiwanaku. In *Arqueología de Lukurmata,* vol. 2, edited by Alan Kolata, pp. 213–236. La Paz: Producciones Puma Punku.

Binford, Michael, Mark Brenner, and Daniel Engstrom

1991   Patrones de sedimentación temporal en la zona litoral del Huiñaimarca. In *El Lago Titicaca,* edited by Claude DeJoux and Andre Iltis, pp. 47–58. La Paz: ORSTOM/HISBOL.

Binford, Michael, Mark Brenner, and Barbara Leyden

1996   Paleoecology and Tiwanaku ecosystems. In *Tiwanaku and its hinterland: Archaeology and paleoecology of an Andean civilization,* vol. 1, edited by Alan Kolata, pp. 89–108. Washington D.C.: Smithsonian Institution Press.

Bingham, Hiram

1922   *Inca land: Explorations in the highlands of Peru.* Cambridge, Mass.: Riverside Press.

Blas Valera. *See* Valera, Blas.

Boulangé, Bruno, and Eleonor Aquize Jaén

1981   Morphologie, hydrographie et climatologie du lac Titicaca et de son bassin versant. *Revue d'Hydrobiologie Tropicale* (Paris) 14 (4): 269–287.

Bouysse-Cassagne, Thérèse

1976   Tributo y etnias en la época del virrey Toledo. *Historia y Cultura* (Lima) 2: 97–113.

1986   Urco and uma: Aymara concepts of space. In *Anthropological history of Andean polities,* edited by John Murra, Nathan Wachtel, and Jacques Revel, pp. 201–227. Cambridge: Cambridge University Press.

1987   Comments on "Lenguas y pueblos altiplánicos en torno al siglo XVI" by Alfredo Torero. *Revista Andina* 5 (2): 377–379.

Bowman, Glenn

1991   Christian ideology and the image of a holy land: The place of Jerusalem pilgrimage in the various Christianities. In *Contesting the sacred: The anthropology of Christian pilgrimage,* edited by John Eade and Michael J. Sallnow. London: Routledge.

Brinton, Daniel Garrison

1891   *The American race: A linguistic classification and ethnographic description of the native tribes of North and South America.* New York: Hodges.

Browman, David

1974   Pastoral nomadism in the Andes. *Current Anthropology* 15: 188–196.

1978   The temple of Chiripa (Lake Titicaca, Bolivia). In *El hombre y la cultura andina,* vol. 2, edited by M. Ramiro Matos, pp. 807–813. Lima: Congreso Peruano III.

1980   Tiwanaku expansion and altiplano economic patterns. *Estudios Arqueológicos* (Universidad de Chile, Antofagasta) 5: 107–120.

1981   New light on Andean Tiwanaku. *American Scientist* 69: 408–419.

1984   Tiwanaku: Development of interzonal trade and economic expansion in the altiplano. In *Social and economic organization in the prehispanic Andes,* edited by David L. Browman, Richard L. Burger, and Mario A. Rivera, pp. 117–142. BAR International Series 194. Oxford: British Archaeological Reports.

1994   Titicaca Basin archaeolinguistics: Uru, Pukina, and Aymara A.D. 750–1450. *World Archaeology* 26 (2): 235–251.

Burger, Richard L., Frank Asaro, Guido Salas, and Fred Stross

1998   The Chivay obsidian source and the geological origin of Titicaca Basin–type obsidian artifacts. *Andean Past* 5: 203–223.

Caballero, Geraldine Byrne de

1984   El Tiwanaku en Cochabamba. *Arqueología Boliviana* (La Paz) 1: 67–72.

Cabello Valboa, Miguel

1951   *Miscelánea antártica, una historia del Perú antiguo* [1586]. Edited by L. E. Valcárcel. Lima: Universidad Nacional Mayor de San Marcos, Instituto de Etnología.

Calancha, Antonio de la

1981   *Corónica moralizada del Orden de San Agustín en el Perú* [1638]. Edited by Ignacio Prado Pastor. Lima: Universidad Nacional Mayor de San Marcos, Editorial de la Universidad.

Callapiña, Supno, and other Quipucamayocs

1974   *Relación de la descendencia, gobierno y conquista de los Incas* [1542/1608]. Edited by Juan José Vega. Lima: Ediciones de la Biblioteca Universitaria.

Chávez Justo, Cecilia

n.d.   Archeological research at the site of Sillumocco-Huaquina, Juli, Peru. Manuscript.

Chávez, Karen L. Mohr

1988   The significance of Chiripa in Lake Titicaca Basin developments. *Expedition* 30 (3): 17–26.

Chávez, Sergio J., and Karen L. Mohr Chávez

1975   A carved stela from Taraco, Puno, Peru, and the definition of an early style of stone sculpture from the altiplano of Peru and Bolivia. *Ñawpa Pacha* 13: 45–83.

Cieza de León, Pedro de

1976   *The Incas of Pedro Cieza de León* [Part 1, 1553, and Part 2, 1554]. Translated by Harriet de Onís and edited by Victor W. von Hagen. Norman: University of Oklahoma Press.

1984   *Crónica del Perú: Primera parte* [1553]. Introduction by Franklin Pease G. Y. and notes by Miguel Maticorena E. Lima: Academia Nacional de la Historia and Pontificia Universidad Católica del Perú.

1985   *Crónica del Perú: Segunda parte* [1554]. Introduction by Franklin Pease G. Y. and notes by Miguel Maticorena E. Lima: Academia Nacional de la Historia and Pontificia Universidad Católica del Perú.

Cobo, Bernabé

1964   *Historia del Nuevo Mundo* [1653]. In *Obras del P. Bernabé Cobo de la Compañía de Jesús*, edited by P. Francisco Mateos. Biblioteca de Autores Españoles (continuación), vols. 91 and 92. Madrid: Ediciones Atlas.

1979   *History of the Inca Empire: An account of the Indians' customs and their origin together with a treatise on Inca legends, history, and social institutions* [1653]. Translated and edited by Roland Hamilton. Austin: University of Texas Press.

1990   *Inca religion and customs* [1653]. Translated and edited by Roland Hamilton. Austin: University of Texas Press.

Coleman, Simon, and John Elsner

1994   The pilgrim's progress: Art, architecture, and ritual movement at Sinai. *World Archaeology* 26 (1): 73–89.

1995   *Pilgrimage: Past and present in the world religions.* Cambridge: Harvard University Press.

Cook, David Noble, editor

1975   *Tasa de la visita general de Francisco de Toledo.* Introducción y versión paleográfica de David Noble Cook. Lima: Universidad Nacional Mayor de San Marcos, Seminario de Historia Rural Andina.

D'Altroy, Terence N., and Ronald A. Bishop

1990   The provincial organization of Inka ceramic production. *American Antiquity* 55: 120–138.

Dearborn, David S. P., Matthew T. Seddon, and Brian S. Bauer

1998   The sanctuary of Titicaca: Where the Sun returns to Earth. *Latin American Antiquity* 9 (3): 240–258.

Dearborn, Davis S. P., and Raymond E. White

1983   The "Torreón" at Machu Picchu as an observatory. *Archaeoastronomy* 5: S37–S49.

Dejoux, Claude, and Andre Iltis

1991   Introduction to *El Lago Titicaca*, edited by Claude Dejoux and Andre Iltis, pp. 11–16. La Paz: ORSTOM/HISBOL.

de la Grasserie, Raoul

1894   *Langues américaines, langue puquina; textes puquina contenus dans le rituale seu manuale peruanum de Gerónimo de Oré.* Paris: Maisonneuve.

de la Vega M., Edmundo

1990   Estudio arqueológico de Pucaras o poblados amurallados de cumbre en territorio Lupaqa: El caso de Pucara-Juli. Tesis de Bachiller, Universidad Católica Santa María, Arequipa, Peru.

1997   Característica de la reocupación Tiwanaku en el sitio de Sillumocco-Huaquina,

Juli (Puno). Tesis de Licenciatura, Universidad Católica Santa María, Arequipa, Peru.

de la Vega M., Edmundo, Kirk L. Frye, Cecilia Chávez J., Mario Núñez M., Fernando Sosa A., David Antesana B., José Núñez, Doris Maldonado A., Norfelinda Cornejo G., Amadeo Mamani M., and Javier Chalcha S.

1995 Proyecto de rescate del sitio arqueológico de Molino Chilacachi (Acora). Proyecto Lupaqa, Universidad Nacional del Altiplano, Instituto Nacional de Cultura-Puno, Peru. Unpublished manuscript in possession of authors.

DeMarrais, Elizabeth, Luis Jaime Castillo, and Timothy Earle

1996 Ideology, materialization, and power strategies. *Current Anthropology* 37: 15–31.

Diez de San Miguel, Garci

1964 *Visita hecha a la provincia de Chucuito por Garci Diez de San Miguel en el año 1567.* Lima: Casa de la Cultura.

d'Orbigny, Alcide Dessaline

1835 *Voyage dans l'Amérique Méridionale.* Paris: Pitois Levrault.

1958 Viaje a la América Meridional [1835]. In *Viajes por América del Sur,* edited by José Alcina Franch. Madrid: Aguilar.

Durkheim, Emile

1965 *The elementary forms of the religious life* [1912]. New York: Free Press.

Duviols, Pierre

1986 *Cultura andina y represión: Procesos y visitas de idolatrías y hechicerías Cajatambo, siglo XVII.* Archivos de Historia Andina Rural 5. Cuzco: Centro de Estudios Rurales Andinos "Bartolomé de Las Casas."

Eade, John, and Michael J. Sallnow, editors

1991 *Contesting the sacred: The anthropology of Christian pilgrimage.* London: Routledge.

Eisleb, Dieter, and Renate Strelow

1980 *Altperuanische kulturen III: Tiahuanaco.* Berlin: Museum für Völkerkunde.

Erickson, Clark

1987 The dating of raised-field agriculture in the Lake Titicaca Basin, Peru. In *Pre-Hispanic agricultural fields in the Andean region,* edited by William Denevan, Kent Mathewson, and Gregory Knapp, pp. 373–384. BAR International Series 359. Oxford: British Archaeological Reports.

1988 An archaeological investigation of raised-field agriculture in the Lake Titicaca Basin of Peru. Ph.D. diss., Department of Anthropology, University of Illinois at Champaign-Urbana. Ann Arbor: University Microfilms.

1993 The social organization of prehispanic raised-field agriculture in the Lake Titicaca Basin. In *Prehispanic water management systems, supplement no. 7,* edited by V. Scarborough and B. Isaac, pp. 369–462. Research in Economic Anthropology. Greenwich, Conn.: JAI Press.

Escalante Moscoso, Javier F.

1994 *Arquitectura prehispánica en los Andes bolivianos.* La Paz: Producción Cima.

Espinal, Manuel de

1959 Relación hecha por el Tesorero Manuel de Espinal al Emperador [1539]. In *Cartas* del Perú (1524-1543), edited by Raúl Porras Barrenechea, pp. 344-367. Colección de Documentos Inéditos para la Historia del Perú, vol. 3. Lima: Edición de la Sociedad de Bibliófilos Peruanos.

Espinoza Soriano, Waldemar

1972a Copacabana del Collao: Un documento de 1548 para la etnohistoria andina. *Boletín del Instituto Francés de Estudios Andinos* 1: 1–16.

1972b Alonso Ramos Gavilán: Vida y obra del cronista de Copacabana. *Historia y Cultura* (Lima) 6: 121–194.

Estete, Miguel de (attributed)

1924 Noticia del Perú [ca. 1535]. In *Historia de los Incas y Conquista del Perú*, vol. 8, edited by Horacio H. Urteaga, pp. 3–56. Colección de Libros y Documentos Referentes a la Historia del Perú, 2d series. Lima: Imprenta y Librería Sanmartí.

Faldín A., Juan D.

1990 La provincia Larecaja y el sistema precolombino del norte de La Paz. In *Larecaja, ayer, hoy y mañana*, pp. 73–89. La Paz: Comité de Cultura.

Fernández de Alfaro, Luis

1904 Relación del oro del Perú que recibimos de Hernando Pizarro que truxo en la nao que era maestre Pero Bernal, para Su Majestad, por el mes de Hebrero del año pasado de mil é quinientos é treinta é cuatro años, pesado por Hernand Alvarez, fiel de los pesos desta cibdad en la forma siquiente . . . [1534]. In *La imprenta en Lima (1584-1824)*, vol. 1, edited by José Toribio Medina, pp. 163–172. Santiago de Chile: Impreso y grabado en casa del autor.

Fifer, Valerie

1974 Introduction to *Report on Bolivia, 1827,* by Joseph Barclay Pentland. Camden Miscellany, vol. 25. London: Royal Historical Society.

Fiske, Alan

1991 *Structures of social life.* New York: Free Press.

Forbes, David

1870 On the Aymara Indians of Bolivia and Peru. *Journal of the Ethnological Society of London,* n.s., 2: 193–305.

Frye, Kirk Lawrence

1997 Political centralization in the Altiplano Period in the southwestern Titicaca Basin. In *Archaeological survey in the Juli-Desaguadero region of Lake Titicaca Basin, southern Peru*, edited by Charles Stanish et al., pp. 129–141. Fieldiana Anthropology, vol. 29. Chicago: Field Museum of Natural History.

Garcilaso de la Vega, Inca

1963 *Comentarios reales de los Incas* [1609]. In *Obras completas del Inca Garcilaso de la Vega.* Biblioteca de Autores Españoles (continuación), vols. 132–135. Madrid: Ediciones Atlas.

1966 *Royal commentaries of the Incas and general history of Peru, parts 1 and 2* [1609]. Translated by H. V. Livermore. Austin: University of Texas Press.

Gasparini, Graziano, and Luise Margolies

1980 *Inca architecture.* Translated by P. J. Lyon. Bloomington: Indiana University Press.

Goldstein, Paul

1993   Tiwanaku temples and state expansion: A Tiwanaku sunken-court temple in Moquegua, Peru. *Latin American Antiquity* 4 (1): 22–47.

González Holguín, Diego

1989   *Vocabulario de la lengua general de todo el Perú llamada lengua Qquichua o del Inca* [1608]. Presentación de Ramiro Matos Mendieta. Prólogo de Raúl Porras Barrenechea. Lima: Universidad Nacional Mayor de San Marcos, Editorial de la Universidad.

Graffam, Gray

1990   *Raised fields without bureaucracy: An archaeological examination of intensive wetland cultivation in the Pampa Koani Zone, Lake Titicaca, Bolivia.* Ph.D. diss., Department of Anthropology, University of Toronto.

1992   Beyond state collapse: Rural history, raised fields, and pastoralism in the south Andes. *American Anthropologist* 94 (4): 882–904.

Gregory, Herbert E.

1913a   A geographical sketch of Titicaca, the Island of the Sun. *Bulletin of the American Geographical Society* 45 (8): 561–575.

1913b   Geologic sketch of Titicaca Island and adjoining areas. *American Journal of Science* 36 (213): 187–213.

Guaman Poma de Ayala, Felipe

1980   *El primer nueva corónica y buen gobierno* [1615]. Edited by J. V. Murra and R. Adorno and translated by Jorge I. Urioste. 3 vols. Mexico City: Siglo Veintiuno.

Gutiérrez de Santa Clara, Pedro

1963   *Historia de las guerras civiles del Perú y de otros sucesos de las Indias* (ca. 1600). Biblioteca de Autores Españoles (continuación), vols. 165–167. Madrid: Ediciones Atlas.

Gutiérrez Flores, Pedro, et al.

1970   Resultas de la visita secreta lega que hicieron en la Provincia de Chucuito del Patrimonio Real de Su Majestad el Licenciado fray Pedro Gutiérrez Flores . . . [1572]. *Historia y Cultura* (Lima) 4: 5–14.

Hastorf, Christine A., ed.

1998   *Early settlement at Chiripa, Bolivia: Research of the Taraco Archaeological Project.* With contributions by Matthew Bandy, Deborah Blom, Emily Dean, Susan deFrance, Melissa Goodman, Christine A. Hastorf, David Kojan, Mario Montaño Aragón, Katherine Moore, José Luis Paz, David Steadman, Lee Steadman, and William Whitehead. Berkeley: University of California Press.

Hernández Príncipe, Rodrigo

1986   Visitas de Rodrigo Hernández Príncipe [1621]. In *Cultura andina y represión: Procesos y visitas de idolatrías y hechicerías Cajatambo, siglo XVII,* edited and transcribed by Pierre Duviols, pp. 461–482. Cuzco: Centro de Estudios Rurales Andinos "Bartolomé de Las Casas."

The Huarochirí Manuscript: A testament of ancient and colonial Andean religion [ca. 1608]

1991   Translation from the Quechua by Frank Salomon and George L. Urioste. Austin: University of Texas Press.

Hyslop, John

1976   An archaeological investigation of the Lupaca kingdom and its origins. Ph.D.
       diss., Department of Anthropology, Columbia University, New York. Ann Arbor:
       University Microfilms.

1990   *Inka settlement planning.* Austin: University of Texas Press.

Janusek, John Wayne

1994   State and local power in a prehispanic Andean polity: Changing patterns of urban
       residence in Tiwanaku and Lukurmata, Bolivia. Ph.D. diss., Department of An-
       thropology, University of Chicago.

Julien, Catherine J.

1983   *Hatunqolla: A view of Inca rule from the Lake Titicaca Region.* Series Publications in
       Anthropology, vol. 15. Berkeley: University of California Press.

1993   Finding a fit: Archaeology and ethnohistory of the Incas. In *Provincial Inca: Ar-
       chaeological and ethnohistorical assessment of the impact of the Inca state,* edited by
       Michael A. Malpass, pp. 177–233. Iowa City: University of Iowa Press.

Kidder, Alfred

1943   *Some early sites in the northern Lake Titicaca Basin.* Papers of the Peabody Museum of
       American Archaeology and Ethnology, vol. 27 (1). Cambridge: Peabody Museum.

Kolata, Alan

1986   The agricultural foundations of the Tiwanaku state: A view from the heartland.
       American Antiquity 51 (4): 748–726.

1992   Economy, ideology, and imperialism in the south-central Andes. In *Ideology and
       pre-Columbian civilizations,* edited by Arthur A. Demarest and Geoffrey W. Con-
       rad, pp. 65–85. Santa Fe, N.M.: School of American Research.

1993   *The Tiwanaku: Portrait of an Andean civilization.* Oxford: Basil Blackwell.

Kolata, Alan, and Carlos Ponce Sanginés

1992   Tiwanaku: The city at the center. In *The ancient Americas: Art from sacred landscapes,*
       edited by Richard F. Townsend, pp. 317–333. Chicago: The Art Institute of Chicago.

La Barre, Weston

1941   The Uru of the Río Desaguadero. *American Anthropologist* 43 (4), part 1: 493–522.

Las Casas, Bartolomé de

1958   *Apologética historia* [ca. 1550]. In *Obras escogidas de Fray Bartolomé de Las Casas,*
       vol. 1, edited by Juan Pérez de Tudela Bueso. Biblioteca de Autores Españoles (con-
       tinuación), vol. 106. Madrid: Ediciones Atlas.

Lee, Vincent R.

1998   Reconstructing the great hall at Inkallacta. *Andean Past* 5: 35–71.

Leyden, Barbara W.

1989   Datos polínicos del período Holoceno tardío en el Lago Titicaca, Bolivia: Una po-
       sible inundación en la Pampa Koani. In *Arqueología de Lukurmata,* vol. 2, edited by
       Alan Kolata, pp. 263–274. La Paz: Producciones Puma Punku.

Lizárraga, Reginaldo de

1908   *Descripción y población de las Indias* [1605]. Edited by Carlos A. Romero. Lima: Im-
       prenta Americana.

Lumbreras, Luis G.

1974a *The peoples and cultures of ancient Peru.* Translated by Betty J. Meggers. Washington, D.C.: Smithsonian Institution Press.

1974b Los reinos post-Tiwanaku en el área altiplánica. *Revista del Museo Nacional* 40: 55–85.

Lynch, Thomas

1981 Recent research. *American Antiquity* 46 (1): 203–204.

MacCormack, Sabine

1984 From the Sun of the Incas to the Virgin of Copacabana. *Representations* 8: 30–60.

1990 *Children of the sun and reason of state: Myths, ceremonies, and conflicts in Inca Peru.* Working Papers, no. 6. College Park: Department of Spanish and Portuguese, University of Maryland.

1991 *Religion in the Andes: Vision and imagination in early colonial Peru.* Princeton, N.J.: Princeton University Press.

Mannheim, Bruce

1991 *The language of the Inka since the European invasion.* Austin: University of Texas Press.

Manzanilla, Linda

1992 *Akapana: Una pirámide en el centro del mundo.* Mexico City: UNAM.

Marroquín, José

1944 Medicina aborigen puneña. *Revista del Museo Nacional* (Lima) 13 (1): 1–14.

Mathews, James Edward

1992 Prehispanic settlement and agriculture in the Middle Tiwanaku Valley, Bolivia. Ph.D. diss., Department of Anthropology, University of Chicago.

McArthur, Mary Anne

1980 The architecture of Pilco-Kayma and Iñak-Uyu in Lake Titicaca. Master's thesis, Department of Art, Tulane University.

McElroy, Keith

1986 Ephraim George Squier: Photography and the illustration of Peruvian antiquities. *History of Photography* 10 (2): 99–129.

Meiklejohn, Norman

1988 *La iglesia y los lupaqas de Chucuito durante la colonia.* Cuzco: Centro de Estudios Regionales Andinos "Bartolomé de Las Casas."

Mesa, José de, and Teresa Gisbert

1966 Arte precolombino en Bolivia. *Anales del Instituto de Arte Americano e Investigaciones Estéticas* (Buenos Aires) 19: 45–71.

1972 La arquitectura incaica en Bolivia. *Boletín del Centro de Investigaciones Históricas y Estéticas* (Caracas) 13: 129–168.

1973 Los Incas en Bolivia. *Historia y Cultura* (La Paz) 1: 15–50.

Métraux, Alfred

1970 *The history of the Incas* [1936]. Translated from the French by George Ordish. New York: Schocken Books.

Middendorf, Ernst F.

1973   *Peru: Observaciones y estudios del país y sus habitantes durante una permanencia de veinticinco años* [1893]. Vol. 3. Lima: Universidad Nacional Mayor de San Marcos.

Miranda, Cristóbal de

1925   Relación hecha por el Virrey D. Martín de Enríquez de los oficios que se proveen en la gobernación de los reinos y provincias del Perú [1583]. In *Gobernantes del Perú: Cartas y papeles del siglo XVI*, vol. 9, edited by Roberto Leviller, pp. 114–230. Madrid: Juan Pueyo.

Molina (el Cusqueño), Cristóbal de

1943   Relación de las fábulas y ritos de los Incas [ca. 1575]. In *Las crónicas de los Molinas*, edited by Carlos A. Romero, Raúl Porras Barrenechea, and Francisco A. Loayza, pp. 7–84. Los Pequeños Grandes Libros de Historia Americana, 1st ser., vol. 4. Lima: Imprenta D. Miranda.

Morales Figueroa, Luis de

1866   Relación de los indios tributarios que hay al presente en estos reinos y provincias del Pirú, fecha por mandado del Señor Marqués de Cañete . . . [1591]. In *Colección de documentos inéditos relativos al descubrimiento, conquista y organización de las antiguas posesiones españolas de América y Oceanía sacados de los archivos del reino*, vol. 6, edited by Luis Torres de Mendoza, pp. 41–63. Colección de Documentos Inéditos de Indias. Madrid: Imprenta de Frías y Compañía.

Morris, Craig, and Adriana von Hagen

1993   *The Inka Empire and its Andean origins.* New York: American Museum of Natural History, and Abbeville Press.

Morris, Craig, and Donald Thompson

1985   *Huánuco Pampa: An Inca city and its hinterland.* London: Thames and Hudson.

Muelle, Jorge C.

1945   Pacarectambo: Apuntes de viaje. *Revista del Museo Nacional* 14: 153–160.

Mujica, Elías

1978   Nueva hipótesis sobre el desarrollo temprano del altiplano, del Titicaca y de sus áreas de interacción. *Arte y Arqueología* (Academia Nacional de Ciencias de Bolivia, La Paz) 5/6: 285–308.

1985   Altiplano-Coast relationships in the south-central Andes: From indirect to direct complementarity. In *Andean ecology and civilization*, edited by Shozo Masuda, Izumi Shimada, and Craig Morris, pp. 103–140. Tokyo: University of Tokyo Press.

1987   Cuspata: Una fase pre-Pukara en la cuenca norte del Titicaca. *Gaceta Arqueológica Andina* 4 (13): 22–28.

1988   Peculiaridades del proceso histórico temprano en la cuenca del norte del Titicaca: Una propuesta inicial. *Boletín del Laboratorio de Arqueología* (Escuela de Arqueología e Historia, Universidad Nacional San Cristóbal de Huamanga, Ayacucho): 75–124.

Murúa, Martín de

1946   *Historia del origen y genealogía real de los reyes Incas del Perú* [1590]. Introduction and notes by Constantino Bayle. Biblioteca "Missionalia Hispánica," vol. 2. Madrid: Instituto Santo Toribio de Mogrovejo.

Niles, Susan A.

1987   *Callachaca: Style and status in an Inca community.* Iowa City: University of Iowa Press.

1988   Pachamama, pachatata: Gender and sacred space on Amantaní. In *The Role of Gender in Precolumbian Art and Architecture,* edited by Virginia E. Miller, pp. 135–151. Washington D.C.: University Press of America.

Núñez M., Mario

1977   Informe: Trabajos arqueológicos en la Isla Esteves. Puno: Instituto Nacional de Cultura. Mimeograph.

Oliva, Juan Anello

1895   *Historia del Perú y varones insignes en santidad de la Compañía de Jesús* [1613]. Lima: Imprenta San Pedro.

Ortloff, Charles, and Alan Kolata

1993   Climate and collapse: Agroecological perspectives on the decline of the Tiwanaku state. *Journal of Archaeological Science* 20: 195–221.

Pardo, Luis A.

1946   La metrópoli de Paccarictambu: El adoratorio de Tamputtocco y el itinerario del camino seguido por los hermanos Ayar. *Revista del Instituto Arqueológico del Cuzco* 2: 2–46.

1957   *Historia y arqueología del Cuzco.* 2 vols. Callao, Peru: Imprenta del Colegio Militar Leonico Pardo.

Patterson, Thomas C.

1985   Pachacamac—an Andean oracle under Inca rule. In *Recent studies in Andean prehistory and protohistory: Papers from the Second Annual Northeast Conference on Andean Archaeology and Ethnohistory,* edited by D. Peter Kvietok and Daniel H. Sandweiss, pp. 159–176. Ithaca, N.Y.: Latin American Studies Program, Cornell University.

Pentland, Joseph Barclay

1827   *Report on the Bolivian Republic* (microfilm 2045). Lima: Great Britain Consulate General, Public Record Office, Foreign Office, file 61/12.

Perrín Pando, Alberto

1957   Las tumbas subterráneas de Wakuyo. In *Arqueología boliviana,* edited by Carlos Ponce Sanginés, pp. 173–205. La Paz: Biblioteca Paceña.

Pizarro, Hernando

1959   Carta a la Audiencia de Sto. Domingo [1553]. In *Cartas del Perú (1524–1543),* edited by Raúl Porras Barrenechea, pp. 77–84. Colección de Documentos Inéditos para la Historia del Perú, vol. 3. Lima: Edición de la Sociedad de Bibliófilos Peruanos.

Pizarro, Pedro

1921   *Relation of the discovery and conquest of the kingdoms of Peru* [1571]. Translated and edited by Philip Ainsworth Means. New York: The Cortés Society.

1986   *Relación del descubrimiento y conquista de los reinos del Perú* [1571]. Lima: Pontificia Universidad Católica del Perú.

Polo de Ondegardo, Juan

1916   *Relación de los fundamentos acerca del notable daño que resulta de no guardar a los indios sus fueros* [1571]. Edited by Horacio H. Urteaga. Colección de Libros y Documentos Referentes a la Historia del Perú, ser. 1, vol. 3, pp. 45–189. Lima: Sanmartí.

Ponce Sanginés, Carlos

1969   *Tunupa y Ekako*. La Paz: Academia Nacional de Ciencias de Bolivia.

1981   *Tiwanaku: Espacio, tiempo y cultura: Ensayo de síntesis arqueológica*. 4th ed. La Paz: Editorial Los Amigos del Libro.

Ponce Sanginés, Carlos, Johan Reinhard, Max Portugal, Eduardo Pareja, and Leocadio Ticlla, eds.

1992   *Arqueología subacuática en el Lago Titikaka*. La Paz: Editorial La Palabra Producciones.

Portugal Ortiz, Max

1988   Excavaciones arqueológicas en Titimani. *Arqueología Boliviana* (La Paz) 3: 51–81.

1992   Un depósito arqueológico de ofrendas subacuáticas en el Lago Titikaka. In *Arqueología subacuática en el Lago Titikaka*, edited by Carlos Ponce Sanginés et al., pp. 531–582. La Paz: Editorial La Palabra Producciones.

Portugal Ortiz, Max, and Dick Edgar Ibarra Grasso

1957   *Copacabana: El santuario y la arqueología de la península e islas del Sol y la Luna*. Cochabamba, Bolivia: Editorial Atlantic.

Porras Barrenechea, Raúl, ed.

1959   *Cartas del Perú (1524–1543)*. Colección de Documentos Inéditos para la Historia del Perú, vol. 3. Lima: Edición de la Sociedad de Bibliófilos Peruanos.

Posnansky, Arthur

1912   *Guía general ilustrada para la investigación de los monumentos prehistóricos de Tihuanacu é islas del Sol y la Luna (Titicaca y Koaty)*. La Paz: Hugo Heitmann.

1933   Precursores de Colón: Las perlas agri y las representaciones sobre tejidos arcaicos como prueba del descubrimiento de América antes de Colón. *Revista de la Sociedad de Historia Argentina* 1: N.p.

1957   *Tihuanacu: The cradle of American man*. Vols. 1–4. Translated by James F. Shearer. La Paz: Ministerio de Educación.

Ramos Gavilán, Alonso

1860   *Historia de Copacabana y de la milagrosa imagen de su virgen*. Edited by Rafael Sans. La Paz: Imprenta de la Unión Católica.

1988   *Historia del Santuario de Nuestra Señora de Copacabana* [1621]. Edited by Ignacio Prado Pastor. Lima: Gráfico P. L. Villanueva.

Ramusio, Giovanni Battista

1550   *Navigationi e viaggi*. Venice: N.p.

Reinhard, Johan

1992a   Investigaciones arqueológicas subacuáticas en el Lago Titikaka. In *Exploraciones arqueológicas subacuáticas en el Lago Titikaka,* edited by Carlos Ponce Sanginés et al., pp. 421–530. La Paz: Editorial La Palabra Producciones.

1992b Underwater archaeological research in Lake Titicaca, Bolivia. In *Ancient America: Contributions to New World archaeology,* edited by Nicholas J. Saunders, pp. 117–143. Oxford: Oxbow Books.

Rivera Sundt, Oswaldo

1984a Pilkokaina e Inakuyu: Hacia la supervivencia de dos monumentos arqueológicos nacionales. *Arqueología Boliviana* (La Paz) 1: 111–114.

1984b La Horca del Inka. *Arqueología Boliviana* (La Paz) 1: 91–101.

Rivero y Ustariz, Mariano Eduardo de, and Johann Jakob von Tschudi

1851 *Antigüedades peruanas.* Vienna: Imprenta Imperial de la Corte y del Estado.

1854 *Peruvian antiquities.* Translated by Francis L. Hawks. New York: Putnam and Co.

Robinson, Martin

1997 *Sacred places, pilgrim paths: An anthology of pilgrimage.* London: Harper Collins.

Roche, Michel A., Jacques Bourges, José Cortés, and Roger Matos

1991 Climatología e hidrología de la cuenca del Lago Titicaca. In *El Lago Titicaca,* edited by Claude Dejoux and André Iltis, pp. 83–104. La Paz: ORSTOM/HISBOL.

Rodríguez Barragán, Juan

1873 Escrito presentado por Juan Rodríguez Barragán para su descargo. In *Colección de documentos inéditos relativos al descubrimiento, conquista y organización de las antiguas posesiones españolas de América y Oceanía sacados de los archivos del reino,* vol. 20, edited by D. Joaquín F. Pacheco, Francisco de Cárdenas, and Luis Torres de Mendoza, pp. 380–485. Colección de Documentos Inéditos de Indias. Madrid: Imprenta del Hospicio.

Rowe, Ann P.

1978 Technical features of Inca tapestry tunics. *The Textile Museum Journal* 17: 5–28.

Rowe, John H.

1954 *Max Uhle, 1856–1944: A memoir of the father of Peruvian archaeology.* University of California Publications in American Archaeology and Ethnology, vol. 46, no. 1. Berkeley: University of California Press.

1979 Standardization in Inca tapestry tunics. In *The Junius Bird Memorial Textile Conference,* edited by A. Rowe, E. Benson, and A. L. Schaeffer, pp. 239–264. Washington D.C.: Dumbarton Oaks.

Rydén, Stig

1947 *Archaeological researches in the highlands of Bolivia.* Göteborg: Elanders Boktryckeri Aktiebolag.

1957 *Andean excavations I.* Publication no. 4. Stockholm: The Ethnographical Museum of Sweden.

Saignes, Thierry

1986 The ethnic groups in the valley of Larecaja: From descent to residence. In *Anthropological history of Andean polities,* edited by John Murra, Nathan Wachtel, and Jacques Revel, pp. 311–341. Cambridge: Cambridge University Press.

Salas, Baltasar de

1901 "Isla de la Luna, Ccoya-ahti (Coatí) con sus misteriosos monumentos explorados en 1618" and "Hallazgo de los restos de la Mama-Huacu-Ojjllo, y de unas láminas hieráticas y apocalípticas en el mismo templo de la Luna año 1618." In *Copacabana de los Incas: Documentos autolingüísticos e isografiados del Ayamaru-Ayamara*, edited by J. Viscarra F., pp. 30–55. La Paz: Plaza Hermanos.

Sallnow, Michael J.

1987 *Pilgrims of the Andes: Regional cults in Cusco*. Washington D.C.: Smithsonian Institution Press.

1991 Pilgrimage and cultural fracture in the Andes. In *Contesting the sacred: The anthropology of Christian pilgrimage*, edited by John Eade and Michael J. Sallnow, pp. 137–153. London: Routledge.

Sancho de la Hoz, Pedro

1898 Relación de la conquista del Perú [1534]. Edited by Joaquín García Icazbalceta, pp. 309–423. Biblioteca de Autores Mexicanos, vol. 8. Mexico City: Imprenta de V. Agüeros.

1917 *An account of the conquest of Peru* [1534]. Translated into English and annotated by Philip Ainsworth Means. New York: The Cortés Society.

Sans, Rafael

1913 Excursión a las islas de Titicaca y Coati en Bolivia. *Boletín de la Sociedad Geográfica de La Paz* 39: 59–122.

Santa Cruz Pachacuti Yamqui Salcamayhua, Juan de

1950 Relación de antigüedades deste Reyno del Perú [1613]. In *Tres relaciones de antigüedades peruanas*, edited by M. Jiménez de la Espada, pp. 207–281. Asunción, Paraguay: Editorial Guaranía.

Santillán, Hernando de

1950 Relación del origen, descendencia política y gobierno de los Incas . . . [1564]. In *Tres relaciones de antigüedades peruanas*, edited by M. Jiménez de la Espada, pp. 33–131. Asunción, Paraguay: Editorial Guaranía.

Santoro, Calagero M., and Lautaro Núñez

1987 Hunters of the dry puna and salt puna in northern Chile. *Andean Past* 1: 57–110.

Santos Escobar, Roberto

1986 Dos testimonios documentales en torno al "hallazgo de un ídolo de oro" en la Isla Titikaka hacia 1740. *Arqueología Boliviana* (La Paz) 1: 107–110.

Sarmiento de Gamboa, Pedro

1906 Segunda parte de la historia general llamada indica . . . [1572]. In *Geschichte des Inkareiches von Pedro Sarmiento de Gamboa*, edited by Richard Pietschmann. Abhandlungen der Königlichen Gesellschaft der Wissenschaften zu Göttingen, Philologisch-Historische Klasse, Neue Folge, vol. 6, no. 4. Berlin: Weidmannsche Buchhandlung.

Schobinger, Juan

1991 Sacrifices of the high Andes. *Natural History* 100 (4): 62–68.

Schreiber, Katharina J.

1992 *Wari imperialism in Middle Horizon Peru.* Anthropological Papers (Museum of Anthropology, University of Michigan) no. 87. Ann Arbor: Museum of Anthropology, University of Michigan.

Seddon, Matthew T.

1998 Ritual, power, and the development of a complex society: The Island of the Sun and the Tiwanaku State. Ph.D. diss., Department of Anthropology, University of Chicago.

Shimada, Izumi, Crystal Barker Schaaf, Lonnie G. Thompson, and Ellen Mosley-Thompson

1991 Cultural impacts of severe droughts in the prehistoric Andes: Applications of a 1,500-year ice core precipitation record. *World Archaeology* 22 (3): 247–270.

Silverblatt, Irene

1987 *Moon, Sun, and witches: Gender ideologies and class in Inca and colonial Peru.* Princeton, N.J.: Princeton University Press.

Solc, Vaclav

1966 *Observaciones preliminares sobre investigaciones arqueológicas en la región de las islas en el Lago Titicaca.* Sonderduck aus Abhandlungen und berichte des Staatlichen Museum für Völkerkunde Dresden, Band 25. Berlin: Staatlichen Museum für Völkerkunde.

Squier, Ephraim George

1877 *Peru: Incidents of travel and exploration in the land of Incas.* New York: Harper and Brothers Publishers.

Stanish, Charles

1985 Post-Tiwanaku regional economies in the Otora Valley, southern Peru. Ph.D. diss., Department of Anthropology, University of Chicago.

1989a Household archaeology: Testing models of zonal complementarity in the south-central Andes. *American Anthropologist* 91 (1): 7–24.

1989b An archaeological evaluation of an ethnohistorical model in Moquegua. In *Ecology, settlement, and history in the Osmore Drainage, Peru,* edited by Don S. Rice, Charles Stanish, and Philip Scarr, pp. 129–166. BAR International Series 545. Oxford: British Archaeological Reports.

1992 *Ancient Andean political economy.* Austin: University of Texas Press.

1993 The Inca occupation of the Juli-Pomata region, Lake Titicaca, Peru. Paper represented at the annual meeting of the Society of American Archaeology, St. Louis, Mo.

1994 Lake Titicaca Basin raised fields in theoretical perspective. *Latin American Antiquity* 5 (4): 312–332.

1997 Nonmarket imperialism in a prehispanic context: The Inca occupation of the Titicaca Basin. *Latin American Antiquity* 8 (3): 195–216.

n.d. Ancient Collasuyu: The evolution of social power in the Titicaca Basin. Manuscript.

Stanish, Charles, Richard L. Burger, Lisa M. Cipolla, Michael Glascock, and Esteban Quelima

1998 Early interregional exchange in the Titicaca Basin: Excavation data from the Island of the Sun, Bolivia. Working Papers of the Programa Collasuyu, no. 2. Manuscript.

Stanish, Charles, and Edmundo de la Vega

1998 Archaeological survey in the northern Titicaca Basin. Working Papers of the Programa Collasuyu, no. 1. Manuscript.

Stanish, Charles, Edmundo de la Vega M., and Kirk Lawrence Frye

1993 Domestic architecture on Lupaqa sites in the Department of Puno. In *Domestic architecture, ethnicity, and complementarity in the south-central Andes,* edited by Mark Aldenderfer, pp. 83–93. Iowa City: University of Iowa Press.

Stanish, Charles, Edmundo de la Vega M., Lee Steadman, Cecilia Chávez Justo, Kirk Lawrence Frye, Luperio Onofre Mamani, Matthew T. Seddon, and Percy Calisaya Chuquimia

1995/1996 Archaeological survey in the southwestern Lake Titicaca Basin. *Diálogo Andino* 14–15: 97–143.

1997 *Archaeological survey in the Juli-Desaguadero region of Lake Titicaca Basin, southern Peru.* Fieldiana Anthropology, n.s., no. 29. Chicago: Field Museum of Natural History.

Stanish, Charles, Edmundo de la Vega M., Lee Steadman, Luperio Onofre, Cecilia Chávez Justo, Percy Calisaya, Kirk Lawrence Frye, and Matthew T. Seddon

1992 Archaeological research in the Juli-Pomata region of the Titicaca Basin, Peru. Final report submitted to the National Science Foundation.

Stanish, Charles, and Lee Hyde Steadman

1994 *Archaeological research at the site of Tumatumani, Juli, Peru.* Fieldiana Anthropology, n.s., no. 23. Chicago: Field Museum of Natural History.

Steadman, Lee Hyde

1994 Ceramic artifacts. In *Archaeological research at the site of Tumatumani, Juli, Peru,* by Charles Stanish and Lee Hyde Steadman, pp. 19–64. Fieldiana Anthropology, n.s., no. 23. Chicago: Field Museum of Natural History.

1995 Excavations at Camata: An early ceramic chronology for the western Titicaca Basin, Peru. Ph.D. diss., Department of Anthropology, University of California, Berkeley.

1999 The ceramics. In *Early settlement at Chiripa, Bolivia: Research of the Taraco Archaeological Project,* edited by Christine Hastorf, pp. 61–72. Contributions of the University of California Archaeological Research Facility, no. 57. Berkeley: University of California.

In press The ceramics from Quelcatani. In *Quelcatani and evolution of a pastoral lifeway,* edited by Mark Aldenderfer. Washington, D.C.: Smithsonian Institution Press.

Terry, Joshua, and Brian S. Bauer

n.d. Pentland's 1827 description of the Islands of the Sun and the Moon and the ruins of Tiwanaku. Manuscript.

Thompson, Lonnie G., M. E. Davis, Ellen Mosley-Thompson, and K-B. Liu

1988 Pre-Incan agricultural activity recorded in dust layers in two tropical ice cores. *Nature* 336: 763–765.

Thompson, Lonnie G., and Ellen Mosley-Thompson

1987 Evidence of abrupt climatic change during the last 1,500 years recorded in ice cores from the tropical Quelccaya ice cap, Peru. In *Abrupt climatic change: Evidence and implications,* edited by Wolfgang H. Berger and Laurent D. Labeyrie, pp. 99–110. NATO ASI Series C, vol. 216. Norwell, Mass.: D. Redel.

Thompson, Lonnie G., Ellen Mosley-Thompson, J. F. Bolzan, and B. R. Koci

1985 A 1500-year record of tropical precipitation in ice cores from the Quelccaya ice cap, Peru. *Science* 229: 971–973.

Thompson, Lonnie G., Ellen Mosley-Thompson, W. Dansgaard, and P. Grootes

1986 The Little Ice Age as recorded in the stratigraphy of the tropical Quelccaya ice cap. *Science* 234: 361–364.

Toledo, Francisco de

1924 Carta de D. Francisco de Toledo, virrey del Perú, sobre la victoria obtenida en Vilcabamba contra los indios, y la prisión de los incas, ejecución de Tupac Amarú y descubrimiento del ídolo Punchau [1572]. In *Gobernantes del Perú: Cartas y papeles, siglo XVI,* vol. 4, pp. 341–345. Documentos del Archivo de Indias. Publicación dirigida por D. Roberto Levillier. Madrid: Colección de Publicaciones Históricas de la Biblioteca del Congreso Argentino, Imprenta de Juan Pueyo.

1975 *Tasa de la visita general de Francisco de Toledo* [1573]. Introducción y versión paleográfica de Noble David Cook y los estudios de Alejandro Málaga Medina y Thérèse Bouysse Cassagne. Lima: Dirección Universitaria de Biblioteca y Publicaciones, Universidad Nacional Mayor de San Marcos, Seminario de Historia Rural Andina.

Torero, Alfredo

1987 Lenguas y pueblos altiplánicos en torno al siglo XVI. *Revista Andina* 5 (2): 329–405.

Trimborn, Hermann von

1967 *Archäologische Studien in den Kordilleren Boliviens.* Berlin: Verlag von Dietrich Reimer.

Tschopik, Marion

1946 *Some notes on the archaeology of the Department of Puno.* Papers of the Peabody Museum of American Archaeology and Ethnology, vol. 27 (3). Cambridge: Peabody Museum.

Turner, Victor Witter

1979 *Process, performance, and pilgrimage: A study in comparative symbology.* New Delhi, India: Concept.

Turner, Victor Witter, and Edith L. B. Turner

1960 *Image and pilgrimage in Christian culture: Anthropological perspectives.* New York: Columbia University Press.

Uhle, Friedrich Max

1903 *Pachacamac: Report of the William Pepper M.D. LL.D. Peruvian Expedition of 1896.* Philadelphia: Department of Archaeology, University of Pennsylvania.

Valera, Blas

1950   De las costumbres antiguas de los naturales del Pirú [ca. 1585]. In *Tres relaciones de antigüedades peruanas,* edited by M. Jiménez de la Espada, pp. 135–203. Asunción, Paraguay: Editorial Guaranía.

Vargas Ugarte, Rubén

1956   *Historia del culto María en iberoamérica y de sus imágenes y santuarios más celebrados.* 2 vols. Madrid: Talleres Gráficos Jura.

Viscarra F., J.

1901   *Copacabana de los Incas: Documentos autolingüísticos e isografiados del Ayamaru-Ayamara.* La Paz: Plaza Hermanos.

Wachtel, Nathan

1986   Men of the water: The Uru problem (sixteenth and seventeenth centuries). In *Anthropological history of Andean polities,* edited by John Murra, Nathan Wachtel, and Jacques Revel, pp. 283–310. Cambridge: Cambridge University Press.

Wallace, Dwight

1957   The Tiahuanaco Horizon styles in the Peruvian and Bolivian highlands. Ph.D. diss., Department of Anthropology, University of California, Berkeley.

Wiener, Charles

1880   *Pérou et Bolivie: Récit de voyage suivi d'études archéologiques et ethnographiques et de notes sur l'écriture et les langues des populations indiennes.* Paris: Hachette et Cie.

Wirrmann, Denis, Philippe Mourguiart, and Luis Fernando de Oliveira Almeida

1990   Holocene sedimentology and ostracods distribution in Lake Titicaca—Paleohydrological interpretations. In *Quaternary of South America and Antarctic Peninsula,* edited by Jorge Rabassa, pp. 89–128. Rotterdam: Balkema.

Wirrmann, Denis, Jean-Pierre Ybert, and Philippe Mourguiart

1991   Una evaluación paleohidrológica de 20.000 años. In *El Lago Titicaca,* edited by Claude Dejoux and Andre Iltis, pp. 61–67. La Paz: ORSTOM/HISBOL.

Xérez, Francisco de

1985   *Verdadera relación de la conquista del Perú* [1534]. Edited by Concepción Bravo. Crónicas de América 14. Madrid: Historia 16.

Ybert, Jean-Pierre

1991   Los paisajes lacustres antiguos según el análisis palinológico. In *El Lago Titicaca,* edited by Claude Dejoux and Andre Iltis, pp. 69–79. La Paz: ORSTOM/HISBOL.

222, 272nn.11–12; Mama Ojlia, 184, 227, 272n.19, 273n.26; Pilco Kayma, 167; Pucara (Island of the Sun), 161; Puncu, 217; Sacred Rock, 73, 179, 201–204; Titinhuayani, 135; visits Tiwanaku, 38, 81. *See also* American Museum of Natural History

Barley, 29

Barreda, Luis Murillo, 10

Battista Ramusio, Giovanni, 55

Beans, 29, 67

Béjar Navarro, Raymundo, 10

Benalcazar, Sebastián de, 56

Bermann, Marc, 41, 92, 95, 141, 271n.18

Betanzos, Juan de, 74, 261–262n.7, 262n.13

Bingham, Hiram, 80, 169, 265nn.11–12

Boats, 30, 31, 103, 202, 218, 247, 248, 268nn.10–11, 275n.10; early technology, 138, 241

Borja, Francisco de, 104

Browman, David, 32, 34, 141, 242

Burger, Richard, 41, 134

Cabello Valboa, Miguel, 257n.5, 262n.13

Cajamarca, 102, 262n.16; on the Island of the Sun, 238–240

Cajatambo, 15

Calancha, Antonio de la, 257n.5, 260n.1

Callapiña, Supno, 57

Camata, 92

Camelids, 26, 33, 38, 43, 270n.7; on the Island of the Sun, 68, 139; silver, 234

Cañares: on the Island of the Sun, 238–240

Canas, 44, 260n.11, 271n.19; on the Island of the Sun, 238–240

Canches, 44, 271n.19; on the Island of the Sun, 238–240

Capachica Pampa, 36

Capancos: on the Island of the Sun, 238–240

Carabaya, 31, 57

Caracollo, 26

Carangas: on the Island of the Sun, 238–240

Cayambis: on the Island of the Sun, 238–240

Ceramics: diagnostic types used, 88–97; earliest production of, 34, 134, 140, 141, 266n.20, 270n.8

Chachapoyas: on the Island of the Sun, 238–240

Challa: bay of, 67, 138, 139, 142, 271n.13; community of, 67, 70, 85, 88, 132, 133, 135, 141, 144, 145, 147, 153, 154, 160, 242, 270n.9; raised fields near, 68, 161–163

Challapampa, 67, 70, 80, 81, 160, 173, 219, 222, 223, 237, 264nn.31,34, 276n.13

Chankas: on the Island of the Sun, 238–240

Charcas, 56

Chávez, Karen, 35, 88, 89, 141, 242

Chávez, Sergio, 35, 242

Chicha, 56, 73, 176, 179, 187, 196, 206, 230, 231, 234, 236, 237, 249, 278n.36

Chichas: on the Island of the Sun, 238–240

Childbirth, offerings made during, 16

Chilques: on the Island of the Sun, 238–240

Chincana, 87, 153, 156, 179, 180, 181, 237, 273n.31; Bandelier at, 187, 191, 194; Cobo describes, 186, 187, 189, 195; Colonial descriptions of, 186–187; function of, 194–196; Pentland at, 191; radiocarbon samples from, 194, 251; Ramos Gavilán describes, 186, 187, 189, 195; research at, 80, 81, 187–196, 273n.30; Squier at, 191; Wiener at, 191, 193, 273n.31

Chinchaysuyos: on the Island of the Sun, 238–240

Chiripa, 35, 36, 89, 90, 135, 141, 150

Chivay, 41

Chosen women. *See* Mamacona

Chucaripupata, 67, 83, 87, 133, 136–138, 144–149, 156, 179, 196, 271n.15; Bandelier at, 136–137, 149, 242, 270n.5; Inca remains at, 196; radiocarbon dates from, 151, 196, 252, 253; Tiwanaku pilgrimage center at, 151–154, 156, 157, 196, 242

Chucuito, city of, 20, 44, 45, 52, 53, 92, 160, 271nn.2,19; lake of, 13, 258

Chullpa, 82

Chumbivilcas: on the Island of the Sun, 238–240

Chuquiabo, 27

Ch'uxuqullu, 87, 88, 132, 133–134, 135, 138, 140, 270n.7; radiocarbon samples from, 134, 138, 251, 252, 269n.1

Cieza de León, Pedro de, 45, 62, 155, 262nn.11,13, 271n.19; Colla on the Island of the Sun, 125; conquest of Collasuyu, 51, 261n.7; emergence of the Sun, 58; first Inca to the Island of the Sun, 53; land of the Colla, 26, 27; Pachacamac, 11, 257n.5; Temples of the Sun, 236

Coati (island). *See* Moon, Island of

Cobo, Bernabé, 45, 52, 202, 229, 237, 268n.9; Andean pilgrimages, 213; approaching the Sacred Rock, 224, 227–230; Chincana, 186, 187, 189, 195; conquest of Collasuyu, 51, 261n.7; Copacabana, 207, 214–216; Coricancha, 9; creation of the Andean world, 49–50; first Incas to the islands, 54–55; growing of coca, 72; Horca del Inca, 207; Inca astronomy, 207; Inca visits between the islands, 100, 101; Island of the Moon, 103, 231–232; Islands of the Sun and the Moon, 13–14, 178; Mamaconas, 187, 196; Manco Capac, 74; Pacariqtambo Origin Myth, 50; Pachacamac, 11; personal history of, 47–48; pilgrimage route, 214–216, 222; re-

moval of island people, 237; Sacred Rock, 206, 226, 230–231, 234; site of Mama Ojlia, 182, 186; statue of the Moon, 101, 102; Topa Inca, 101, 219, 222; use of Molina, 258n.13; use of Pizarro, 268n.6; use of Ramos Gavilán, 48, 54, 100, 186, 224, 257n.1, 278n.26, 280n.39; veneration of the islands, 1, 2, 62

Coca, 76, 233; on the Island of the Sun, 72

Cochabamba, 31, 41, 42, 153

Coipaso, 23

Colca, valley of, 134, 135; storage houses, 215–216

Coleman, Simon, 248

Colla, 26, 44, 51, 52, 56, 82, 155, 222, 230, 262n.8, 271n.19; labor used from, 53, 125

Collaguas: on the Island of the Sun, 238–240

Collao, 55, 56, 58, 62, 261n.7; ceramic style, 97

Collasuyu, 82; Inca conquest of, 51, 245, 247; village of, 240

Colliyungas: on the Island of the Sun, 238–240

Constantine, 20, 22

Cook, David Noble, 32

Copacabana, 13, 17, 19, 23, 24, 30, 47, 62, 65, 70, 71, 80, 103, 147, 220, 262n.14, 264n.30, 274n.8, 280n.45; astronomical work near, 207–212, 216; Cobo describes, 214–216; *doctrina* of, 102; *encomienda* of, 57–58, 216, 237–238; Inca divisions of, 56, 216, 271n.2; Inca materials at, 160; Inca sites near, 216; Lupaqa at, 155; *mitimaes* at, 54, 59, 155, 238–240, 280n.47; part of pilgrimage, 211–218, 247–249; pilgrims arrive at, 22; population of, 238, 240; Ramos Gavilán at, 48, 98, 129; Ramos Gavilán describes, 155, 215–216, 263n.25;

rock deposits on, 117, 274n.45; modern occupations on, 69–71; modern rituals on, 75–78; myths about, 48–51; objects taken from, 59–62, 80, 81–83, 264n.34, 266nn.16,18; offerings made on, 232–235, 264n.34; pre-Inca history of, 132–157, 241–243; 245; previous research on, 78–83; Ramos Gavilán describes, 53–54, 72, 98–101, 178–180, 182, 186, 187, 189, 195, 206, 208, 215–217, 222, 224–230, 233, 234, 237–240; Ramos Gavilán visits, 48; Sanctuary area on, 66, 136, 179–207, 247–249; Tiwanaku materials on, 132, 133, 136–138, 144, 145, 147–154, 196, 242–243, 245, 248, 266n.18, 270n.2, 271nn.16–17; Tiwanaku pilgrimages to, 150–155, 243, 246, 247; visits to, 48, 53–54, 62

Tambos, 215, 222, 260n.8
Tambo Tocco, 49, 131
Taquile, 23
Taraco, 36, 38
Temple of the Sun. *See* Coricancha
Tikani, 87, 179; marks June solstice, 208
Titicaca, Island. *See* Sun, Island of
Titicaca, Lake, 258n.8, 262n.13; altitude of, 241; changing levels of, 27–29, 260n.9; characteristics of, 23–33; cores from, 28; creation takes place at, 15; cultural chronologies of, 33–46; depth of, 64; ecological zones of, 29–33; first description of, 55–56; first Europeans at, 13, 98, 102, 263n.17; Inca activities in the region of, 47–55, 244–249; Inca expansion to, 4, 22, 45–46, 51–55, 128, 261n.7, 132, 196, 245, 271n.19; location and size of, 5, 23, 24; myths about, 48–51; offerings found in, 84, 150, 151, 269nn.19,23,31, 274n.42; population of region, 259n.4; sacred islands of, 64, 132; shrine complex at, 21; temperature near, 27

Titikala. *See* Sacred Rock
Titimani, 35, 36
Titinhuayani, site of, 67, 87, 132, 135–136, 138, 140, 141, 145, 146, 147, 149, 270n.2, 271n.14
Tito Yupanqui, Francisco, 59, 263n.22, 264n.27, 268n.12, 280n.45
Tiwanaku, 30, 79, 81, 109, 123; capital city of, 38, 152, 242; ceramic styles of, 89–95; development and collapse of, 35–43, 136, 147, 149, 151–156, 243, 248; materials on the Island of the Moon, 104, 109, 114, 119, 121–124, 128–129; 147, 150, 154, 242–243, 245, 248, 266n.18; materials on the Island of the Sun, 132, 133, 136–138, 144, 145, 147–154, 196, 242–243, 245, 248, 266n.18, 270n.2, 271nn.16–17; materials recovered, 84, 150, 151, 260n.10, 269nn.19,23,31; pilgrimage to the islands, 150–155, 243, 246, 247; Squier at, 38; visited by various Incas, 51–52
Toledo, Francisco de, 15, 58, 59, 259n.4, 264nn.27,33
Topa Inca, 4, 6, 261–262n.7, builds a royal palace, 178, 222; builds a town, 219, 222; visits the Islands of the Sun and the Moon; 53–54, 62, 98, 99, 101, 123; visits Pachacamac, 11
Totora reeds, 30, 31, 139
Tschudi, Johann Jakob von, 79, 109, 165, 269n.21
Tumatumani, 35, 41, 134, 135, 144, 270n.11
Turner, Victor: theory of pilgrimage, 20, 21, 75, 244, 246

Uhle, Max: on the Islands of the Sun and the Moon, 80, 147, 266n.18; visits Tiwanaku, 38; work at Pachacamac, 12
Uila Peki, 99, 125, 126, 128, 129
Umasuyu, 225, 260n.11, 277n.24
Urcosuyu, 260n.11, 277n.24
Uro-Chipaya, 32